SERFDOM AND SOCIAL CONTROL
IN RUSSIA

MAP I: European Russia. From George Yaney, *The Urge to Mobilize: Agrarian Reform in Russia, 1861–1930,* copyright © 1982 by the University of Illinois Press.

SERFDOM
AND
SOCIAL CONTROL
IN RUSSIA
Petrovskoe, a Village in Tambov

STEVEN L. HOCH

THE UNIVERSITY OF CHICAGO PRESS
CHICAGO AND LONDON

The University of Chicago Press, Chicago 60637
The University of Chicago Press, Ltd., London

LIBRARY OF CONGRESS CATALOGING IN PUBLICATION DATA

Hoch, Steven L.
    Serfdom and social control in Russia.

    Bibliography: p.
    Includes index.
    1. Serfdom—Russian S.F.S.R.—Tambovskaîa
oblast'—History. 2. Social structure—Russian
S.F.S.R.—Tambovskaîa oblast'—History.
3. Tambovskaîa oblast' (R.S.F.S.R.)—Social conditions.
I. Title.
HT807.H63 1986   306'.365'094735   86-6915
ISBN 0-226-34583-1 (cloth)
ISBN 0-226-34585-8 (paper)

To H., M., and E.

CONTENTS

ACKNOWLEDGMENTS

TO ALL WHO HAVE HELPED ME BRING THIS BOOK INTO BEING, I am sincerely grateful, and I wish to express my thanks. Research was undertaken primarily in the Library of Congress, the Slavonic Division of Helsinki University Library, the V. I. Lenin State Library, and the Central State Archives of Ancient Acts in Moscow. To the staffs of these institutions I am greatly indebted.

As a French Government Fellow at the Ecole des Hautes Etudes en Sciences Sociales in Paris, I was able to attend the seminars of Louis Henry in historical demography and Emmanuel Le Roy Ladurie in rural history. Their influence should be evident. The International Research and Exchanges Board, through its sponsorship and financial support, made possible my research in the Soviet Union. My graduate advisors at Princeton University, Cyril Black and Jerome Blum, and my advisor at Moscow State University, V. A. Fedorov, must receive particular thanks for their guidance, patience, and encouragement.

Adele Lindenmeyr of Carnegie-Mellon University, Moshe Lewin of the University of Pennsylvania, Richard Hellie of the University of Chicago, Daniel Field of Syracuse University, editor of the *Russian Review,* Richard Stites of Georgetown University, Orest Pelech, formerly the Slavic bibliographer at Princeton University, Michael Paul Sacks of Trinity College, Thomas Christofferson and Philip Peek of Drew University, Simon Dixon, Sandra Holscher, and Harriet Ritter all read the manuscript and contributed numerous helpful suggestions. E. Brooke Anthony, Linda Connor, and Beth Hogan, student assistants, relieved me of much of the drudgery involved in demographic calculations and computer programming. My wife Eeva has read the manuscript more times than I can recall. To all these people I am most appreciative.

One comment on mechanics is necessary. I have followed

the Library of Congress system of transliteration from Russian, though most plurals have been anglicized. Nouns ending with a soft sign have had this diacritical mark deleted in the anglicized plural to avoid confusing the non-Russian reader.

INTRODUCTION

PEASANTS ARE BY DEFINITION EXPLOITED, WHETHER FREEMEN, serfs, or slaves. This is what ties them to a larger culture.[1] Thus it is necessary to understand the structure of that exploitation, given biological and ecological determinants and seigneurial and cultural influences. The problem of exploitation is essentially social, not political or economic: to exploit one must exercise authority. Though serfdom differs economically from the exploitation of slaves and free peasants, the key problem of establishing and maintaining authority determines much peasant behavior and accounts for the similarities of behavior and attitude in many peasant societies. How did landlords and bailiffs in imperial Russia get the serfs to work and behave as desired?

One of the major weaknesses of the historical literature on Russian serfdom has been its inability to deal with this question and to probe beyond the broad legal and economic aspects of serf life. Although the legal history of serfdom has received much attention, in reality the state played a minor role in maintaining this institution. Clearly, the Russian autocracy was one of the primary beneficiaries of serfdom, if not its initiator. But the social structures that emerged in serf society reflected the extremely limited part the state played in upholding this institution. Rural Russia in the first half of the nineteenth century was not merely undergoverned, it was largely ungoverned. The state was able to collect its taxes and conscript its sailors and soldiers. The militia could suppress local disturbances and catch many runaways. But this was largely the extent of effective government involvement in rural society.

Beginning in the late eighteenth century, the autocracy did try to smooth some of the sharper edges of serfdom. Over the course of years it was made easier for persons wrongfully enserfed to sue for their freedom. New laws were passed that

1. Eric Wolf, *Peasants* (Englewood Cliffs, N.J., 1966), 4, 11.

facilitated the manumission of serfs. Restrictions were placed on their sale, who could purchase them, the amount of time they could be required to work for their lord, and the minimum amount of land to which they had to be attached. In addition, the autocracy in the nineteenth century stopped the growth of serfdom. In 1811 there were 10.5 million male serfs, just over half the total male population. As a result of government policies, their number barely increased over the next fifty years, while their proportion in the total population declined to just over 37 percent.[2]

Although legislation checked the growth of serfdom and attempted to place it in a more humane light, distinguishing serfs, at least in law, from mere chattels or slaves, this meant little to those in servitude. It was not merely a question of the enforcement of the rule of law, though often there was little of that. Rather, society was atomized into virtually autonomous units and severely constrained by ecological factors. With few exceptions, village life was all of life. The world, whether fearful or joyful, was small, and these little societies were held together from within. In Russian the word for the peasant commune, *mir*, also meant the universe and, in a variant spelling, the world. Similarly, it was the presence of a church that gave a village a history and its inhabitants a sense of identity. A village with a church was a *selo*, which meant not merely to settle and take root, but to inspire and instill.

In the small rural worlds of servile Russia, dearth and disease were far more potent forces than czar or landlord. Climate and geography were determining features of life. Epidemics and bad harvests were the greatest of fears. But serfdom was not simply imposed over a fixed ecology; it interacted with the environment, and both were changed.

Structures of authority, in this instance controls for serf behavior, are best viewed on a microcosmic level. There is of course no typical serf village; microecologies and varying seigneurial policies can create noticeable differences even among neighboring settlements. However, the historian's task is not to

2. Steven L. Hoch and Wilson R. Augustine, "The Tax Censuses and the Decline of the Serf Population in Imperial Russia," *Slavic Review* 38 (1979): 406.

generalize but to integrate. If the world is intricate and complex, that must be appreciated and not made to yield to a broad but distorted overview. Yet serf villages were not radically individualistic in resolving tensions and conflicts, responding to servitude, controlling access to productive resources, and establishing family patterns without reference to broader ecological constraints, biological limitations, historical and cultural traditions, and to a lesser extent legal and political structures.

Soviet scholars have produced a number of case studies on serf life in Russia, relying on the archives of the estate offices of such prominent noble families as the Kurakins, Vorontsovs, Sheremetevs, Iusupovs, and Gagarins, the last being the owners of Petrovskoe, the focus of this book. Such magnate families, whose serfs numbered in the tens of thousands and whose lands covered hundreds of thousands of acres, had holdings scattered throughout the empire. Yet a single estate of more than five thousand serfs was rare, and this of necessity would be further divided into separate villages to reduce the distance to outlying fields. Though the figures available are not very reliable, we can roughly state that perhaps no more than 4 percent of all the serfowners possessed 54 percent of the serfs. Systematic records for the estates of the vast majority of petty landlords probably were rarely kept and are even less likely to have been preserved. Thus, of their serfs it may never be possible to say much beyond what can be adduced by analogy.

The case studies available, along with more general surveys of serf life by both Soviet and Western scholars, have in some instances followed the traditions of prerevolutionary researchers and largely discussed legal history. More often, emphasis has been on the economically exploitative aspects of serfdom. Such historians have provided a broad understanding of how the peasants used the land. They have analyzed the economics of peasant and manorial farming and detailed the serfs' obligations to the landlord.[3] But though serfdom was a human

3. Geroid T. Robinson, *Rural Russia under the Old Regime* (New York, 1932); Jerome Blum, *Lord and Peasant in Russia from the Ninth to the Nineteenth Century* (Princeton, 1961); K. N. Shchepetov, *Krepostnoe pravo v votchinakh Sheremetevykh* (Moscow, 1947); K. V. Sivkov, *Ocherki po istorii krepostnogo khoziaistvo i krest'ianskogo dvizheniia v Rossii v pervoi polovine XIX veke* (Moscow, 1951); E. I. Indova, *Krepostnoe khoziaistvo v nachale*

institution, it was substantially confined by ecological determinants. Serf behavior and attitudes were in fact an integrated human response to the ecological constraints at work in the society and to the inhuman degradation of being reduced to property.

Soviet historians follow an unusually narrow line of interpretation, taken directly from Lenin, regarding developments in Russian peasant society between 1800 and 1860. Not only do they confine their analyses largely to either economic questions or peasant movements, but they unanimously see a growing crisis during the last years of what they call the "feudal-serf system," that is, before the capitalist period, which is said to begin with the emancipation of 1861. Declining peasant living standards, reduced landlord profits, greater socioeconomic differentiation within serf society, increased intrusion of capitalist relations into the countryside, and heightened class conflict are virtual clichés in Soviet historical literature. The Petrovskoe estate itself has been the subject of such an analysis as part of a broader study on the Gagarin family holdings by the now prominent Soviet historian I. D. Koval'chenko in his first book, published in 1959.

It is not my purpose to engage in an ideological dispute with Soviet historians. Nor am I interested, as they often are, in revealing the so-called laws of history and the regularity of historical development. Rather, I wish to tell quite a different story, about the structure of serf life. I differ rather sharply with Koval'chenko over two key issues, the serfs' standard of living and the extent of socioeconomic differentiation. I am critical of both the measures he uses and his interpretation of the data that follow. These differences will be considered at some length, but on other issues such discussion does not seem appropriate. For example, the evidence Koval'chenko puts forth to show that the serfs of Petrovskoe suffered a negative natural growth rate ignores the incidence of emigration, mainly in the

---

XIX veka po materialam votchinnogo arkhiva Vorontsovykh (Moscow, 1955); I. D. Koval'chenko, Krest'iane i krepostnoe khoziaistvo Riazanskoi i Tambovskoi gubernii v pervoi polovine XIX veka (Moscow, 1959); and I. D. Koval'chenko, Russkoe krepostnoe khoziaistvo v pervoi polovine XIX veka (Moscow, 1967).

form of recruitment. Given the sources he used, the soul-tax registers, this was virtually impossible to overlook. This negative growth rate was a point Koval'chenko so wished to emphasize that he italicized the text, yet to my mind rebuttals to such errors would only be a distraction.[4] For this and similar reasons, Soviet historiography was only of limited help in my work, and therefore I have not relied heavily upon Soviet studies.

The estate of Petrovskoe, the property of the princely noble family the Gagarins, consisted in the nineteenth century initially of six and later of eight separate but neighboring settlements along the Vorona River in the southern part of Tambov province. The two main villages were Petrovskoe, from which the estate took its name, and Kanin. Each had its own church. The estate had a total population of about 3,500 serfs, all under the same manorial authority.

For the historian what distinguishes Petrovskoe is its documents. From the early nineteenth century to the 1860s, the Gagarin family, like many others, maintained a central estate office in Moscow to administer its holdings throughout the empire. For most of the period a bailiff hired by the Gagarins was present on the estate in Tambov. The correspondence and documents exchanged between the bailiffs of the Petrovskoe estate and the Moscow administrators of the Gagarin properties are the documentary basis of my research.

Concern for the good management of serf estates and the proper keeping of manorial records, particularly where large numbers of serfs were involved, became increasingly common in Russia in the latter half of the eighteenth century. Bailiffs were often given lengthy written instructions on serf management. The Free Economic Society for the Encouragement of Agriculture and Household Management in Russia published numerous sets of model instructions, including translations of many works on farm management by German and English agronomists and landed aristocrats.[5] The archives of serf es-

---

4. Koval'chenko, *Krest'iane i krepostnoe khoziaistvo*, 168.
5. V. A. Aleksandrov, *Sel'skaia obshchina v Rossii (XVII–nachalo XIX v.)* (Moscow, 1976), and Michael Confino, *Domaines et seigneurs en Russie vers la fin du XVIIIe siècle* (Paris, 1963).

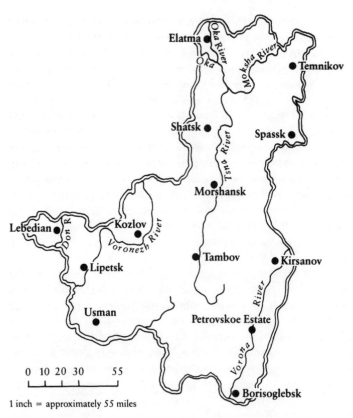

MAP 2: Historic province of Tambov, with the twelve uezd centers.

tates belonging to many prominent Russian noble families reflect this change in record keeping. Peasant household inventories (*podvornye opisi*), financial records for the estate and peasant commune (*prikhodskie i raskhodskie knigi*), manuals of discipline (*shtrafnye knigi*), weekly bailiff's reports, grain inventories, sowing and harvest records, land surveys, estate inventories, and recruitment lists, all thought to be attributes of a well-run estate, were the kinds of documents normally kept.

The expansion and development of true manorial regimes in the eighteenth century forced this introduction of detailed record keeping. Earlier, when it was often simply a matter of collecting money dues, the management of most estates was rather simple. Even on corvée estates, few records seem to have been kept. But with more opportunities to market grain during the eighteenth century, greater profit possibilities in the more fertile south, and the influence, albeit limited, of foreign ideas on estate administration, mainly seen in the rise of professional managers, bookkeeping became more elaborate. At Petrovskoe records were made of all revenues and expenditures, though whether some of the money was spent as stated must remain in doubt. Manuals of discipline were supposed to be evidence that order was being maintained, and they were used during recruitment levies to rid the estate of undesirables. The weather, the progress of work, peasant petitions, and any special problems were detailed in reports the bailiff sent to Moscow every week or two.

For the historian the most important documents are the peasant household inventories. The earliest ones for serf estates in Russia date from the seventeenth century, and landlords used them primarily for tax purposes. During the course of the eighteenth century there was added to these tax records information on land allotments, livestock holdings, corvée obligations, and grain reserves. In time they permitted landlords and bailiffs to assess the productive capacity of individual peasant households, which made them useful for an estate like Petrovskoe.[6] Along with the resources and reserves of each household were listed the age, sex, marital status, and estate labor obligations of each household member. At a glance a bailiff could see whether a particular household was in a position to meet its responsibilities, whether it was capable of utilizing its resources fully, or whether it would need assistance from the estate or peasant commune.

Peasant household inventories on the Gagarin estates and elsewhere were compiled irregularly, and often it is not clear why they were taken when they were. In some instances an inventory was drawn up shortly after a crop failure or epidemic so as to assess the damage and redistribute taxes and dues.

---

6. B. G. Litvak, *Ocherki istochnikovedeniia massovoi dokumentatsii XIX nachala XX v.* (Moscow, 1979), 60–74.

When an estate passed to an heir, an inventory was usually made. But for many inventories the only reason seems to be the ongoing need to evaluate household utilization of land, labor, and livestock.

For the social historian these peasant household inventories are exciting sources. From the standpoint of historical demography, they are nominative lists. They reveal the age distribution and family structure of the population, and a series of inventories lets us trace changes in these over time. Moreover, if we can determine the fate of all persons between consecutive compilations, as was possible for Petrovskoe between 1850 and 1856, then an examination of mortality is possible. No less intriguing is to follow households over time, to determine their life cycle, and to undertake a dynamic analysis of economic mobility within the society.

The difficulties encountered in carrying out this study, in addition to the general methodological problems of using these household inventories, included the restrictions of working in Soviet archives. Because photocopying was not permitted and microfilming was limited to a very small number of frames, the documents had to be hand copied. There were 3,500 serfs on the estate, and with nine inventories, many other materials in the archives to read, and only nine months of research time as a participant on the academic exchange, I had to restrict the sample. Consequently, data from the nine inventories were collected only for the largest settlement on the estate, the village of Petrovskoe, whose population fluctuated from 523 to 762 serfs. Though it seems small, this is adequate for the demographic and economic analyses undertaken here. From a statistical standpoint, only a sample of under five hundred would have posed problems. Bear in mind, however, that only with the household inventories was it necessary to restrict the research in this manner. All other archival materials, and the discussion that flows from them, relate to the estate as a whole—to all eight settlements and the entire population.

Good management of a serf estate involves the proper use of capital, in this instance primarily land, livestock, and agricultural implements, and the institution of effective labor policies. Historians generally agree that Russian serfowners were notoriously poor estate managers. In spite of the efforts of the

Ministry of State Domains, the Free Economic Society, and other regional agricultural organizations, the level of agricultural technology remained low. The three-field system of crop rotation, with its adverse effect on pastureland and animal husbandry, predominated. Increases in cereal production were achieved by enlarging the area sown at the expense of forest, meadows, and pastures. Feed grasses for livestock were not introduced as a means of increasing the supply of manure for the fields and thus raising grain yields per unit of arable land. Little attempt was made to improve the strains of cereals grown. Serfowners preferred to consume the income from their estates; only rarely did they invest in them, and when they did it was only in rather particular ways. The peasants continued to use the crudest of implements, and they divided the fields into long, narrow strips, a method sharply criticized by contemporary agronomists, who understood little of its benefits, as an extremely inefficient utilization of the land. Yet given the depressed nature of the grain market in Russia, these may all have been very sensible policies.

In spite of the technological stagnation, a substantial improvement in record keeping took place. Indeed, good management in Russia was often equated with good record keeping of the kind described above. But Russian landlords were very concerned about the supervision of their labor supply, the serfs. Order, discipline, subordination, and routine coupled with a feeling of paternalistic dependence were values deeply engrained in the Russian service nobility and were the principles they, as landlords, sought to apply to rural life. Often Russian serfowners hired bailiffs of Prussian or Baltic origin, feeling that they embodied these virtues.[7] Thus the primary function of a bailiff was not so much to manage an agricultural enterprise as to see that the serfs correctly fulfilled their labor or quitrent obligations and acted according to desired social norms. Many Russian serfowners, not only unwilling to invest large amounts of capital in their estates but little interested in agriculture itself, hoped that the proper control and regulation of the serfs, which required minimal expenditure, would ensure the reve-

7. Confino, *Domaines et seigneurs*, 259–61.

nues they desired. This emphasis on labor management to the detriment of agricultural improvement was an important aspect of the legacy of serfdom in the postemancipation years.

Of course, serf estates in imperial Russia were not prisons or concentration camps. It is true that bailiffs and landlords did have almost unlimited legal power over the peasants, for the state did little to regulate the relationship between masters and serfs.[8] But the economic success of an estate and the viability of serfdom as an institution did not rest upon the exercise of total power, literally forcing the serfs to fulfill their obligations. In fact, the total domination of man by man is an expensive undertaking requiring trained guards, numerous administrators, and an elaborate physical plant. And even in these circumstances the desired results are rarely obtained.[9]

On serf estates in Russia expenses were generally kept to a minimum. There were no walls and no armed guards. Often one bailiff singlehandedly managed an estate, and his power over the serfs can hardly be described as total in practice. Even if power is defined as only the likelihood that the serfs would correctly fulfill their labor or quitrent obligations and adhere to certain social norms, then the extent of rule violation in servile Russia reveals that the relationship of bailiffs and serfs was one of conflict and compromise, not supremacy. For all peasants, and especially for those in servitude, noncooperation, apathy, mischief making, and negligence are common responses to their plight.

It is difficult to see why serfs would have had any internalized sense of duty toward their obligations, even though they did accept many of the norms of serf life.[10] Consequently, serf administrators were forced to rely upon an elaborate system of rewards and punishments to ensure the financial success

---

8. Blum, *Lord and Peasant,* 422.
9. Gresham Sykes, *The Society of Captives* (Princeton, 1958), 40–52.
10. For quite similar behavior on the part of prison inmates, patients in mental hospitals, and American Negro slaves see Sykes, *Society,* 48–62; Erving Goffman, *Asylums: Essays on the Social Situation of Mental Patients and Other Inmates* (Garden City, N.Y., 1961), 206–7, 308; and George M. Fredrickson and Christopher Lasch, "Resistance to Slavery," *Civil War History* (December 1967), reprinted in *The Debate over Slavery,* ed. Ann Lane (Urbana, Ill., and Chicago, 1971), 231–32.

of an estate and the economic viability and productivity ᴑ̣ᵢ every serf household. Ecological and demographic structures largely determined the material base of serf society and thus the rewards and punishments available to the bailiff. In effect, ecology and demography restricted the nature of the authority the bailiff exercised.

The first chapter examines this material base, in particular the peasants' diet and housing. In "normal" years the serfs of Petrovskoe, though by no means unique in the region, were rather well off by the standards of most preindustrial, peasant societies, but subsistence crises and epidemics were beyond the control of the estate's administrators. The various stewards of the Petrovskoe estate during the course of the nineteenth century did not ruthlessly exploit the peasants for short-run gains. Rather, the bailiffs recognized that the profitability of the estate was directly related to the peasants' material well-being. Thus, tied to this virtual slave regime were paternalistic attitudes and a welfare system that, though often put forth by supporters of serfdom as evidence of its humaneness and beneficence, were more self-serving than benign.

Upon this material base of relative prosperity rested family structures markedly different from household patterns found in contemporary western Europe. As I will show in the second chapter, most households at Petrovskoe were large, consisting of three generations and two or more conjugal family units, essentially the function of early and universal marriage, high fertility, and careful control of household division. And, I shall argue, it was primarily through this patriarchal household that authority was maintained, power was distributed, and rewards and punishments were dispensed.

The last three chapters each confront one broad aspect in the structure of social control, the system of reward and punishment. Chapter 3 presents evidence that exploitation at Petrovskoe was largely a social problem resolved by a conjunction of interests fusing the power of serf patriarchs and peasant functionaries with the authority of the bailiff. Patriarchy defined reward, even outside the household. Privileges were awarded to village elders in their roles as serf overseers and drivers. The bailiffs upheld patriarchal power by limiting socioeconomic differentiation to reduce conflict among heads of household and by regulating household division to ensure the elders a labor supply to exploit. The regular redistribution of arable land and the custom of bride-price were key factors lessening stratification.

In chapter 4 the peasant commune is viewed as an institution reflecting this endemic intergenerational conflict and representing the collective interests of the patriarchs. The commune controlled social deviance and was the key institutional support for patriarchs who confronted recalcitrant family members. In the final chapter the weaknesses and inefficiencies in this system of control are discussed. In spite of the rewards to patriarchs and the powers of the commune, rule violation was widespread, tension between serfs the norm, and punishment commonplace. The bailiff had to intervene almost daily to maintain a work regime and a semblance of social order.

In the records of the Petrovskoe estate, the peasants rarely spoke for themselves, and to resurrect the thoughts of those who did not record them directly is necessarily a difficult task. But many of the documents report serf behavior from which attitudes may be inferred and mentalities reconstructed. The picture presented, however, is neither unbiased nor complete. Many of the documents concentrate on disorder, dysfunction, and disharmony. There is far less on the forces that bound this little society together than on the coercive pressures necessary to keep it from flying apart. Little mention is made of peasant religious practices, festivals, or the role of the parish church. None of the bailiffs seemed concerned with the serfs' religious life or their adherence to Orthodox rituals. In addition, kinship ties, so crucial in many peasant societies, are difficult to trace because the peasants lack surnames. Consequently their importance at Petrovskoe, if any, is barely seen.

Finally, a few comments are in order about the Gagarin family, the owners of Petrovskoe, and the estate's setting approximately 330 miles southeast of Moscow, in the central agricultural region. Prince Sergei Sergeevich Gagarin (1745–98) and his wife, Princess Varvara Nikolaevna Gagarina, were the first owners of record for about half of the estate, situated in Borisoglebsk district in the southernmost part of Tambov province. They acquired an adjacent tract of land with its serf population, including the village of Petrovskoe, in 1797.

This area was a rather newly settled region. Tambov, the provincial capital, was founded in 1636 and Borisoglebsk, the district seat, ten years later. Both were originally little more than forts to help contain the nomadic Tatars.[11] It was only in the 1700s that this part of Russia was opened up to agriculture, and even at the end of the eighteenth century there remained a considerable amount of unsettled land.[12] The Gagarins were still transferring large numbers of serfs to Petrovskoe from their other estates in the early nineteenth century.

Once secure from the threat of nomadic raids, this fertile area developed quickly. The rich black earth, the longer growing season, and the ease of moving grain along the Tsna, Oka, and Volga rivers to the major cities of the north let agriculture flourish. Still, the extent of trade should not be exaggerated. The Petrovskoe estate was approximately 150 miles by road from Morshansk, the southernmost navigable point on the Tsna and a major grain-marketing center. For peasants carting cereals, it took roughly two weeks to make the round trip.

In 1813 the estate passed into the hands of Prince Nikolai Sergeevich Gagarin (1784–1842), and it is from this date that systematic record keeping begins. In 1842 Nikolai's elder son Nikolai Nikolaevich (1823–1902) inherited the estate. All matters, however, were handled by the family estate office in Moscow, and it is not even certain that any of the Gagarins ever visited Petrovskoe. They were as far removed from the life of their serfs as contemporary society permitted. Both Sergei Sergeevich and Nikolai Sergeevich held court appointments and rose to the very highest of positions, *hofmeister*, master of the court. Nikolai Sergeevich, the owner of Petrovskoe for much of the period under consideration, was actually born in London, and from 1832 he served as director of the imperial glass and porcelain factory. His murder on 25 July 1842 by a disgruntled Finnish forest guard who worked on factory-owned lands was said to have had a depressing effect on all of Saint Petersburg society. The Finn, who shot Gagarin in the

11. Stephan Berenegovskii, "Nekotoryia istoricheskiia i statisticheskiia zamechaniia o Tambovskoi gubernii," *Izvestiia Tambovskoi Uchenoi Arkhivnoi Komissii* 55 (1913): 33.

12. Koval'chenko, *Krest'iane i krepostnoe khoziaistvo,* 69.

neck just outside his office, was sentenced to run the gauntlet of one thousand men six times and then, should he survive, to be stripped of his civil rights and exiled to Siberia.

Petrovskoe was very profitable, providing an average annual net income of over 61,000 rubles assignats between the years 1845 and 1860, though this was not the most successful of the Gagarins' properties.[13] But there is little to suggest that the estate was unique for the region. In fact, a detailed land survey of Borisoglebsk district taken in 1837 stated that the level of well-being at Petrovskoe was "average," below the 5 percent of the villages in the district cited as "good." No settlements were found to be poverty-stricken.[14]

Serfdom was, of course, economically exploitive. It existed, after all, to support serfowners. But while serfdom was imposed from above, it had to be maintained from below. It was far more than a legal and economic structure. Simply put, serfdom was a highly integrated social system, a careful but despicable balance of ecological, demographic, economic, social, and political forces.

13. Ibid., 128.
14. TsVIA, f. VUA, ed. khr. 19079.

I

THE MATERIAL BASE

OVER FORTY-FIVE YEARS AGO MARC BLOCH WROTE, "IT IS very naive to claim to understand men without knowing what sort of health they enjoyed. But in this field the state of the evidence, and still more the inadequacy of our methods of research, are inhibitive."[1] Since then, medical research on developing countries has tremendously increased the knowledge of subsistence requirements and of the physiological and psychological effects of insufficient calories, an unbalanced diet, or unsanitary living conditions. And historians have made valuable use of this work. To cite one important result, it is now clear that improvements in diet and better public sanitation were the primary factors causing the steady decline in noninfant mortality throughout much of Europe during the nineteenth century.[2] But higher mortality is not the sole consequence of malnutrition or undernourishment. People may live for years on an inadequate diet, and the Food and Agriculture Organization of the United Nations has described such a community: "The whole manner of life is adapted to an insufficient supply of calories, with results that are socially undesirable: lack of drive and initiative; avoidance of physical and mental effort; excessive rest."[3] Starvation, it is now known, is rarely a direct cause of death. But were the serfs of Petrovskoe malnourished or undernourished, thereby either falling prey to sickness and disease or necessarily behaving listlessly? Did their housing adversely affect their physical and mental well-being?

To examine these questions we must investigate all aspects of serf agriculture, the basis of the peasants' standard of living. Adult serfs in Petrovskoe were in effect bound to the person of their lord, exchanging their labor (*barshchina*) for the

1. Marc Bloch, *Feudal Society,* trans. L. A. Manyon (Chicago, 1961), 1:72.
2. E. A. Wrigley, *Population and History* (New York, 1969), 164–80.
3. Cited in C. Clark and M. Haswell, *The Economics of Subsistence Agriculture* (New York, 1967), 19.

right to work an allotment of plowland, to share communal pastures and meadows, to possess a home and an adjacent garden, and to have limited access to estate woodlands. The somewhat unique but well-known aspect of peasant life in Great Russia, which existed in Petrovskoe as well, was that husband and wife work teams (*tiaglos*), or more rarely single or widowed male serfs, enjoyed the full use of plowland only as long as they fulfilled labor obligations in estate grainfields.[4] Thus the right to a particular plot of arable land or to even any plowland at all did not belong to a household (*dvor*) or to its head in perpetuity as was the case throughout much of Europe and in Little and White Russia as well. Rather, the plowlands were periodically redistributed and therefore held only temporarily. The harvest from these fields, however, was the common property of the entire household. In contrast to the plowlands, the lands immediately surrounding a farmstead and the buildings on them were held in perpetuity and never reapportioned. And everyone in the village had equal right to common pastures, hayfields, and estate forests.

At Petrovskoe, adult males no longer able to work in estate fields were generally still obligated to perform other labor services, though this did not entitle them to any plowland. Their wives, however, and all widows seem to have been exempt. At least there is no mention of any such obligations in estate records. Elderly persons living alone were supplied with grain from communal reserves, though there were very few such cases on the estate. Also, during the 1850s widows of working age had access to a "widow's allotment," which they cultivated with the assistance of the commune. Apparently this plot adequately met their household needs. Soldiers' wives (*soldatkas*), which in the years following high recruitment levies could be a substantial proportion of young females (see table 18), were roughly equivalent in status to widows because of the twenty-five-year terms their husbands had to serve. Generally soldatkas continued to live on the estate with their husbands'

---

4. Blum, *Lord and Peasant*, 7. In many places corvée was commuted to a quitrent, though this was not the case in Petrovskoe or the surrounding region.

families. But under the law they were free persons, and consequently they received no land or other benefits from the estate.

None of this, however, applied to a special category of serfs whose status was usually hereditary, the *dvorovye liudi*, frequently translated as household serfs. Yet these serfs were rarely in domestic service and worked rather as scribes or skilled craftsmen carrying out some of the more specialized functions needed on a large agricultural estate. The estate strove to be as self-sufficient as possible, not only training its own serfs as blacksmiths, carpenters, and saddlemakers but also teaching some of them to keep the estate's books. Many of the household serfs simply served as a ready supply of unskilled labor, usually performing the least desirable functions in the stables. In fact it has been shown conclusively that household serfs were far more numerous on corvée (barshchina) estates than on quitrent (*obrok*) manors. The existence of a demesne created greater administrative demands and required some serfs to devote full time to inventorying, storing, and marketing grain.[5] And the presence of directly cultivated estate lands made some limited commercial animal husbandry possible, which engaged about thirty to forty of the household serfs at Petrovskoe (see table 1).

These serfs and their families were entirely supported by the estate. They did not work the demesne or an allotment of peasant land but instead received a monthly grain ration. Most working males were also given one and a half to two rubles a month for *kharchi* (nongrain food purchases), an annual salary, and a sheepskin coat and caftan every three years. Female household serfs were often required to spin flax, for which they were paid. A number of their children also worked in the estate cloth factory until it ceased operating in the 1820s. Widows on rare occasions served as shepherds. The diet of the household serfs was supplemented from their own household gardens, and housing and outbuildings were provided by the estate. These serfs were also permitted to raise livestock, though they had little need for horses and at one time were prohibited from hav-

---

5. B. G. Litvak, *Russkaia derevnia v reforme 1861 goda: Chernozemnyi tsentr, 1861–98 gg.* (Moscow, 1972), 46–50.

TABLE I

Occupations of Household Serfs (Males Only)

Occupation	1815	1827	1858
Assistant bailiff	1	1	—
Bookkeeper	1	1	1
Scribe	4	6	9
Overseer	—	2	—
Police official (*pristav*)	5	—	—
Assistant doctor	—	1	2
Forest guard	—	3	4
Carpenter	4	3	5
Blacksmith	—	3	—
Horse doctor	—	1	—
Saddlemaker	—	1	—
Stableman	27	38	16
Shepherd	9	11	—
Weaver	7	—	—
Machinist	—	—	1
Office guard	—	—	1
Various duties	4	1	15
Young or elderly with no specific duties	—	—	50
In service to the bailiff	—	3	2

Sources: TsGADA, f. 1262, op. 4, ch. 1, ed. khr. 74, 1815–16; ed. khr. 377,
September 1827; ch. 2, ed. khr. 862, June–August 1858.

ing them. Feed, mostly hay or grain husks and stalks, was supplied by the estate.

Though the household serfs were only 7 percent of the estate population (approximately 230 persons), they are of considerable interest because much is known about their diet and living conditions since the estate kept very detailed records of its grain and cash expenditures. These data both complement and confirm information about the life of the *krest'iane,* the field serfs, who were the overwhelming majority of the estate population.

Virtually all adult household serfs, including elderly persons and widows, received on a strict per capita basis two *puds* (72.2 pounds; one *pud* equals 36.1 pounds) of rye flour and one-quarter *chetverik* (a volume measure, one-quarter of which is approximately equal to 9 pounds) of either buckwheat groats or ground millet a month. Their children between the ages of six and sixteen, including orphans, got half that amount, but for those below age six no food was provided. Except for times of crisis, this was the standard food allotment and did not otherwise vary over the years for which estate records have been preserved.[6] Only two persons received any additional foods, one overseer and the bookkeeper being supplied with some wheat, oats, peas, and hempseed.

These rations supplied by the estate provided every household serf with 607 pounds of rye flour and 76 pounds of buckwheat groats or ground millet per year, after recalculating for the young children and few adults not given any grain directly. It has been estimated that on a diet consisting solely of coarsely ground cereal approximately 470 pounds of milled grain per person per year is the subsistence minimum, providing not only adequate carbohydrates but most essential protein as well.[7] The household serfs of Petrovskoe with their allowance of 1.9 pounds of milled cereal per day were thus well above this minimum, consuming per capita at least 2,100 calories in grain alone.

Unfortunately, there is no detailed information on the livestock holdings of the household serfs, but it is certain that they were able to supplement their diet either by purchasing meat and other food products or by investing their salaries in domestic animals. In the early part of the nineteenth century usually only widows and orphans were given an additional monthly cash allowance to purchase foods other than grain. But beginning in 1819 most adult males received a cash allowance for nongrain food purchases, a policy that then persisted on the estate for over forty years. In 1827 the estate paid out 3,096 rubles in salaries to these male and female serf workers and an additional 1,608 rubles for buying food, or a per capita

6. TsGADA, f. 1262, op. 4, ch. 1, ed. khr. 20, 1811–12; ed. khr. 29, 1812–13; ed. khr. 44, 1813–14; ed. khr. 58, 1814; ed. khr. 61, 1814–15; ed. khr. 74, 1815–16; ed. khr. 137, 1819–20; ed. khr. 210, 1822–23; ed. khr. 233, 1823–24; ed. khr. 377, 1827; ed. khr. 415, 1828–29; ch. 2, ed. khr. 649, l. 46–47, 1855; and ed. khr. 866, l. 62–65, 1859.

7. Clark and Haswell, *Economics*, 53–54. See also E. C. Albritton, ed., *Standard Values in Nutrition and Metabolism* (Washington, D.C., 1954), tables 27–32, 68, 72, 80.

TABLE 2

Number of Household Serfs (Male and Female) Receiving Salaries and Kharchi, with Mean and Median Ruble Levels (by Agricultural Year)

	Salaries			Kharchi		
	Number of Household Serfs	Rubles per Year		Number of Household Serfs	Rubles per Year	
Years	Receiving Salaries	Mean	Median	Receiving Kharchi	Mean	Median
1811–12	—	—	—	14	17.13	10.80
1812–13	80	10.98	3.00	—	—	—
1813–14	54	17.53	10.00	16	13.18	19.80
1814–15	63	15.40	10.00	6	12.60	16.20
1815–16	63	14.00	10.00	4	14.40	10.80
1819–20	125	26.25	20.00	59	16.10	6.00
1822–23	159	38.28	10.00	78	22.42	24.00
1823–24	122	42.40	12.00	75	23.33	18.00
1827	86	36.01	30.00	66	24.36	24.00

Sources: TSGADA, f. 1262, op. 4, ch. 1, ed. khr. 20, 1811–12; ed. khr. 29, 1812–13; ed. khr. 44, 1813–14; ed. khr. 61, 1814–15; ed. khr. 74, 1815–16; ed. khr. 137, 1819–20; ed. khr. 210, 1822–23; ed. khr. 233, 1823–24; and ed. khr. 377, 1827.
Note: A number of children were employed in the estate cloth factory when it was first established sometime between 1816 and 1819, which accounts for the sharp increase in the total number of persons receiving salaries. In 1826 the factory was moved to another Gargarin estate, and the children therefore were no longer paid.

average of 19.76 rubles for each of the 238 household serfs, including children and the elderly (see table 2). In 1854 the income (salaries and kharchi) per capita for household serfs was 22.71 rubles.[8] This money, of course, was in addition to grain and clothing allowances. The household serfs did not pay any taxes themselves, since the financial obligations levied per soul were redistributed among the field serfs. This was a common practice on serf estates because the government held the owner responsible only for the total amount of taxes due. Although the assessment was made per soul, the state seemed little concerned with how the taxes were actually collected, in sharp contrast to the original intent of the law enacted by Peter

8. TsGADA, f. 1262, op. 4, ch. 1, ed. khr. 377, 1827; and ed. khr. 649, 1854–55.

the Great. Thus the figures above are for disposable in.....
and with a mean household size of 7.9 persons these serfs had
over 150 rubles to spend annually per household.

The records of the estate give little indication of what the
household serfs did with their money, though clothes, bast for
shoes, household implements, and church offerings were necessary expenses. Also, most of these serfs raised livestock, a form
of savings that provided them with eggs, milk, butter, and
meat.[9] Information on local commodity prices suggests that
with their ruble income the household serfs would certainly
have been able to balance their predominantly cereal diet with
more than adequate amounts of fats and meat protein. In fact
meat and poultry prices were low, with beef, mutton, and
whole slaughtered pigs per pud only two to four times the cost
of rye flour (see table 3). Elsewhere in Europe meat prices were
often twelve times those of cereal. With a per capita kharchi of
6.76 rubles in 1827, even if every household serf used only half
that amount to buy meat, each could have purchased approximately forty to fifty pounds annually. In all likelihood, consumption of meat was much higher. By way of comparison, in
the first half of the nineteenth century annual per capita meat
consumption in the area of the future German empire was no
more than thirty-five pounds.[10]

At Petrovskoe, fats and oils were the most expensive nutrients required for a balanced diet, but since only small
amounts were needed daily, the household serfs should have
suffered no deficiency, especially given the availability of salt
pork. However, imported luxuries such as sugar and tea were
very costly and probably used rarely if at all. Finally, it should
be kept in mind that the garden adjacent to every farmstead
provided fruits and vegetables as well as hempseed for oil.

For the field serfs, 93 percent of the estate population, it
is much more difficult to evaluate food intake, though there are
generally good data on grain yields, land allotments, and livestock holdings.

---

9. TsGADA, f. 1262, op. 4, ch. 2, ed. khr. 862, 1856, l. 6.
10. H. J. Teuteberg, "The General Relationship between Diet and Industrialization," in *European Diet from Pre-Industrial to Modern Times*, ed.
Elborg Forster and Robert Forster (New York, 1975), 77.

TABLE 3
Local Prices by Agricultural Year (in Assignats/Pud unless Specified)

Product	1811–12	1812–13	1813–14	1814–15	1815–16	1816–17	1817–18	1818–19	1819–20	1820–21	1821–22	1822–23	1823–24	1824–25	1825–26	1826–27	1827–28
Rye/chetvert'	7.00	4.70			6.60		4.60	(7.75)			10.00	(4.80)	2.60	(4.20)	(3.00)	(4.30)	(3.78)
Rye flour					0.88		1.00	1.53	1.00				0.50				
Millet/chetvert'					17.11	7.00	10.00	(12.00)	15.00		20.00	16.00	8.00	12.00	8.70	9.50	8.90
Buckwheat/chetvert'	(5.50)	(8.00)		(4.90)	4.45				5.00	(8.50)				(3.85)			
Oats/chetvert'	3.21	4.00			4.90		4.23	2.75	3.10		5.58	2.46	2.40	1.80	2.80	3.90	4.00
Hay	0.45	0.33					0.55	0.42	0.85		0.48	0.43	0.40	0.40	0.37	0.43	0.45
Beef							2.26	2.62									2.16
Ham			6.00		6.00	6.00	5.33	4.00	7.33		5.89	6.00	6.00				
Slaughtered pig	3.58	3.00										6.06					
Mutton				4.15			4.00	2.00	2.40		1.12	1.60					
Hemp oil					10.75	10.00	14.27	12.00									
Butter			11.50					10.00					8.80	7.20		8.66	
Salt	1.00	1.25	0.93	1.10	1.20	1.10	1.22	1.13	1.53		1.50	1.70	1.72			2.00	
Sugar/funt							1.60	1.53	1.60			1.25					
Tea/funt	3.50	3.50	9.50				9.00	9.50	7.50				4.20				
Sheep/head								7.25									
Chicken/head			0.20				0.30					0.25					
Geese/head							0.60										
Turkey/head							0.80										
Duck/head							0.40										
Linen/arshin	0.60					0.25	0.25										
Coarse, heavy cloth/arshin		0.57						0.59									
Wool					11.50	11.50	10.25	9.37			6.50	5.45	2.70				
Boots/pair	7.00									6.50	6.00			5.40			

Source: TsGADA, f. 1262. op. 4, ch. 1, ed. khr. 20, 29, 44, 61, 74, 94, 101, 123, 137, 190, 210, 233, 273; for the data in parentheses, Kh. Kozlov, "Tseny raznykh produktov v 1796–1856 godakh," *Ekonomicheskii ukazatel'*, no. 35 (1857): 805–12. Kozlov's prices are for Borisoglebsk district in Tambov.

It was widely agreed that in the six provinces of the central agricultural region two *desiatinas* of plowland per *tiaglo* (usually a husband and wife work team) in each of the three fields (winter, spring, and fallow) was the standard peasant allotment. Unfortunately, there were two kinds of desiatinas commonly used as land measures in nineteenth-century Russia, *desiatinas kazennye,* or *ukaznoi mery* (state or statutory measure), equal to 2,400 square *sazhens* (2.7 acres in all), and *desiatinas khoziaistvennye* (agricultural), which were one-third larger (3.6 acres). Desiatinas of statutory measure were often called desiatinas of thirty, since they were usually 30 sazhens in width and 80 in length, whereas agricultural desiatinas were 40 sazhens wide. Frequently, contemporaries confused these two land measures or failed to distinguish between them.[11]

The confusion arose because in practice a desiatina was often simply ten strips of land, though this does not seem to have been its original meaning. According to one observer, when the peasants met to distribute the plowlands, they divided themselves into groups of ten to facilitate the process. First lots were drawn by group for desiatinas, then within each group for strips.[12] If the fields permitted, the length of a strip was fixed at roughly 80 sazhens (560 feet), supposedly the distance a horse could plow without having to stop for rest. But the width of a strip—the number of furrows—could vary, though by the nineteenth century strips of 3 to 4 sazhens (21 to 28 feet) were most common.

The Lebedian Agricultural Society, established in 1847 and chartered to operate in Tambov, Voronezh, Tula, Orel, and Riazan' provinces, took a great interest in the size of peasant allotments and demesne obligations. When the society sent out a questionnaire to its members, one landlord wrote back in 1848: "Under the local conditions of Tambov province, Borisoglebsk district, one peasant tiaglo cultivates in each field for itself and for the lord four desiatinas (30 *meras*) without

---

11. D. P. Zhuravskii, *Ob istochnikakh i upotreblenii svedenii* (Kiev, 1846), 115.
12. V. Babarykin, "Sel'tso Vasil'evskoe, Nizhegorodskoi gubernii, Nizhegorodskago uezda," *ES* 1 (1853):12–13.

any exhaustion."¹³ Thus a peasant tiaglo would have six desiatinas (16.2 acres) including the two in the fallow field, each
of 2,400 square sazhens, on which to support itself, while tilling an equal amount for the lord. At the society's annual meeting in 1850, the unanimous opinion of the persons present was
that "two desiatinas of thirty in a field per tiaglo is customary"; "a two-desiatina proportion between peasant allotment
and demesne is common in our region and is accepted as the
norm by all landlords"; "in our black-earth provinces, we find
a two-desiatina proportion in each field correct"; and "two
desiatinas per field is customary everywhere, but where land is
abundant the lords give the peasants somewhat more."¹⁴ By
1857, however, these evaluations were slightly modified. On
rich, black lands that were easy to plow and required no manuring, it was now felt that one tiaglo could easily work three
desiatinas (each of 2,400 square sazhens) for the lord and three
for itself per field. Only if the land were naturally less fertile
and needed manuring once every nine to twelve years—in rotation, of course—would a reduction to two desiatinas per field
be necessary.¹⁵ Therefore, according to the society, which used
the smaller, statutory desiatina as the basis for measurement, in
any one year a tiaglo could be cultivating from 10.8 to 16.2
acres for its own use, excluding the field lying fallow.

However, two statutory desiatinas per field per tiaglo was
more probably the minimum peasant allotment than the mean.
In 1858 one landlord living in a district bordering that of the
Petrovskoe estate noted: "Almost all the peasants of Tambov
district on corvée receive 2.5 statutory desiatinas in each field
from their lords, very rarely two and, some are even given three
desiatinas."¹⁶ For the serfs of the neighboring district of Kirsanov, just a few miles from Petrovskoe, five statutory de-

13. Kh. Kozlov, "Khoziaistvennye voprosy," *ZLOSKh za 1848* (1849),
89.
14. *ZLOSKh za 1850* (1851), 90–91.
15. *ZLOSKh za 1857* (1858), 247–48. See also *Obozrenie Deistvii
Lebedianskago Obshchestva Sel'skago Khoziaistva za pervoe desiatiletie s
1847 po 1857 god* (Moscow, 1858), 21.
16. I. R. Gruzinov, "Byt krest'ianina Tambovskoi gubernii," *Zhurnal
zemlevladel'tsev* 2, no. 5, part 6 (1858):7; see also idem, "Vozmozhnost'" uluchsheniia byta pomeshchich'ikh krest'ian (Tambovskoi gubernii)," *Zhurnal
zemlevladel'tsev* 4, no. 13, part 4 (1858):20–21.

siatinas per tiaglo in all three fields was considered insufficient to support a serf household. Six desiatinas (16.2 acres) was common, but only on estates where land was not plentiful. Seven was thought adequate, eight comfortable, and more than eight was unknown.[17] Peasants in the village of Tarbeevka, Spassk district, Tambov province, received three desiatinas in each field per tiaglo from their lord. The parish priest of the villages of Golun' and Novomikhailovskoe, 220 miles directly west of Petrovskoe in Tula province, wrote that serf tiaglos there had two agricultural desiatinas in each field, or 14.4 acres for cultivation, with another 7.2 in the fallow field.[18]

In the early 1820s, on the estate of M. S. Lunin in Kirsanov district, just twenty-five miles from Petrovskoe, the peasants had access to 7.26 desiatinas per tiaglo in three fields from their lord. But the serfs rented an additional 1.7 desiatinas of arable land per tiaglo from nearby lords, though the three-field system was not always observed on these lands. Unfortunately the author of the article on this estate, the historian B. D. Grekov, who later confined his scholarship to the medieval period, never stated which of the two types of desiatinas he was referring to. But because he was researching estate records, especially of the 1820s, and not government documents or official publications, it is more likely that the larger agricultural desiatina was the basis of measurement. Thus Lunin's peasants were probably tilling a total of 17.4 acres of land in the winter and spring fields, with 8.7 acres of fallow, not including the plowlands they leased. If the statutory desiatina was the measure, then the correct acreage under crops would be 13.1, with another 6.5 fallow.[19] Similarly, the Soviet historian A. N. Nasonov, writing about the estates of the Iusupov family in Kursk, Voronezh, Kharkov, and Poltava provinces, states that the average serf holding per tiaglo fluctuated from 6.24 to 8.40

17. M. N. Kishkin, "Dannye i predpolozheniia po voprosu ob uluchshenii byta krest'ian v Kirsanovskom uezde, Tambovskoi gubernii," *Sel'skoe blagoustroistvo,* no. 1 (1859):234–35.
18. *ZLOSKh za 1851* (1852), 390–92; A. Rudnev, "Selo Golun' i Novomikhailovsloe, Tul'skoi gubernii, Novosil'skago uezda," *ES* 2 *(1854):106.*
19. B. D. Grekov, "Tambovskoe imenie M. S. Lunina v pervoi chetverti XIX v. (material k voprosu o razlozhenii krepostnoi sistemy khoziaistva," *Izvestiia,* Akademiia Nauk SSSR, *Otdelenie obshchestvennykh nauk,* ser. 7, no. 6 (1933):489–90.

desiatinas between the years 1831 and 1846, without specify-
ing the precise land measure.[20]

However, all these statements on the size of peasant allotments, though in all probability reasonably accurate, mask the
confusion in the fields that was the logical result of strip farming, the periodic redistribution of both peasant plowlands and
the demesne, and poorly and infrequently surveyed estates. In
Petrovskoe, at least, the bailiffs were never sure precisely how
much land the peasants had. Surveys were made irregularly,
with intervals as long as seventeen years, and the results invari-
ably showed that the bailiffs had underestimated serf holdings
by 5 to 10 percent. Obviously, over the years the peasants wid-
ened their strips at the expense of adjacent demesne, pasture,
and long-fallow land. As late as 1837 the bailiff of Petrovskoe
was pleading with his superiors in Moscow: "A surveyor is
vitally needed on this estate, for the estate fields are so mixed
up with those of the peasants that even the very sowers of estate
cereals scarcely know what's what."[21] Twenty years later, in
1857, another surveyor was requested for the same reason.[22]

On a few occasions, documents summarizing land usage
on the Petrovskoe estate simply noted that each tiaglo was
given the requisite six agricultural desiatinas (21.6 acres) to
cultivate for itself in all three fields as estate policy dictated.[23]
But after every detailed land survey it became clear that the
serfs regularly had access to 6.2 to 6.6 agricultural desiatinas
(22.3 to 23.8 acres) per tiaglo, including at least some long-
fallow lands, arable lands not part of the three-field rotation.

20. A. N. Nasonov, "Khoziaistvo krupnoi votchiny nakanune os-
vobozhdeniia krest'ian v Rossii," *Izvestiia,* Akademiia Nauk SSSR, *Otdelenie
Gumanitarnykh nauk,* ser. 7, nos. 4–7 (1928):346–47. See also A. N. Nasonov,
"Iz istorii krepostnoi votchiny XIX veka v Rossii," *Izvestiia,* Akademiia Nauk
SSSR, ser. 7, nos. 7–8 (1926):505–6.

21. TsGADA, f. 1262, op. 4, ch. 1, ed. khr. 558, 14 June 1837.

22. TsGADA, f. 1262, op. 4, ch. 2, ed. khr. 846, 15 October 1857 and 20
May 1858.

23. TsGADA, f. 1262, op. 4, ch. 1, ed. khr. 121, 1 January 1818, l. 60–
61; ed. khr. 161, 19 July 1820, l. 1–2; ch. 2, ed. khr. 906, 1848, l. 44–48; ed.
khr. 866, 22 May 1859. The Petrovskoe documents clearly state that agricultural desiatinas are the measure being used. Even if this were not so, it would
be obvious from the sources, since fractions of statutory desiatinas could not
exceed 2,400 square sazhens, while agricultural desiatinas could have as many as
3,200 square sazhens.

Thus, in 1810 the actual allotment was 6.6 desiatinas; in 1827, 6.3; in 1843, 6.3; in 1849, 6.25; and in 1859, 6.6.[24] Only once is there any evidence that serf holdings ever fell below 6 agricultural desiatinas per tiaglo. In 1857 a surveyor hired by the estate was instructed to allot the peasants only 5.75 desiatinas, though within a few months each tiaglo was given an additional quarter-desiatina.[25] Nevertheless, even after the land survey, the situation in the fields remained confusing. During the spring planting of 1858 the bailiff discovered, much to his surprise, an excess of more than 440 desiatinas (almost 1,600 acres) of arable land after providing each tiaglo with the requisite amount of demesne and peasant land. And as it turned out, most of this extra land the serfs cultivated for themselves. The source of the problem was the nonstandardized desiatina, which persisted in being ten strips rather than a fixed area of land. "The division of land into desiatinas is very irregular in the peasants' fields," the bailiff wrote in 1859, again requesting permission to hire a surveyor.[26]

It should be kept in mind, however, that "very irregular" was in fact an error of only 5.3 percent on an estate with over 27,000 acres of arable land. The total income lost to the estate could, of course, be substantial or the benefits to each serf household significant. But the bailiffs always had a very good idea, though never an exact one, of how much land was being tilled for the lord and for the support of the peasants. On the whole, it does not seem unreasonable to conclude that between the years 1810 and 1859 the serfs of Petrovskoe annually cultivated no less than 14.4 acres of plowland per tiaglo and no more than 15.8, not counting the fallow, or from 21.6 to 23.8 acres in all, including the fallow. These figures assume minimum and maximum allotments of 6.0 and 6.6 agricultural desiatinas per tiaglo in all three fields combined. Clearly, there

---

24. TsGADA, f. 1262, op. 4, ch. 1, ed. khr. 256, 1 May 1810; op. 4, ch. 1, ed. khr. 369, 1827–28; ed. khr. 615, December 1843–April 1844, l. 5–11; op. 1, ch. 1, ed. khr. 2830a, 1849, l. 2–3; op. 4, ch. 2, ed. khr. 866, 22 May 1859. The sources from which these figures are drawn are land surveys of the estate and detailed inventories made either upon the passing of the estate to an heir or upon the owner's attaining his majority.

25. TsGADA, f. 1262, op. 4, ch. 2, ed. khr. 846, 22 May 1858.

26. TsGADA, f. 1262, op. 4, ch. 2, ed. khr. 866, 22 May 1859.

was no shortage of arable land on the estate, with slightly more than 500 agricultural desiatinas of long-fallow land during the 1820s and over 800 during the 1840s, the only times for which data were available. Thus Petrovskoe serfs were adequately provided with land, and their allotments were well in line with serf holdings elsewhere in the region.[27]

The archives of the Petrovskoe estate provide no information on grain yields for peasant lands. However, for the demesne it is possible to determine not only seed/yield ratios but yields in terms of quintals and hectoliters per hectare, these being better indicators of the level of agricultural intensification, though some error necessarily ensues given the inadequacies of land surveying. Table 4 presents the yields on estate grainfields for the period 1811–60, using all three measures. Tables 5 and 6 compare these yields with published data for other serf manors or peasant villages in the southern districts of Tambov province or the southern part of the central agricultural region.

The figures reveal both sharp annual fluctuations and marked local differences within the region. For example, the yields reported for the village of Mokhovoe in neighboring Tula province were more than double those of Petrovskoe and Vataryno in Tambov. Nevertheless, the data from these eleven

27. By way of further comparison, data collected by the government just before the emancipation on the twenty-nine barshchina estates in Borisoglebsk district with over one hundred male serfs reveal the following: on seventeen estates, the serfs had from 16.2 to 18.9 acres of arable land per tiaglo (including the fallow); on five estates, from 19.0 to 21.6 acres per tiaglo; and on seven estates over 21.6 acres per tiaglo. The circumstances in which these data were collected, however, encouraged landlords and stewards to understate the true amount. The managers of the Gagarin estates viewed the government's request for information on peasant land usage with great suspicion, though they mistakenly believed it was related to state mortgage loans against Petrovskoe and not to the impending emancipation. The bailiff of Petrovskoe misreported to the government that peasant allotments of arable land were only 16.2 acres per tiaglo in all three fields, approximately one-third less than the true amount. Perhaps all that can be said for these official figures is that taken together they might show the upper limits of peasant allotments, since presumably some landlords must have told the truth. *Prilozheniia k trudam Redaktsionnykh komissii dlia sostavleniia Polozheniia o krest'ianakh, vykhodiashchikh iz krepostnoi zavisimosti. Svedeniia po pomeshchich'im imeniiam*, vol. 3 (Saint Petersburg, 1860). Tambovskaia guberniia, 12–17, and TsGADA, f. 1262, op. 4, ch. 2, ed. khr. 846, 1857, l. 4; ed. khr. 862, 1858, l. 3.

TABLE 4
Estate Grain Yields, 1811–60

Years	Rye			Oats			Buckwheat			Millet
	Seed/Yield	Quintals/Hectare	Hectoliters/Hectare	Seed/Yield	Quintals/Hectare	Hectoliters/Hectare	Seed/Yield	Quintals/Hectare	Hectoliters/Hectare	Seed/Yield
1811–20	4.9	6.4	9.5	4.6	7.1	18.5	4.8	5.2	8.6	—
1821–30	7.4	9.9	14.5	5.9	9.2	23.7	5.0	5.4	9.0	—
1831–40	5.7	7.6	11.1	4.3	6.7	17.2	4.6	4.9	8.2	—
1840–49	6.5	—	—	5.5	—	—	6.3	—	—	22.6
1851–52, 1855–60	6.5	8.7	12.8	4.4	6.9	17.9	3.1	3.4	5.7	—
Average	6.2	8.2	12.0	4.9	7.5	19.3	4.8	4.7	7.9	—

Sources: Data for 1840–49 from TsGADA, f. 1262, op. 1, ch. 1, ed. khr. 283oa (1849). For the other years, the figures are from the annual harvest records of the estate. See I. D. Koval'chenko, *Krest'iane i krepostnoe khoziaistvo Riazanskoi i Tambovskoi gubernii v pervoi polovine XIX veka* (Moscow, 1959), 83.

Note: Except for 1840–49, seed yield ratios assume that 1.36 chetverts of rye, 2.81 of oats, and 1.25 of buckwheat were sown per agricultural desiatina. These figures are the mean sown per agricultural desiatina for seven years between 1816 and 1858. Also, since grain was measured in chetverts, a volume measure, weight per chetvert' varied depending upon the cereal and seed size. Over the years, rye averaged 143 kilograms per chetvert', oats 81 kilograms, and buckwheat 126 kilograms.

TABLE 5

Average Grain Yields (Hectoliters/Hectare)

Locality	Years	Yields		
		Rye	Oats	Buckwheat
Petrovskoe, Borisoglebsk district, Tambov province	1811–60	12.0	19.3	7.9
Vataryno, Lebedian' district, Tambov province	1825–50	10.3	20.7	9.0
Nizhedevits district, Voronezh province	1843–49	14.1	29.9	8.2
Mokhovoe, Novosil' district, Tula province	1834–49	23.6	49.0	19.5

Sources: Table 4 and *Zapiski Lebedianskago obshchestva sel'skago khoziaistva za 1850* (1851), 204–5; *za 1851* (1852), 26–29; *za 1852*, (1853), 86.

localities, including Petrovskoe, reflect a level of agricultural productivity common throughout much of contemporary Europe. A 1:6–7 return on rye or a harvest of 8–9 quintals per hectare was the average in Denmark and France in the eighteenth century and in Germany to the mid-nineteenth century. For oats, a seed/yield ratio of 5 was the norm during the 1700s in Germany and not unheard of in France, though by the 1820s yields had improved to over 7.[28]

For those familiar with the history of Russian agriculture, the grain yields observed for Petrovskoe and elsewhere may seem surprisingly high. But in fact the belief that Russia suffered from relatively low agricultural productivity, with average yields of 3.5, "lower than those of any European nation," is quite simply incorrect.[29] Most such assessments, especially by Soviet historians eager, it seems, to minimize seed/yield ratios, have relied upon official data annually reported by the governor of each province. Some Western scholars have accept-

28. B. H. Slicher van Bath, *The Agrarian History of Western Europe, A.D. 500–1800* (London, 1963), 280–81, 331–33; Jerome Blum, *The End of the Old Order in Europe* (Princeton, 1978), 144–45.
29. Blum, *Lord and Peasant*, 330.

TABLE 6

Seed/Yield Ratios (1:x) (Nongovernment Published Sources)

	Rye			Oats			Buckwheat			Millet			Period of Observation
	Avg.	Min.	Max.	Avg.	Min.	Max.	Avg.	Min.	Max.	Avg.	Min.	Max.	
Tambov province													
Petrovskoe, Borisoglebsk district[a]	6.2	—	—	4.9	—	—	4.8	—	—	—	—	—	1811–60
Borisoglebsk district[b]	14.0	—	—	—	—	—	—	—	—	—	—	—	1853, 1855–56
Tambov district[c]	9.3	—	—	8.8	—	—	9.1	—	—	25.7	—	—	Not specified
Lunin estate, Kirsanov district[d]	8.6	7.2	9.6	5.2	2.7	8.0	5.8	0.3	12.0	24.9	13.9	40.6	1823–25
Kirsanov district[e]	8.0	—	—	4.6	—	—	7.0	—	—	—	—	—	Not specified
Voronezh province													
Nizhedevits district[f]	8.0	—	—	—	—	—	8.0	—	—	15.0	—	—	Not specified
Kursk province													
Iusupov estates[g]	6.4	2.0	10.8	5.4	2.0	8.0	3.9	0.0	9.5	—	—	—	1831–59
Oboian' district[h]	—	—	15.0	—	—	13.0	—	—	12.0	—	—	60.0	Best years

[a]See table 4.

[b]Zapiski Lebedianskago obshchestva sel'skago khoziaistva za 1853 (1854), 196–97; za 1855 (1856), 270–73; za 1856 (1857), 81–83.

[c]I. R. Gruzinov, "Byt krest'ianina Tambovskoi gubernii," Zhurnal zemlevladel'tsev 2, no. 5, part 6 (1858): 8.

[d]B. D. Grekov, "Tambovskoe imenie M. S. Lunina v pervoi chetverti XIX v.," Izvestiia, Akademiia Nauk SSSR, Otdelenie obshchestvennykh nauk, ser. 7, no. 6 (1933): 493.

[e]M. N. Kishkin, "Dannye i predpolozheniia po voprosu ob uluchshenii byta krest'ian v Kirsanovskom uezde, Tambovskoi gubernii," Sel'skoe blagoustroistvo, no. 1 (1859): 229.

[f]P. Malykhin, "Byt krest'ian Voronezhskoi gubernii, Nizhnedevitskago uezda," Etnograficheskii sbornik 1 (1853): 229.

[g]A. N. Nasonov, "Khoziaistvo krupnoi votchiny nakanune osvobozhdeniia krest'ian," Izvestiia, Akademiia Nauk SSR, Otdelenie gumanitarnykh nauk, ser. 7 nos. 4–7 (1928): 350.

[h]Mashkin, "Byt krest'ian Kurskoi gubernii, Oboianskago uezda," Etnograficheskii sbornik 5 (1862): 95–96.

ed these figures as well.[30] But numerous bureaucrats, landlords, and contemporary scholars were extremely critical of the governors' figures or other official data.[31] Many landlords, fearful of increased military demands for cereals and forage, purposely underestimated the size of the harvest, a practice particularly widespread in the central agricultural region.[32] The local police, responsible for the collecting of official data from sample areas, viewed this as a duty of secondary importance[33] and in all likelihood were easily bribed. Equally, the governors' reports, which were due on 1 January each year, failed to include grain threshed after the New Year, often a considerable portion of the harvest.[34]

There was, indeed, virtually universal agreement among contemporaries that government figures were too low. According to the results of the 1765 questionnaire of the Free Economic Society, the average yield in European Russia was 4.9.[35] Subsequent articles in the society's *Transactions* (*Trudy*) sug-

---

30. A. S. Nifontov, *Zernovoe proizvodstvo Rossii vo vtoroi polovine XIX veka* (Moscow, 1974), 61, 72–76, 121–23, 275, in a detailed study of governors' reports and data of the Ministry of Internal Affairs and Ministry of State Domains for the 1850s, estimates a seed/yield ratio of 3.5 for all European Russia. Between the years 1780 and 1796 (minus 1781 and 1784) the average ratio in Russia was 3.2, according to the governors' reports. N. A. Rubinshtein, *Sel'skoe khoziaistvo Rossii vo vtoroi polovine XVIII v.* (Moscow, 1957), 355–56. For the intervening years see Koval'chenko, *Russkoe krepostnoe khoziaistvo,* who shows rather constant yield ratios of 3.4 for over half a century. Similar results, using the governors' reports, can also be found in V. K. Iatsunskii, "Izmeneniia v razmeshchenii zemledeliia v Evropeiskoi Rossii s kontsa XVIII v. do pervoi mirovoi voiny," in *Voprosy istorii sel'skogo khoziaistva, krest'ianstva, i revoliutsionnogo dvizheniia v Rossii* (Moscow, 1961); V. A. Fedorov, *Pomeshchich'i krest'iane tsentral'no-promyshlennogo raiona Rossii kontsa XVIII–pervoi poloviny XIX v.* (Moscow, 1974), 39. See also N. M. Druzhinin, *Gosudarstvennye krest'iane i reforma P. D. Kiseleva* (Moscow, 1958), 2:350, and P. I. Liashchenko, *Istoriia narodnogo khoziaistva SSSR* (Moscow, 1947), 1:522, for identical estimates of grain yields.

31. See Nifontov, *Zernovoe proizvodstvo,* 16–34, for an overview of nineteenth-century opinion on the validity of government agricultural statistics.

32. Zhuravskii, *Ob istochnikakh,* passim; Rubinshtein, *Sel'skoe khoziaistvo,* 358.

33. N. S. Golitsyn, "O merakh k ustroistvu statisticheskikh istochnikov i rabot v Rossii," *ZhMVD* 3 (1860):9; Zhuravskii, *Ob istochnikakh,* 157.

34. Kuz'min, *Voenno-statisticheskoe obozrenie Rossiiskoi Imperii,* vol. 13, part 1, *Tambovskaia guberniia* (Saint Petersburg, 1851), 63.

35. Rubinshtein, *Sel'skoe khoziaistvo,* 355–56.

gest an average seed/yield ratio of 5.[36] Similarly, the topographical descriptions compiled by the army during the 1780s show an average harvest of 5.[37] During the nineteenth century D. V. Bludov and P. A. Valuev, both ministers of internal affairs, as well as P. P. Semenov, director of the Central Statistical Committee, expressed serious doubts about the accuracy of official agricultural data.[38] I. I. Vil'son, editor of a widely cited agricultural-statistical atlas first published in the early 1850s, felt that while the governors' reports might be used to determine general trends in grain yields, the reported absolute levels for cereals sown and harvested were dubious, with figures for the black-earth region in particular much too low. In other words, the governors consistently underestimated yields by roughly the same proportion. In the fourth edition of his atlas, Vil'son assumed a seed/yield ratio of 4.5 for winter cereals and 4 for spring crops as the average for European Russia during the 1850s and 1860s in attempting to calculate the size of the total harvest.[39] In studies of various provinces by the General Staff of the army, official figures were also repeatedly criticized for underestimating grain yields.[40] The statistician L. V. Tengoborskii claimed government estimates of the harvest should be increased by approximately 10 percent.[41] Nevertheless, table 7 shows that for Tambov province the General Staff and

36. See Confino, *Domaines et seigneurs,* 124–25.
37. Rubinshtein, *Sel'skoe khoziaistvo,* 355–56.
38. See Nifontov, *Zernovoe proizvodstvo,* 17–21, 25–26.
39. I. I. Vil'son, *Ob'iasneniia k khoziaistvenno-statisticheskomu atlasu Evropeiskoi Rossii,* 4th ed. (Saint Petersburg, 1869), 75–113.
40. Glavnyi General'nyi Shtab, *Materialy dlia geografii i statistiki Rossii, sobrannye ofitserami General'nago Shtaba,* 25 vols. (Saint Petersburg, 1859–69). M. Domontovich, *Chernigovskaia guberniia* (1865), 183; A. Zashchuk, *Bessarabskaia oblast'* (1862), 230, 233–34; I. Zelenskii, *Minskaia guberniia* (1864), part 2, 14; A. Korevo, *Vilenskaia guberniia* (1861), 443 and 451; A. Lipinskii, *Simbirskaia guberniia* (1868), 336, 400; V. Mikhalevich, *Voronezhskaia guberniia* (1862), 77; and M. Tsebrikov, *Smolenskaia guberniia* (1862), 193.
41. L. V. Tengoborskii, *O proizvoditel'nykh silakh Rossii* (Moscow, 1854), 1:198–99. See also K. S. Veselovskii, "Neskol'ko dannykh dlia statistiki urozhaev i neurozhaev v Rossii," *ZhMGI* 52, part 1 (1857):26–27, who thought that long-run analyses of various estate records would give a more accurate idea of grain yields than would data supplied by the Ministry of State Domains.

TABLE 7

Seed Yield Ratios, Tambov Province (Archival and Official Government Sources)

Source	Winter Cereals	Spring Cereals	All Cereals
Annual governors' reports[a]			
1806–15	4.03	3.47	3.75
1841–50	4.09	3.58	3.85
1851–60	3.89	3.20	3.45
Partial land survey,[b]			
Borisoglebsk district (34 estates and villages)	7.5	8.4	

Source	Rye		Oats		Buckwheat		Millet	
	Avg.	Max.	Avg.	Max.	Avg.	Max.	Avg.	Max.
Journal of the Ministry of Internal Affairs[c] (15–20-year averages)								
Northern districts	—	7	—	—	—	—	—	—
Southern districts	—	10–12	—	—	—	5	—	25
All districts	5	—	<5	10+	5	11+	25	70+

	Rye			Winter Wheat			Oats			Buckwheat			Millet		
	Avg.	Min.	Max.	Avg.	Min.	Max.	Avg.	Min.	Max.	Avg.	Min.	Max.	Avg.	Min.	Max.
Army General Staff[d]															
Northern district	—	—	6–7	—	—	—	—	—	—	—	—	—	—	—	—
Southern district	—	—	10–12	—	—	—	—	—	—	—	—	—	—	—	—
Governors' reports	4.9	—	—	—	—	—	3.3	—	—	—	—	—	—	—	—
Estate records	5.5	1.5	12	5.8	1.3	11	4.9	2.5	10	4.7	0.0	10.3	25.5	0.0	65
(13–23-year averages)															

[a] I. D. Koval'chenko, *Krest'iane i krepostnoe khoziaistvo Riazanskoi i Tambovskoi gubernii v pervoi polovine XIX veka* (Moscow, 1959), 39.

[b] TsGADA, f. 1357, op. 4, ed. khr. 1/211. Compiled between 1850 and 1853.

[c] "Ocherki Tambovskoi gubernii v statisticheskom otnoshenii," *ZhMVD*, no. 7, part 3 (1858): 41.

[d] Kuz'min, *Voenno-statisticheskoe obozrenie Rossiiskoi imperii*, vol. 13, part 1 (Saint Petersburg, 1851), 59–62.

the unknown author of an article in the official *Journal of the Ministry of Internal Affairs* held that seed/yield ratios were in fact from 25 to 40 percent above the figures reported by the governors and the Ministry of State Domains.[42] According to the so-called Mende Land Survey of the early 1850s, jointly conducted by the surveying corps of the Ministry of Justice, the Russian Geographic Society, and the General Staff, the average yield on thirty-four estates and villages in Borisoglebsk district (where Petrovskoe was situated) was 7.5 for winter crops and 8.4 for spring cereals, including millet. For Petrovskoe, the average seed/yield ratio was 8.5.[43] This figure, which is considerably above the observed level of estate grain yields presented in table 4, may reflect the effects of the much expanded cultivation of higher-yielding strains of wheat taking place at this time. Or quite simply, the time period the mean return was based on may have been rather short and coincidentally limited to above-average yields.

To conclude, official estimates for grain yields simply cannot be relied upon. For Russia as a whole, government figures consistently underestimated yields by as much as 30 percent. In the fertile grain-producing region where Petrovskoe was situated, the error was even greater. Data from individual serf estates, the Free Economic Society, the army, and the Russian Geographic Society all suggest yields comparable to those found in many places in Europe in the late eighteenth and early nineteenth centuries.

The bailiffs of Petrovskoe kept no records on the amount of peasants' arable land assigned to each of the various cereals the serfs cultivated for their own maintenance. But household grain inventories, though crudely measured in stacks or shocks, are a fair indicator of land usage (see table 8). Rye, a winter crop, was the peasants' main food and must have occupied most, if not all, of the winter field. Oats and millet, the pre-

---

42. Similarly, for Riazan' province, northwest of Tambov, the governors' reports show an average seed/yield ratio of 3.3 for the years 1841–59. But a landlord living in Ranenburg district, a fertile grain-producing region though not part of the rich steppe, wrote that the very worst return was 1:3. M. Semenov, "Khoziaistvennyia oshibki ot neurozhaia," *Zemledel'cheskii zhurnal* no. 6 (1840):448.

43. TsGADA, f. 1357, op. 4, ed. khr. 1/211, l. 3–4.

TABLE 8

Total Serf Household Grain Inventories, Village of Petrovskoe
(Measured in Stacks)

Grain	2 October 1813	1 January 1818	1 November 1856
Rye	2,114	1,680	4,166
Wheat	177	55	0
Oats	1,663	1,304	798
Millet	627	425	822
Buckwheat	152	10	15

Sources: TsGADA, f. 1262, op. 4, ch. 1, ed. khr. 41, 121; ch. 2, ed. khr. 822.
Note: In 1856 the spring cereal harvest, especially for buckwheat, was extremely poor
because of an August hailstorm. Besides the unthreshed cereals, for 1856, 922
puds of rye flour and 34.4 chetverts of ground millet were cited in the inventory—
very small amounts in relation to the rye and millet in stacks.

dominant spring cereals, could serve as both food and feed. Buckwheat, eaten as porridge, was probably more important than table 8 indicates, in all likelihood occupying as much as one-quarter of the spring field during the 1850s, but this remains uncertain. Peas and potatoes, which were raised in very small quantities on estate plowlands by midcentury, if cultivated by the serfs, were confined to the kitchen garden, along with vegetables and possibly flax. Hemp was grown in special enclosures adjoining each homestead, these being considered part of the household plot (*usad'ba*) as distinct from the allotted arable land.

Wheat, as is well known, was not a significant item in the diet of the nineteenth-century Russian peasant. Nevertheless, in October 1813 almost one-third of all the households in the village of Petrovskoe had some wheat, which was probably sown in the winter field.[44] In a 1 January 1818 inventory only five households possessed any wheat, though most of the small amounts that were grown may have already been sold or eaten by this time of year.[45] After 1818 there is no further evidence of wheat cultivation by the serfs on their allotted plowlands. A

44. TsGADA, f. 1262, op. 4, ch. 1, ed. khr. 41.
45. TsGADA, f. 1262, op. 4, ch. 1, ed. khr. 121.

grain inventory form used in February 1834 did not even provide a column for wheat as had the two previous inventory
documents.[46] A 1 November 1856 grain inventory showed no
wheat stored by any serf household on the entire estate.[47]

Though any conclusions must be tentative, since the evidence is far from conclusive, wheat, which was probably a cash
crop early in the century, rather quietly disappeared from the
serfs' fields for reasons that remain unclear. By the 1850s and
1860s few observers make any mention of serf wheat cultivation in the central agricultural region.[48] This decline in the
peasants' use of wheat, especially for cash income, is rather
surprising, since beginning in the 1830s this cereal became a
major source of revenue for the landlords of this region, largely
owing to the increased export of wheat from Black Sea ports.[49]
In 1854–55 wheat on the Petrovskoe estate was expected to
account for 32 percent of all cereal revenues, second only to
rye.[50] Equally surprising are the data, though scanty, suggesting that peasants in the more northern provinces of Iaroslavl'
and Nizhegorod, and possibly elsewhere, continued to grow
some spring wheat well into the 1850s, with yields averaging
1:4–5.[51]

This decline in wheat cultivation by the Petrovskoe serfs
is difficult to evaluate. If the serfs ate the wheat, the nutritional
effects of its being eliminated from their diet would have been
slight. In any case it is doubtful that the first decades of the
nineteenth century were witness to either a short-lived attempt

46. TsGADA, f. 1262, op. 4, ch. 1, ed. khr. 515.
47. TsGADA, f. 1262, op. 4, ch. 2, ed. khr. 822.
48. Semenov, "Khoziaistvennyia," 445–46; Kuz'min, *Voenno-statisticheskoe*, 61; P. Malykhin, "Byt krest'ian Voronezhskoi gubernii, Nizhnedevitskago uezda," *ES* 1 (1853):8; Kishkin, "Dannye i predpolozheniia," 234–40;
and Grekov, "Tambovskoe," 491. For Kursk province, see Mashkin, "Byt
krest'ian Kurskoi gubernii, Oboianskago uezda, *ES* 5 (1862):94.
49. Nasonov, "Khoziaistvo," 352–57; D. I. Ablov, "Razsuzhdenie
Vitse-Prezidenta Obshchestva Dmitriia Ivanovicha Ablova, o stoimosti ozimago
khleba," *ZLOSKh za 1847* (1848), 95–99; Khr. Kozlov, "Khoziaistvennye
voprosy," *ZLOSKh za 1852* (1853), 141–42.
50. TsGADA, f. 1262, op. 4, ch. 1, ed. khr. 649, l. 93.
51. Babarykin, "Sel'tso," 16–17; A. Arkhangel'skii, "Selo Davshino,
Iaroslavskoi gubernii, Poshekhonskago uezda," *ES* 2 (1854):44; and A. Preobrazhenskii, "Volost' Pokrovsko-Sitskaia, Iaroslavskoi gubernii, Molozhskago uezda." *ES* 1 (1853):80–82.

to improve the quality of life by "whitening" bread or the ultimate conclusion of a long-run decline in wheat cultivation. Rather, it is more likely that the estate wished either to prevent serf competition in the wheat market[52] or to force the peasants to use their plowland for cultivating rye, a heartier cereal that guaranteed a more regular return. Finally, the serfs may have found livestock a safer and more rewarding investment, thereby expanding oat production at the expense of wheat. But all these explanations are little more than speculation. Nevertheless it is far from sure that the end of serf wheat cultivation signified a net decline in cash income, adversely affecting the standard of living of the Petrovskoe peasants.

To return to the peasants' use of their allotted arable land, a study of the serfs of Kirsanov district, Tambov province, states that peasants with access to seven or eight statutory desiatinas (18.9 to 21.6 acres) of plowland per tiaglo would sow two desiatinas of rye, two of oats, and one of buckwheat or millet. Similarly, in Nizhedevits district, Voronezh province, 240 miles west of Petrovskoe, serfs with rather small allotments of six statutory desiatinas per tiaglo would plant 2 of rye, 1.5 of oats, and 0.5 of buckwheat or millet. Grain yields, it should be noted, in both these districts were on the average slightly higher than those of Petrovskoe.[53] The household of Feodor Nepriakhin, a "typical" serf living in Tambov district, cultivated per tiaglo 2.5 statutory desiatinas of rye, 1.5 of buckwheat, 0.5 of oats, 0.3 of millet, and 0.2 of flax, though his yields were 50 to 90 percent above those observed on estate lands at Petrovskoe.[54]

Household inventories from the village of Petrovskoe for 1813 and 1818 suggest an allocation of arable land not unlike that found in Kirsanov and Nizhedevits districts, though rather different from Nepriakhin's use of the spring field in Tambov. The poor harvest of spring cereals at Petrovskoe during the fall of 1856 makes it difficult to evaluate the distribution of cereals on the spring field for that year on the basis of the inventories,

52. Nasonov, "Khoziaistvo," 343.
53. Kishkin, "Dannye i predpolozheniia," 234–38; Malykhin, "Byt," 232–33.
54. Gruzinov, "Byt," 7–8.

though rye alone occupied the winter field. Nevertheless, with allotments of 6.0 to 6.6 agricultural desiatinas per tiaglo on the Petrovskoe estate, it seems reasonable that each tiaglo would have assigned at a minimum approximately 7.3 acres to rye, designated an equal area fallow, and split the spring field two or three to one in favor of oats over millet and buckwheat combined. For the earlier period, it is unclear whether wheat was raised as a spring or winter cereal.

If the Petrovskoe serfs, in sowing roughly 7.3 acres of rye, 5.1 of oats, and 2.2 of buckwheat and millet together, had yields similar to those on estate lands, then on the average each tiaglo would have produced 24.2 quintals of rye, 15.6 of oats, and at least 3.2 of buckwheat (or millet).[55] This assumption on yields is not unreasonable given that the peasants used the same implements and draft animals on both their fields and the demesne and that there were no differences in the strains of seed sown. Neither the demesne nor peasant land was manured. Even more important, the estate worked on the *brat na braty* system, common on most barshchina lands, whereby each day only half the work teams were assigned to the demesne, the others being free to work their own fields. In this way the estate did not take advantage of better weather, the most important factor that could have contributed to higher estate grain yields. Rather, it split the meteorological risks and environmental uncertainties with the peasants. In general, claims by serfowners that their grain yields were higher than the peasants', though common, were more fanciful than real. At Petrovskoe, and presumably elsewhere, the demesne and peasant fields were so intermingled that yield differentials may well have been physically impossible.

Subtracting the seed needed for the following year from the figures given above and allowing for a milling off of as much as 15 percent by weight of rye and buckwheat, the net

55. Because precise data were not available for the amounts of arable land used for growing either buckwheat or millet, to calculate a minimum estimate of serf grain production per tiaglo I will assume that buckwheat alone was planted. This cereal had a much lower return than millet, even though the latter, when ground, lost almost 40 percent in weight. *Polnaia entsiklopediia russkago sel'skago khoziaistva i soprikasaiushchikhsia s nim nauk*, 12 vols. (Saint Petersburg, 1900–1912), 3:1035.

yield would be 17.2 quintals of rye flour and 2.7 of buckwheat groats (or ground millet). If the serfs working land consumed as much as the household serfs with their annual ration of 607 pounds of rye flour and 76 pounds of groats or millet per person, then with an average harvest the arable land allotted each tiaglo would have provided enough rye flour for 6.2 persons and buckwheat or millet for 7.8 persons. The millings, along with 12.4 quintals of oats, could be used to support livestock. Also, it should be noted that the figures above assume an allotment of only 22 acres per tiaglo including the fallow, though frequently the serfs had access to as much as 1.8 acres more. In sum, a husband and wife work team cultivating a full unit of land could readily support itself and more than four nonworking persons while maintaining sizable livestock holdings. At the bare subsistence level, 470 pounds of milled grain per person per year, one tiaglo could, if necessary, feed 9.3 persons without their having to consume oats. The key point, however, is that the productive capacity of the village could support very high levels of fertility, permitting high consumer/worker ratios. In other words, almost half the population could consist of pre-working-age children.

Actually, between 1810 and 1856 one tiaglo maintained on the average from 4.6 to 5.5 serfs (based upon thirteen years of data), or 2 working adults and only 2.6 to 3.5 additional persons. Table 9 shows that only one-fifth to one-third of the village population lived in households having tiaglo/person ratios that would have caused grain production to fall below the per capita level consumed by the household serfs. Only 4.4 to 12.5 percent of the Petrovskoe serfs were members of households producing below the subsistence level, including all those with no working-age couples—households of widows, soldiers' wives, and elderly persons, all frequently with children. Rarely did the number of persons in the village belonging to households that had workers yet produced below the grain subsistence level exceed 4.5 percent of the total population. Thus only a small number of persons would have needed assistance from the village commune or the estate. In fact, most Petrovoskoe households apparently raised excess cereal, and that part over the ration established for the household serfs was available to meet tax obligations and other money dues, to pur-

TABLE 9

Households with a Low or Inadequate Number of Tiaglos per Person

| | 1813 | | | | 1814 | | | | 1818 | | | |
| | Households | | Persons | | Households | | Persons | | Households | | Persons | |
Tiaglo/Person Ratio	N	%	N	%	N	%	N	%	N	%	N	%
1:7.0–9.5	14	21.9	132	25.2	7	10.8	61	11.4	10	15.6	100	17.5
1:9.5+	4	6.3	43	8.2	2	3.1	21	3.9	1	1.6	10	1.7
No tiaglos	4	6.3	7	1.3	2	3.1	5	0.9	4	6.3	18	3.1
Total	22	34.5	182	34.7	11	17.0	87	16.2	15	23.5	128	22.3

| | 1821 | | | | 1824 | | | | 1826 | | | |
| | Households | | Persons | | Households | | Persons | | Households | | Persons | |
	N	%	N	%	N	%	N	%	N	%	N	%
1:7.0–9.5	10	14.5	93	16.9	12	16.2	101	17.6	16	21.3	143	24.0
1:9.5+	2	2.9	20	3.6	3	4.1	23	4.0	1	1.3	10	1.7
No tiaglos	10	14.5	35	6.4	7	9.5	23	4.0	5	6.7	16	2.7
Total	22	31.9	148	26.9	22	29.8	147	25.6	22	29.3	169	28.4

	1827				1834				1856			
	Households		Persons		Households		Persons		Households		Persons	
	N	%	N	%	N	%	N	%	N	%	N	%
1:7.0–9.5	14	18.4	123	20.6	9	11.5	93	14.6	7	5.6	59	8.3
1:9.5+	3	3.9	24	4.0	4	5.1	28	4.4	2	1.6	16	2.2
No tiaglos	4	5.3	12	2.0	4	5.1	12	1.9	26	20.8	73	10.3
Total	21	27.6	159	26.6	17	21.7	133	20.9	35	28.0	148	20.8

Source: TsGADA, f. 1262, op. 1, ed. khr. 1495; op. 4, ch. 1, ed. khr. 41, 59, 121, 186, 344, 357, 515; ch. 2, ed. khr. 822.

Note: A tiaglo/person ratio of lower than 7 in a household would mean that its members would have less grain per capita, excluding oats, to consume than the household serfs. A ratio lower than 9,5 would mean that a household was not producing at a subsistence level and would require assistance if it were to survive. A household with no tiaglos had no labor obligations or land allotment other than a widow's allotment or similar small plot from the commune.

chase farm implements, draft animals, and household goods, to provide a cushion against below-average harvests, and to provide a standard of living higher than that of the household serfs.

Virtually all of the rye, buckwheat, and millet the serfs raised was for consumption, only a small portion being marketed to permit various purchases, most notably alcohol. Taxes were largely met by carting estate cereals to market in winter, when the peasants had much free time. Though the horses required oats rather than simply hay or straw for such strenuous trips, this did not affect the serfs' consumption. Moreover, cartage insulated the serfs from sharp price fluctuations. Otherwise—during the 1820s, for example—a work team would have had to sell, depending upon prevailing prices, anywhere from 1 to 3.7 *chetverts* of rye (315 to 1,164 pounds) to meet its annual tax and money dues. On average, taxes and dues would have amounted to 22 percent of the net rye yield (after seed). So cartage, though burdensome, had its benefits. As for other possible expenditures, the peasants generally bred what livestock they needed. Tools and agricultural implements were crude and easily made at home.

The extent of serf wealth on the Petrovskoe estate is best indicated by the size of peasant livestock holdings. After land, livestock was the most crucial element in serf life. Without a horse or an ox, a serf could not work his fields; without sheep, he could not clothe himself or his family; without cows, pigs, and domestic poultry, he could not break the endless monotony of a cereal diet and have access to high-protein foods. Land, moreover, was rarely a variable commodity in the serf economy, while livestock, especially that raised for personal consumption, necessarily responded quickly to changes in the serfs' fortunes.

Besides the allotted arable land, the serfs of Petrovskoe were provided with common pastures (*vygon*) and meadows (*senokos* or *lug*) to support their livestock. But unlike the plowlands, which were distributed estatewide, thereby assuring each tiaglo an equal amount of land, as a matter of convenience the pastures and hayfields were apportioned among each of the eight villages separately, though used communally within each village. Over the years, substantial differences developed in the amounts of such lands per tiaglo in the various villages. In 1857, for example, the village of Petrovskoe, one of the two oldest settlements of the estate, had only 120 agricultural desiatinas (432 acres) of common pasture for 156 tiaglos (125 households). But the village of Viktorovna, established in 1848, had roughly the same amount of land for half the number of tiaglos and households.[56] A new land survey undertaken in 1858 corrected these inequities, allotting each village one agricultural desiatina (3.6 acres) of both common pasture and hayfield per tiaglo, though these lands continued to be used jointly by the inhabitants within the village.[57] During the first half of the nineteenth century, the total amount of pasture and meadows available to the peasants of the Petrovskoe estate was approximately the same, but it fluctuated from 2.2 to 8.3 acres per tiaglo in the various villages, with greater discrepancies in the distribution of common pasture than in the distribution of hayfields.[58]

Therefore hay, oats, chaff, and tailings were all sources of feed, supplemented by the grass and stubble of the common pasture, fallow field, and forest. With these feeds, the peasants of the village of Petrovskoe were able to maintain the per capita levels of livestock shown in table 10. Domestic poultry— mostly chickens, some geese and ducks, and occasionally turkeys—was also raised. Data on these were available only for 1843, when there averaged more than two fowls per person.[59]

Additional sources suggest that such livestock holdings were common in the region surrounding the Petrovskoe estate. Kh. Kozlov was marshall of the nobility in Borisoglebsk and the author of numerous articles on the economic life of this district. In 1848, in an essay intended for entry in a competition organized by the Scientific Commission of the Ministry of State Domains, he wrote:

> The number of horses in the district is almost equal to the number of males because each tiaglo must have a working

56. TsGADA, f. 1262, op. 4, ch. 2, ed. khr. 846, 15 October 1857.
57. Ibid., 20 May 1858.
58. TsGADA, f. 1262, op. 1, ch. 1, ed. khr. 256, 2830a, and 2833; op. 4, ch. 1, ed. khr. 589 and 615.
59. TsGADA, f. 1262, op. 4, ch. 1, ed. khr. 615.

TABLE 10

Livestock per Capita, Village of Petrovskoe

	Horses			Cows			Sheep	Pigs	Beehives
	Working	Colts	Total	Mature	Calves	Total			
May 1810	.40	.17	.57	.24	.17	.41	1.56	.69	.81
October 1813	—	—	.43	.24	—	—	1.80	.55	.33
April–May 1814	—	—	.41	.25	—	—	1.60	.48	.30
January 1818	.37	.17	.54	—	—	.40	1.89	.65	.23
April 1821	.40	.19	.59	.23	.21	.44	1.55	.38	.40
Fall 1823	.37	.10	.47	.27	.16	.43	1.11	.47	.36
May 1824	.38	.09	.47	.27	.14	.41	1.17	.47	.38
May 1826	.35	.13	.48	.26	.16	.42	1.32	.52	.45
May 1827	.35	.14	.49	.26	.16	.42	1.32	.52	.43
February 1834	.33	.16	.49	.19	.10	.29	1.06	.28	.29
November 1856	.38	.12	.50	.18	.11	.29	1.36	.43	.12

Source: TsGADA, f. 1262, op. 1, ch. 1, ed. khr. 256, 1495; op. 4, ch. 1, ed. khr. 41, 59, 121, 186, 249, 344, 357, 515; ch. 2, ed. khr. 822.

horse and a colt, which pulls the harrow; but there are many heads of household who have for each male worker, not including colts, two working horses, one of which they sell off every third or fourth year. . . . It is not possible to calculate exactly the number of cattle, but it is possible to say that each family, consisting of five male souls, has from one to three cows plus young calves. . . . The number of sheep reaches as high as five head for each male soul. . . . The number of pigs reaches as high as two head per male soul.[60]

By these standards the serfs of Petrovskoe, though substantially below the maxima observed by Kozlov for sheep and pigs, had almost exactly the average number of horses and were well provided with cows. Similarly, a topographical description of Tambov province published by the General Staff of the army in 1851 noted that nearly all peasant households had from two to seven horses, one to five cows, and five to ten sheep along with an unspecified number of pigs and domestic poultry.[61] In the village of Feodor Nepriakhin, the "typical" serf of Tambov district, the richest households had six horses and fifty sheep per male worker, the poorest, only two horses and five sheep per male worker. Nepriakhin himself, described as neither rich nor poor, with two male and three female workers in his household of sixteen persons, had nine working horses, five colts, two milk cows, one heifer, forty sheep, nineteen pigs, forty chickens, ten geese, three turkeys, and twenty-five beehives.[62] Certainly his family was much better off than most households in the village of Petrovskoe. Finally, a tiaglo in Nizhedevits district, Voronezh province, consisting of approximately five persons of both sexes, could usually support three horses, one colt, one cow, two heifers, seven sheep, and four pigs.[63] These figures are not much higher than those for Petrovskoe.

60. Kh. Kozlov, "Sel'sko-khoziaistvennaia statistika Borisglebskago uezda," *Izvestiia Tambovskoi Uchenoi Arkhivnoi Komissii* 29 (1890):86–89.
61. Kuz'min, *Voenno-statistcheskoe,* 67–78.
62. Gruzinov, "Byt," 6–8.
63. Malykhin, "Byt," 232–33.

The abundance of livestock in the village of Petrovskoe and the persistently low prices at local markets for meat, poultry, and eggs throughout the first half of the nineteenth century[64] make it unlikely that the serfs regularly suffered protein deficiency, especially lysine inadequacy. Though there are no data on the amount of meat eaten annually by the field peasants of Petrovskoe, with two chickens, almost one and a half sheep, and half a pig per capita, some form of meat was certainly available weekly, if not daily. Contemporary observers of peasant life in southern Tambov province and the surrounding region agree that meat was found on most peasant tables for major religious holidays, parish festivals, wedding days, and funerals. Only the very poor were unable to have meat on these occasions. In Kirsanov district, prosperous peasants ate meat daily, purchasing fresh and salted beef in autumn and winter, slaughtering sheep in the summer, and never being without eggs, cream, or oil.[65] Nepriakhin's family put a chicken in its cabbage soup every Sunday and ate 578 pounds of salted beef, 12 lambs, 18 geese, 3 fattened pigs, and 20 piglets during the course of the year—well over 100 pounds of meat per person.[66]

Fruits, vegetables, and oils, the remaining essential nutrients for a balanced diet, came from the kitchen garden, of which as much as half was devoted to hemp, a source of oil and livestock feed. Unfortunately, estate records for Petrovskoe provide no information on the subdivision of farmsteads (usad'bas) by the amount of land allocated to dwelling space, outbuildings, livestock stalls, threshing floor, and kitchen garden. It is clear, however, that peasant farmsteads even within the same village of the Petrovskoe estate were not uniform in size, though those in older settlements tended to be larger.[67] In 1848 the 522 farmsteads of the estate occupied a total of 298 agricultural desiatinas, the average size of a household plot being 2.1 acres or, in the village of Petrovskoe, 2.4 acres.[68]

64. See table 3 and Kozlov, "Sel'sko-khoziaistvennaia statistika," 87–89.

65. Kishkin, "Dannye i predpolozheniia," 231.
66. Gruzinov, "Byt," 10–11.
67. TsGADA, f. 1262, op. 4, ch. 2, ed. khr. 846, l. 65.
68. TsGADA, f. 1262, op. 4, ch. 2, ed. khr. 902, l. 44–45.

Similarly, in 1862, as a result of the emancipation, the land settlement in the village of Petrovskoe provided for household plots averaging 2.4 acres.[69] Thus the land reform avoided the enormous difficulties involved in reapportioning household plots, which in the past had always been exempt from periodic redistribution.[70]

Kishkin reports that in Kirsanov district a household plot of 600 square sazhens (0.7 acre), equally divided among buildings, threshing floor, and garden, was considered sufficient. But the amount of land given to the serfs in the district for farmsteads was far from equal. Plots of 1,200 square sazhens (1.4 acres) were not uncommon, all of the additional land being used to expand the size of the garden. With a small garden of 200 square sazhens (0.23 acre), a household could produce 200 heads of cabbage, 27 pounds of hemp oil, seed for next year's hemp crop, and an undetermined amount of other vegetables.[71] Cabbage and cucumbers were the most important vegetables, sharing the kitchen garden with smaller quantities of onions, beets, Russian turnips, carrots, radishes, potatoes, and an occasional apple tree or gooseberry bush.[72] Per capita intake of such produce, however, is impossible to estimate.

To sum up the dietary regime of the peasants of Petrovskoe, the daily per capita consumption of rye, buckwheat,

69. Ibid., l. 41.

70. In documents prepared for the Editing Commissions in 1858, which were drafting plans for the emancipation of the serfs, the 630 households of the Petrovskoe estate were said to occupy 642 statutory desiatinas, or 2.8 acres per plot. TsGADA, f. 1262, op. 4, ch. 2, ed. khr. 862, l. 4, and published in *Prilozheniia k trudam Redaktsionnykh komissii* 3:12–17. For three other estates in Borisoglebsk district having more than one hundred male souls and for which it is clear that hemp gardens were included in the totals for household plots, the average size of an usad'ba was 3.8 acres, according to documents from the Editing Commissions. The remaining twenty-four estates of the district, with over one hundred souls and no indication whether hemp gardens were included in usad'ba totals, had a mean household plot size of 2.2 acres, a median of 1.6 acres. As I stated above, the veracity of these materials has been seriously challenged, and data submitted by the bailiff of the Petrovskoe estate to the commissions contained information he knew was inaccurate. See Litvak, *Russkaia derevnia,* 34–36.

71. Kishkin, "Dannye i predpolozheniia," 230, 235–36.

72. Kuz'min, *Voenno-statisticheskoe,* 65; Kishkin, "Dannye i predpolozheniia," 237; Mashkin, "Byt," 97; and P. Troitskii, "Selo Lipitsy i ego okrestnosti, Tul'skoi gubernii, Koshirskago uezda," *ES* 2 (1854):84–85.

and millet of the household serfs was 1.9 pounds (860 grams), and the evidence suggests a comparable if not slightly higher level for the field peasants. Potato consumption, generally linked to a "certain relative pauperization" in western Europe during the eighteenth century, was a minor nutritional component in the diet of the Petrovskoe serfs.[73] When cultivated, the potato was confined to the kitchen garden, having made no inroads as an open field crop. In contrast, the absence of wheat from the serfs' diet is of no significance in terms of nutrition. Of much greater importance, both the mythical family pig of French peasant households and the "self-same chicken" that was "plucked for the last two centuries" of the Ancien Régime were quantifiable realities in Petrovskoe between 1810 and 1856.[74] And, with one mature milch cow for every four to five persons, even if average annual milk production per cow was as low as an unlikely five hundred liters, milk, butter, and other dairy products must have been readily available.

Excluding for the moment years of agricultural crisis, the peasants of Petrovskoe were therefore better nourished than their French and Belgian counterparts at the turn of the nineteenth century and certainly had a better diet than most persons living in developing countries today.[75] The process of "depecoration," that is, growing meatlessness, that characterized much of Europe after the sixteenth century was certainly much less in evidence at Petrovskoe. While it is unlikely that the serfs ate meat at the same high rate as medieval Europeans had done, approximately 220 pounds per person per year, it is not inconceivable that they ate half that amount, three times more than their contemporaries to the west. Clearly, the serfs of Petrovskoe suffered less imbalance between proteins, especially those derived from animal products, and carbohydrates than

73. M. Morineau, "The Potato in the Eighteenth Century," in *Food and Drink in History,* ed. R. Forster and O. Ranum (Baltimore, 1979), 31–32. Originally published in *Annales, E.S.C.* 25 (November–December 1970).

74. J. Hemardinquer, "The Family Pig of the Ancien Régime: Myth or Fact?" in *Food and Drink in History,* ed. R. Forster and O. Ranum (Baltimore, 1979), 58–59, 66–72. Originally published in *Annales, E.S.C.* 25 (November–December 1970).

75. M. Burk and M. Ezekiel, "Food and Nutrition in Developing Economies," in *Agricultural Development and Economic Growth,* ed. H. M. Southworth and B. F. Johnston (Ithaca, N.Y., 1967), 334–37.

many French, Belgian, or German peasants, for whom meat was limited to special feasts, no more than a few pounds per capita per year. And the effects of their more balanced diet would necessarily be manifested in increased biological resistance and less vulnerability to epidemic disease.[76] In essence, the serfs were a healthier lot. Nevertheless, this more favorable nutritional standing is relative and should not be exaggerated. According to modern schemes of analysis, the dietary regime of the Petrovskoe peasants fits into the broad cereal-based category, in which approximately half of all proteins (42–66 percent) are derived from various cereals, a characteristic of virtually all of western Europe from the Middle Ages into the nineteenth century and in most parts even later.[77] Yet, though within the confines of the same dietary structure, the serfs of Petrovskoe were normally better off.

But in an "abnormal year," usually the result of a crop failure, these serfs suffered a miserable, pathetic existence. In Petrovskoe, throughout the period under consideration, subsistence crises and epidemic diseases repeatedly assumed catastrophic proportions. The age distribution for the village of Petrovskoe for 1850 reveals the devastating effects that the famine and cholera epidemic of 1848–49 had on the very young. According to a household list compiled that year, only 20.1 percent of the village population was aged 0–9 years, though this age cohort averaged over 29 percent between the years 1813 and 1827. In effect, approximately one-third of this age group was lost to the village as a result of the 1848–49 crisis, a combination of sharply increased infant and child mortality, delayed marriages, and in all likelihood, delays in ovulation resulting from famine. Similar though less severe effects on the age structure of the village population are visible after the bad harvest of 1821. The age group 5–9 in 1827, which was 0–4 years old during the winter of 1822 when food was in short supply, represented only 10.7 percent of the total population,

76. E. Le Roy Ladurie, *The Peasants of Languedoc*, trans. John Day (Urbana, Ill., and Chicago, 1974), 103.
77. M. Aymard, "Toward the History of Nutrition: Some Methodological Remarks," in *Food and Drink in History*, ed. R. Forster and O. Ranum (Baltimore, 1979), 5. Originally published in *Annales, E.S.C.* 30 (March–June 1975).

down from an average 14.6 percent between the years 1813 and 1824. (See figs. 1 and 2.)

Following the crop failure late in the summer of 1833, the weekly reports of the bailiff provide a detailed account of the deprivation that resulted. As early as mid-September, the bailiff prohibited the serfs from selling their own grain and requested the burmeister, a serf functionary, to make the rounds of neighboring bazaars to ensure that this order was not violated.[78] In mid-October the bailiff wrote to his superiors in Moscow: "With every passing day the peasants come more and more to the estate administration with requests for grain for food, which the administration somehow avoids giving out, though some millet mixed with rye is given to the very needy and the poorest."[79]

Beginning in November the monthly rye ration for household serfs was reduced 25 percent, from 50.6 to 38.0 pounds per capita.[80] In mid-December estate grain reserves were

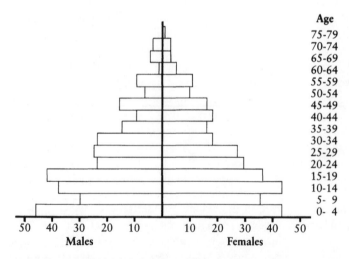

FIGURE 1: Pyramid of ages, village of Petrovskoe (1827).

78. TsGADA, f. 1262, op. 4, ch. 1, ed. khr. 496, 17 September 1833.
79. TsGADA, f. 1262, op. 4, ch. 1, ed. khr. 496, 17 October 1833.
80. TsGADA, f. 1262, op. 4, ch. 1, ed. khr. 496, 14 October and 2 November 1833.

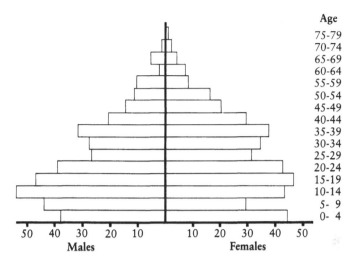

Age
75-79
70-74
65-69
60-64
55-59
50-54
45-49
40-44
35-39
30-34
25-29
20-24
15-19
10-14
5- 9
0- 4

50 40 30 20 10   10 20 30 40 50
      Males   Females

FIGURE 2:   Pyramid of ages, village of Petrovskoe (1850).

opened to the neediest households, and on 28 December every serf on the estate began receiving a monthly ration. To cite again the bailiff's weekly report: "For the distribution of food grain to the peasants, respected peasant functionaries have been selected, and they have taken an oath in the church of God, because the bailiff and the burmeister cannot attend to all this. They were directed to give each person from the eldest down to 2 years old one chetverik [of rye] each month."[81]

One chetverik of rye is the equivalent of 38 to 40 pounds of grain, which would permit a daily ration of slightly more than 1.2 pounds per capita, only 63 percent of the normal daily allowance for the household serfs. Estate reserves, however, were not the only source of grain at this time, since the serfs had not yet exhausted their own supplies.

With the new year, however, the situation became more critical. In January the parish priest buried serfs to whom he had not been able to administer the final sacrament because of so many calls for his services. That indicates a significant in-

81. TsGADA, f. 1262, op. 4, ch. 1, ed. khr. 496, 14 December and 28 December 1833.

crease in mortality.[82] On 8 February the bailiff entered in his report: "The peasants are in extreme need of feed for their livestock, they even strip the thatch from the roofs of their houses; nowhere can they find any to buy."[83] To keep the Moscow office accurately informed of the dimensions of the crisis, in late February the bailiff inventoried peasant grain and livestock holdings. In the village of Petrovskoe, two-thirds of the households were found to be completely without grain; over three-fourths had no rye. The inventory revealed only 243 chetverts of milled and unmilled cereal and no more than 358 quintals of various grains. Over half was oats, and this was only one-third of the amount needed for seed in the spring. Supplies of buckwheat and millet were virtually exhausted, leaving nothing to sow in May. Livestock holdings per capita of sheep, pigs, and milch cows were at the lowest level ever observed in the village, though the number of horses had held up remarkably well (see table 10).[84] Certainly the normally abundant livestock resources of the peasants mitigated the effects of the crisis by providing high-protein foods. But the serfs were consuming their savings by eating more meat and poultry, undermining the quality of their diet for years to come because they had no alternative. By late March the depletion of estate grain reserves forced a further reduction in food assistance to the serfs, and for the first time the lack of feed had an effect on draft animals. The bailiff reported on 22 March:

> As regards supplying food to the peasants, each family has been personally inspected and many of them were found to be in a most sorry state, not having the means to feed themselves, [and thus] for four and more days have been without food. Compassion and the cries of children have required that all possible measures be taken for the benefit of His Excellency . . . out of necessity the monthly ration was fixed at 30 *funts* [one funt equals 0.9 pound] per adult, 10 funts per child. Moreover, the taking of a household inventory was ordered for an accurate evalua-

82. TsGADA, f. 1262, op. 4, ch. 1, ed. khr. 507.
83. TsGADA, f. 1262, op. 4, ch. 1, ed. khr. 496, 8 February 1834.
84. TsGADA, f. 1262, op. 4, ch. 1, ed. khr. 515, February 1834.

tion [of the situation], because it has been found that many [households] do not have any horses.[85]

Regrettably, no copy of this inventory was found in the archives of the estate, though the need for a second report within the span of a month to determine the level of peasant well-being can only suggest, in light of the comments above, a substantial worsening of the situation since February. The monthly ration for adults now stood at 27.1 pounds of cereal per capita. With very few households able to supplement this ration with their own grain stores, for most persons daily consumption of grain was limited to 0.7 pound, just 37 percent of the normal daily per capita intake of grain by the household serfs. This is fewer than 800 calories per day, far below any subsistence minimum, and it is inconceivable that an increased consumption of meat or poultry could make up for the substantial deficiency in food energy. Presumably the remaining livestock was weak and emaciated and continued to be adversely affected by the crisis until pasture or other grazing lands became available sometime in early spring. In addition, either slaughter or starvation had reduced the number of workhorses on the estate, leaving numerous households with no means of cultivating their fields.

By April, insufficient calorie intake undermined the serfs' ability to work. Undernourishment, for some in its sixth month, hindered the preparation of the spring fields. In April the bailiff noted, "many [serfs] do not worry about the future." To him the peasants appeared irresponsible and "lazy," especially "when they give their own lands over to strangers [nonestate peasants] to sow."[86] The bailiff's concern was genuine given the serfs' negligent attitude toward their own well-being. The estate manager felt that the peasants were "more accustomed to take out loans [of food grain] than repay debts, being convinced that their master would feed them, even if they were more lazy."[87] But such languid and listless behavior as occurred during the spring of 1834 should be understood as a

85. TsGADA, f. 1262, op. 4, ch. 1, ed. khr. 496, 22 March 1834.
86. TsGADA, f. 1262, op. 4, ch. 1, ed. khr. 496, 12 April 1834.
87. TsGADA, f. 1262, op. 4, ch. 1, ed. khr. 518, September 1834.

symptom of prolonged undernourishment, from which these serfs were undoubtedly suffering.

The inability of Russian society to eliminate the "great crises" of 1821–22, 1833–34, and 1848–49 as witnessed in Petrovskoe was one of the major features separating eastern and western Europe of the nineteenth century. Indeed, more than anything else, the lowering of "the peaks rather than the plateau of mortality" constituted the vital revolution of the eighteenth century and early nineteenth century: "In other words, it was not so much a reduction of mortality in 'normal' years that produced the downward secular trend of the death rate, but an unmistakable abatement of the 'great crises.' The disappearance of the plague above all, but also very sensible mitigation of subsistence crises seem to have been chiefly responsible for the increase in life expectancy."[88]

On the Petrovskoe estate, the old demographic world was not dead. Subsistence crises persisted, and in the nineteenth century they were accompanied by a new infectious invader, cholera. Thus the comparative success of the Petrovskoe serfs in exploiting their agricultural resources, which normally yielded foods in greater abundance and of higher protein quality than were available to their peasant neighbors in the West, nevertheless failed to break the cycle of dearth and famine, even though such crises may have been somewhat mitigated by the generally higher level of well-being.

Whereas sudden crop failures and epidemics completely disrupted the pattern of life of the Petrovskoe serfs, housing deficiencies and poor sanitary conditions were persistent features of existence on the estate. And they greatly affected the serfs' lives, for interpersonal relations among household members were very much determined by the confined space in which all the peasants lived.

The major factor contributing to the poor quality of housing was the lack of forestlands capable of supplying cheap and abundant construction materials. Borisoglebsk district was

88. K. F. Helleiner, "The Vital Revolution Reconsidered" in *Population in History*, ed. D. V. Glass and D. E. C. Eversley (London and Chicago, 1965), 85. See also Wrigley, *Population*, 165, and J. D. Chambers, *Population, Economy, and Society in Pre-industrial England* (Oxford, 1972).

on the edge of the steppe. Most woodlands were of inferior quality, more shrubs than trees, and forests that were cut down did not recover.[89] In 1848 the average price for a desiatina of plowland, meadowland, virgin steppe, hemp field, long-fallow field, or land for a household plot on the Petrovskoe estate was estimated to vary from 60 to 70 silver rubles. Standing timber suitable for construction, however, was valued at three times that amount.[90]

The Petrovskoe estate was unique in having a forest reserve of 1,200 agricultural desiatinas (4,320 acres) of construction timber, almost two-thirds of which was alder, the remainder consisting of slightly more aspen than oak. In addition there were 500 desiatinas (1,800 acres) of forest suitable for firewood, and over 270 desiatinas of scrub. From this estate reserve, worth over 276,000 rubles, the serfs of Petrovskoe were supplied with logs, lumber, firewood, and *luchinas* (torches for lighting their huts) as needed. In return, during haymaking and harvest time, those tiaglos that had made use of estate woodlands worked up to eight extra days per year or, as it was actually carried out, sixteen days on which only half of all work teams were called upon to perform corvée obligations.[91]

There is no evidence that this arrangement was particularly advantageous for the Petrovskoe serfs, though the proximity of forestlands undoubtedly made it easier for them to steal wood. Thatch was the main fuel used to heat peasant huts (*izbas*). Felling trees for firewood was permitted only in years of crop failure. Luchinas generally came from birch or otherwise useless scrub. In any case, both firewood and luchinas were frequently pilfered, Thus, the peasants' basic need was for construction timber, which was more difficult to steal, and much of its cost was met by the additional labor obligations. Certainly the size of peasant huts at Petrovskoe suggests that the serfs were not able to benefit much from this estate resource.

89. Kozlov, "Sel'sko-khoziaistvennaia statistika," 85; Kishkin, "Dannye i predpolozheniia," 229; Gruzinov, "Byt," 3; *ZLOSKh za 1855*, ch. 1, pp. 92–96; *Obozrenie Deistvii*, 53; L. R. Keller, "Opisanie krest'ianskoi izby s glinosolomennymi stenami i svodom," *ZhMGI* 29, no. 4, part 3 (1848):1–3.

90. TsGADA, f. 1262, op. 1, ch. 1, ed. khr. 2833, l. 38–54.

91. TsGADA, f. 1262, op. 4, ch. 2, ed. khr. 862, l. 7.

Peasant homesteads were usually laid out in twos adjoining one another, sharing a common wall or fence and thus saving wood. The peasants' huts, built of logs, would be situated next to the road, but between them there would be two *sens,* covered shelters attached to each of the huts. Therefore the common wall of the two homesteads was perpendicular to the road and separated the sens, with a hut on each end. Most often sens were as deep as the hut, though the side next to the road was slightly shorter, from fifteen to twenty-six feet in length.[92] Inside the sens were one or two *chulans,* large areas partitioned off for storage of food and clothes or for sleeping during the summer. Access to the hut was through the sen' and never directly from the street. Rather, one or two ornately decorated windows looked onto the road, and that side of the hut was known as the "face" (*litso*).

The hut was a family's main living space, especially in wintertime, since it was the only structure that was heated. But the peasants had to share their hut with domestic fowl and young livestock for at least four months of the year to protect them from the cold. At times of extremely low temperature, mature animals had to be brought in as well.

The archives of the Petrovskoe estate reveal little about these peasant huts. Inventories of estate property taken in 1819 and 1849 disclose that most of the huts for the household serfs were between 200 and 600 square feet in area (see table 11). The few very large huts on the estate, those over 600 square feet, were for the bailiff and other nonserf employees of the estate or served as bunkhouses for unmarried household serfs who had been brought to Petrovskoe from other estates. Though the table suggests that the average size of peasant huts was somewhat smaller in 1849 than in 1819, this was because the larger bunkhouses had been torn down. Otherwise there seems to be little change over the years. Undoubtedly the huts of the field serfs were quite similar.

With most huts on the Petrovskoe estate less than 500 square feet in area, of which 10 to 20 percent was lost to the stove, space was at a premium, furniture sparse, and, in winter,

92. TsGADA, f. 1262, op. 4, ch. 1, ed. khr. 150 (1 September 1819), l. 8; and op. 1, ch. 1, ed. khr. 2833 (29 January 1849), l. 59–64.

TABLE 11

Size of Peasant Huts (Izbas) for Household Serfs, Petrovskoe Estate

Area (square feet)	1819	1849
< 200	0	2
200–299	1	4
300–399	5	8
400–499	8	19
500–599	5	4
> 600	9	2
Total	28	39

Sources: TsGADA, f. 1262, op. 4, ch. 1, ed. khr. 150, l. 1–8 (1 September 1819); op. 1, ch. 1, ed. khr. 2833, l. 59–64 (29 January 1849).

privacy virtually unknown. And these were the circumstances of life in many neighboring villages as well. Indeed, one progressive serfowner felt that a hut of 73.5 square *arshins* (400 square feet) would be an improvement for a household of ten persons, though it would have allowed less than 4.5 square yards per person. Generally, it seems, most huts in the region varied in size from 195 to 440 square feet, quite similar to the situation at Petrovskoe.[93]

In 1813, of the sixty-four households in the village of Petrovskoe, forty-seven (73 percent) had only one hut, though six of these also had a *gornitsa,* a separate adjoining hut for family use but with no sleeping benches. It is unclear if the gornitsas were heated or if they could be used for preparing meals and eating. Fourteen households had two huts (22 percent), and for three households there was no information.[94] In 1856 the situation was virtually identical. The village now consisted of 126 households. Ninety-four homesteads (75 percent) had one hut,

93. Ia. P. Bakhtearov, "Dvoinyia krest'ianskiia izby s odnoiu topkoiu," *ZLOSKh za 1857* (1858), 131; Gruzinov, "Byt," 3; Kishkin, "Dannye i predpolozheniia," 230–31; and O. P. Semenova-Tian-Shanskaia, *Zhizn' "Ivana." Ocherki iz byta krest'ian odnoi iz chernozemnykh gubernii, Zapiski Imperatorskago russkago geograficheskago obshchestva po otdeleniiu etnografii, 39* (Saint Petersburg, 1914), 79–83.
94. TsGADA, f. 1262, op. 4, ch. 2, ed. khr. 41 (October 1813).

twenty-eight (22 percent) had two, and one had three. (Three cases were unknown.)[95] Households with two izbas would have a sen' connecting these huts. Inside the hut, usually in the right corner of the wall opposite the door, was the stove. There was a brick factory on the estate, and a small part of its output was used by the peasants, suggesting that some stoves were made of brick and had chimneys, rather than of clay without chimneys.[96] Nevertheless, most of the huts in the region lacked chimneys, so that they were *chernye* or *kurnye izbas*, always sooty and smoky. In these huts smoke and ash drifted along the ceiling and exited through a hole in the wall, blackening the inside, or were cleared by simply opening the door. Both the Ministry of State Domains and the Lebedian Agricultural Society repeatedly pointed out to landlords the discomfort and danger to health resulting from constant exposure to smoke and soot. Physicians claimed this was the principal cause of blindness. By the mid-nineteenth century *belye izbas,* clean huts with brick chimneys, were becoming more common, possibly as a consequence of these concerns.[97]

There were, however, a number of drawbacks to having a chimney. Belye izbas required more fuel, for much heat went up the chimney. In regions where straw was used instead of firewood, as in Petrovskoe, a chimney considerably increased the possibility of fire, since burning straw could easily go up the flue and land on the thatched roof. The extra bricks used to construct the chimney increased the cost of building a hut, and the chimney had to be cleaned frequently and repaired occasionally. In a word, it took additional work.[98]

95. TsGADA, f. 1262, op. 4, ch. 2, ed. khr. 822 (November 1856).
96. TsGADA, f. 1262, op. 4, ch. 1, ed. khr. 615 (April 1844), l. 9; V. I. Semevskii, "Domashnii byt i nravy krest'ian vo vtoroi polovine XVIII v.," *Ustoi,* no. 1 (1882): 112–13; and V. A. Aleksandrov et al., eds., *Russkie: Istoriko-etnograficheskii atlas,* 2 vols. (Moscow, 1967–71), map 26.
97. A. Dmitriukov, "Nravy, obychai, i obraz zhizni v Sudzhanskom uezde, Kurskoi gubernii," *Moskovskii telegraf,* no. 10 (1831):264; Kishkin, "Dannye i predpolozheniia," 229–30; Malykhin, "Byt," 208–11; Bakhtearov, "Dvoinyia krest'ianskiia izby," 127–28; P. I. Kushner, ed. *The Village of Viriatino,* trans. Sula Benet (New York, 1970), 58–60; Mashkin, "Byt," 4–6; and Semenova, *Zhizn' "Ivana,"* 79–83.
98. Bakhtearov, "Dvoinyia krest'ianskiia izby," 127–28; Semevskii, "Domashnii byt," 112–13.

There was no room for beds in these small huts, so the peasants constructed *polati*, high platforms over the stove and along the walls. Fresh straw was brought in each evening to serve as mattresses and was burned the following morning. When no straw was available, the peasants simply slept on their clothes. The huts lacked any foundation, and floors were almost always of dirt. Even in the northern parts of Russia where lumber was abundant, only rich peasants had floorboards. Furniture consisted of a table and a few stools, usually placed in the near or far left corner from the door under the icon, along with a cupboard or two for storing dishes and cooking utensils.

Households with two or more huts generally had one with a chimney and one without. Nevertheless, in wintertime all household members crowded into the *chernaia*, which was cheaper to heat. The clean hut was used only in warm months, providing a more pleasant place to cook, eat, and sleep. Thus, with a mean household size in the village of Petrovskoe between 1782 and 1856 (based upon twelve years of observation) of 7.9 persons (see table 12), peasant huts of 500 square feet,

TABLE 12

Mean Household Size, Village of Petrovskoe

Year	Number of Households	Males	Females	Total	Mean Size
1782	72	304	304	608	8.4
1810	92	358	355	713	7.7
1813	64	257	266	523	8.2
1814	65	260	273	533	8.2
1818	64	273	300	573	9.0
1821	69	258	293	551	8.0
1824	74	267	306	573	7.7
1826	75	277	320	597	8.0
1827	76	283	315	598	7.9
1834	78	—	—	638	8.2
1850	104	365	397	762	7.3
1856	126	351	364	715	5.7

Sources: Besides the nine household lists, TsGADA, f. 1355, op. 1, ed. khr. 1575 (1782?), l. 6; TsGADA, f. 1262, op. 1, ch. 1, ed. khr. 256 (1 May 1810); op. 4, ch. 1, ed. khr. 515 (February 1834).

larger than most, after subtracting a minimal 10 percent for the stove, had only 6.3 square yards per person. And most of the peasants experienced even more confining conditions.

The full extent of these wretched hovels in which the serfs lived can now be appreciated. Inside the huts, the air was fetid from animal and fowl excreta. The walls and ceiling were covered with soot and ash. Smoke, especially in the morning when the stove was lit, filled the top half of the izba. In the evening, soot from the luchinas stung the eyes. The dirt floor was always damp, and in the spring and autumn it was muddy. It was impossible to keep cockroaches out of the food; they even became a symbol of abundance and material wealth and a sign of good luck. In fact, when moving to a new home, the head of the household would bring a few roaches with him and let them loose. These were the conditions under which all the serfs lived for at least a third of the year.[99]

In contrast, the warm months brought considerable relief from the squalor of the hut, and the psychological effect must have been substantial. Livestock, of course, was moved outside. The stove was heated less often and in summer was used only for cooking. More hours of sunlight reduced the need for luchinas. Animal feces were removed from the hut, though with warm weather came the stench of decomposing manure piled in the yard. The serfs were no longer confined to their huts for hours on end, often with little to do. Life moved not only outdoors, but into the belye izbas for those who had them and into the numerous unheated parts of the home for most. At least one-third of the homesteads in the village of Petrovskoe had a *klet'*, a shed behind the hut for storing holiday clothes and other personal items. In summer a married couple would sleep there, and some households had a klet' for each conjugal pair. In all, thirty-three homesteads in Petrovskoe, with 61 percent of the village population, had at least two huts or a hut with a gornitsa or klet'. Virtually all households had sens. Nev-

99. Rudnev, "Selo Golun'," 101; V. Bondarenko, "Pover'ia krest'ian Tambovskoi gubernii," *Zhivaia starina* 1, part 2, no. 3 (1890): 118–19; *ZLOSKh za 1855* (1856), part 1, pp. 92–96; Kishkin, "Dannye i predpolozheniia," 229–30; Semevskii, "Domashnii byt," 112; Malykhin, "Byt," 208–9; Troitskii, "Selo Lipitsy," 83–84, and Semenova, *Zhizn' "Ivana.,"* 73–83.

ertheless, the huts, sens, sheds, and gornitsas should not be thought of as separate residences. They were all attached to one another, though not always connected by a door, and ethnographers consider them all part of the peasant home. These structures shared the same thatched roof, under which the peasants ate out of a common pot.[100]

Most outbuildings were constructed immediately adjacent to the hut and summer sleeping structures, though during the course of the nineteenth century they were increasingly separated off as a precaution against fire. In 1813, fifty-seven homesteads in Petrovskoe (90 percent) had granaries for storing cereals. These small granaries were constructed of logs, much like the huts, and often had elaborate wood carvings on the outside. The granary was an important structure to which the peasants devoted much time, for survival depended upon keeping their grain dry and safe from rodents and other small animals. In contrast, sarais, storage barns for agricultural equipment and carts as well as hay and chaff, were much cruder. The sarai was essentially a covered threshing floor, often enclosed only by a wattle fence. Over 60 percent of the households had at least one sarai.

Seventy percent of the homesteads in Petrovskoe were completely enclosed; that is, all the structures adjoined so only a solid facade of logs and planks was visible from outside. This afforded a large measure of privacy for households, and it also made it more difficult for members of different families to steal from one another. In addition, the layout of the homesteads discouraged much public life and socializing even when the peasants were not confined to the izba, as in the winter. Thus the household was a world apart from the village, having clearly separated itself off from the community at large, in the process minimizing communal interference or control of household matters.

At the far end of the household plot, some distance from the hut and other outbuildings and often even behind the kitchen garden, peasants built *ovins* and *banias*. Rye, millet, and

---

100. E. E. Blomkvist and O. A. Gantskaia, "Tipy russkogo krest'ianskogo zhilishcha serediny XIX–nachala XX v.," in *Russkie: Istoriko-etnograficheskii atlas*, ed. V. A. Aleksandrov et al. (Moscow, 1967), 1:131–49.

buckwheat were dried in sheaves in *ovins,* kilns; other cereals were winnowed by the wind. Kilns posed a substantial hazard and were frequently associated with village fires and accidental deaths in spite of their location. Nevertheless, over half the homesteads in Petrovskoe had kilns, and presumably those that did not would borrow or rent one from their neighbors. Finally, though Petrovskoe was situated on a river from which the peasants drew water, sixteen households, one-quarter, had *banias,* Russian baths. Here the peasants washed and steamed themselves. Those without banias simply turned their izba into steambaths, a luxury that only squalor would permit.[101]

To draw an overall assessment of the material base of life in Petrovskoe is difficult. Although quantifiable measures are useful in evaluating diet from a physiological standpoint, the pleasures of variety in food or the psychological benefits of an additional square yard of living space, though very real, cannot be so readily counted. Nevertheless, a number of points are worth noting.

It has been shown that there was nothing unique about the size of land allotments, grain yields, livestock holdings, or dwellings of the Petrovskoe serfs. The general level of prosperity, even if surprising, was not confined to this estate but prevailed throughout the region. Underneath the serfs was a paternalistic but limited welfare system. Yet this was a fragile and tenuous wealth, quickly lost in times of crisis, from which recovery must have been slow.

The household was physically cut off from the community and was the emotional center for much of life. The vast majority of households were self-supporting in food production, though all serfs lived in wretched housing. Still, the serfs of Petrovskoe were farmers with large amounts of land, even if used extensively, and large numbers of livestock compared with many of their European contemporaries. And thus it was on a base of relative, if tenuous, prosperity that the institution of serfdom, the degradation of man into property, existed.

101. TsGADA, f. 1262, op. 4, ch. 1, ed. khr. 41.

2

The Demographic Framework

FROM THE PRODUCTIVE CAPACITY OF THE ESTATE OF PETROV-skoe to support very large numbers of pre-working-age children emerges one of the fundamental bases of social control—the carefully regulated large, patriarchal household. In essence, the material base and the demographic framework of life at Petrovskoe provided the essential supports for all aspects of life. The household, however, was the function of a complex of demographic determinants that need to be analyzed first.

Because bailiffs of the Petrovskoe estate were periodically required to compile household inventories (*podvornye opisi*), it is possible to study the demographic characteristics of the estate population. These inventories specified the age, sex, marital status, and labor obligations, if any, of each household member. In addition, livestock holdings, housing and storage facilities, and grain reserves were recorded for every household. Thus the main estate office of the Gagarin family in Moscow could readily assess the productive capacity of the estate and judge the level of serf well-being according to the unit of production and consumption—the serf household. With the household inventories, the central administrators of the family's holdings could check on the bailiff in the field, seeing that he assigned the serfs adequate amounts of corvée without undermining the peasants' long-run capability to perform labor services.

The bailiffs, with their assistants and scribes, were certainly capable of recording this information correctly, given their extensive experience in bookkeeping. Internal demographic tests on the data show them to be extremely accurate. Blending procedures reveal little heaping in the reporting of ages. The age distribution of the population suggests little or no underenumeration of infants or children, a problem frequently encountered in historical demography. The results from the household lists conform to biological determinants affecting human populations and fall within anticipated demographic parameters for a premodern peasant society. Also, the data are consistent over the years, though they span the tenure of several bailiffs.

The only instance where any of the demographic data themselves raise a question is with the equal sex ratios evident in 1782 and 1810 (table 12). These figures come not from the household inventories, however, but from summary data provided by the bailiff. This unexpected balance in the sex ratios was probably the result of a heavier in-migration of males during this period, offsetting the effects of military recruitment. Migratory movements tend to be disproportionately male, and in the early years of Gagarin ownership serfs were being transferred to Petrovskoe from other family estates. There was certainly a greater need for males during these years to work as scribes, carpenters, and stableboys. This in-migration, which ended in the early nineteenth century, would also explain the previously noted decline in bunkhouses between 1819 and 1849.

The archives of the Petrovskoe estate contain nine household inventories, seven of which were compiled between 1813 and 1827. The remaining two date from 1850 and 1856.[1] If other inventories were compiled, they have been lost. It was not possible to gather demographic data for the entire estate given the constraints of working in Soviet archives. Therefore in this chapter the village of Petrovskoe, the largest of the eight settlements on the Petrovskoe estate, is the basis of analysis. The village had a population of from 523 to 762 serfs, and this sample is adequate for the demographic analysis undertaken here.

The household inventories did not include all the inhabitants of the estate, but only the servile population, thereby excluding the bailiff, the estate horse breeder and doctor, soldiers who had fulfilled their military obligations and returned home, all clergymen, and their nonserf families. The one exception was the wives of serfs recruited into the army (*soldatkas*) and any of their illegitimate children; though free persons, they were included in the first seven lists if they continued to reside

1. TsGADA, f. 1262, op. 1, ch. 1, ed. khr. 1495; op. 4, ch. 1, ed. khr. 41, 59, 121, 186, 344, 357, ch. 2, ed. khr. 822.

66

on the estate with serf relatives, as was usually the case. Only the last two lists were cross-referenced, making it possible to trace the fate of every serf between the years of 1850 and 1856. On the earlier lists, although immigration is obvious, it is impossible to distinguish between emigration and deaths taking place during the intervening years between compilations.

Monthly summary data from the registration of all births, deaths, and migration were also found in the archives for the years 1854–58.[2] The figures, however, cannot be verified and must be taken at face value. Nevertheless, they are of considerable interest, since they provide an independent confirmation of the nominative lists and in themselves are revealing.

Because the household inventories, or for demographic purposes nominative lists, of 1850 and 1856 were cross-referenced, they permit the calculation by sex of age-specific death rates. These rates, in turn, can easily be converted into mortality rates, from which an estimate of the expectation of life at birth can be determined. Table 13 gives the age-specific death rates, the mortality rates, and the estimates for life expectancy at birth for the village of Petrovskoe. Because the time period is short and the sample small, ten-year age intervals have been used. A comparison of the observed mortality rates with model life tables, in this case the Princeton "West" tables, produces the estimates for life expectancy.[3]

The mean of the estimates for the expectation of life at birth during the six-year period under consideration is 24.8 for females and 29.8 for males, discounting the male age interval 20–29, which, if included, would push the estimate up an additional 3.1 years. It has been excluded because in all likelihood the data for males of this age group are distorted by the heavy recruitment levies for the Crimean War. Between 1850 and 1856, twenty-two serfs from the village were drafted, eighteen of whom were in their twenties. One possible explanation for

2. TsGADA, f. 1262, op. 4, ch. 2, ed. khr. 652, 800, 823, 842.

3. The "West" tables were chosen because they have been found to be more applicable at high levels of mortality and because they encompass a greater range of variants than the other three models. A. J. Coale and P. Demeny, *Regional Model Life Tables and Stable Populations* (Princeton, 1966), part 1, p. 35, and part 2, pp. 4–7; T. H. Hollingsworth, *Historical Demography* (London, 1969), 342.

TABLE 13

Mortality Rates and Estimated Expectation of Life at Birth:
Village of Petrovskoe, 1850–56

Age	Population			Total Deaths	Death Rate	Mortality $(10qX)$	Estimated Expectation of Life at Birth (e_0^0)
	1850	1856	Mean				
Females							
10–19	71	70	70.5	4	9.5	91.3	29.3
20–29	63	52	57.5	6	17.4	161.7	24.2
30–39	67	59	63.0	8	21.2	193.9	25.1
40–49	50	54	52.0	9	28.8	255.2	20.6
Males							
10–19	83	78	80.5	4	8.3	80.1	27.2
20–29	56	69	62.5	3	8.0	77.4	(42.5)[a]
30–39	56	42	49.0	5	17.0	158.3	30.7
40–49	35	49	42.0	6	23.8	215.4	31.4

Source: TsGADA, f. 1262, op. 4, ch. 2, ed. khr. 822.
[a]Excluded from calculations; see explanation in text.

the high estimate of life expectancy for this age cohort is that the bailiff and the village commune, in filling draft quotas, rid the estate of serfs in ill-health or from poorer households, who were likely to have experienced higher rates of mortality had they remained in the village. This would have been a sensible policy. In fact the reason the estimates of male life expectancy exceed those of female life expectancy for all but the youngest age group is probably partly due to recruitment, though higher female mortality resulting from complications associated with childbirth is obviously a much more significant factor.

In spite of the problem posed by recruitment, the overall expectation of life at birth in the village based upon all persons aged 10–49 (except for males aged 20–29) can be calculated and was found to be 27.3 years. This estimate, however, should not be taken to mean that few serfs survived beyond age 30. A life expectancy of this sort implies high infant and child mortality. Perhaps as many as 450 out of every 1,000 persons born died before reaching age 5. In contrast, the average age of persons dying after age 5 was approximately 40 years. Similarly, persons 20 years old could expect, on the average, to live an additional 32 years.

Such circumstances were common throughout much of preindustrial Europe and are even encountered in developing countries today. Although by 1850 many Europeans and Scandanavians could anticipate living 41.6 years, this was a recent development.[4] In England and Wales, between 1781 and 1821, life expectancy remained relatively stable at 31.5 years.[5] In France at the end of the eighteenth century, the expectation of life was 28.8 years.[6] In both instances, however, local and regional variations were substantial, and the figures cover all social classes.

Expectation of life at birth is a useful measurement because it summarizes mortality conditions, although a complex of factors affect mortality, diet and private and public hygiene being the most important. For Petrovskoe, all that can be said is that the observed level of mortality was neither high nor low by the standards of Europe before 1800. There is no evidence that serfdom had a markedly adverse affect on mortality. In this regard the demographic data support the conclusions reached earlier. It appears that the marginally better diet of the Petrovskoe serfs was balanced by the extremely poor sanitary conditions, producing mortality levels roughly equivalent to those experienced by many peasants elsewhere in Europe. Nevertheless, since there are at present no comparable data for other estates in Russia, the question of the relation between serfdom and mortality must remain open. It is clear, however, that the demographic changes that took place throughout many parts of Europe during the first half of the nineteenth century had not reached Petrovskoe by 1856.

Combining the observed level of mortality with data from the household lists showing the age distribution of the village population makes it possible to estimate crude birthrates and death rates, though the latter are subject to a wide margin of

---

4. Wrigley, *Population*, 169–75.
5. Hollingsworth, *Historical Demography*, 346–48.
6. Wrigley, *Population*, 131.

error. To estimate these vital rates, however, requires the application of stable population theory, which poses a number of problems, since the population of Petrovskoe did not grow at a constant rate and the age structure changed over the years. In particular, the bad harvests of 1821 and 1848 coincided with mortality rates considerably above the norm. These demographic crises clearly destabilized Petrovskoe's population, complicating the use of stable population models. Sudden jumps in mortality will lower the estimate of the birthrate for the age groups most affected. But under more stable conditions, fertility is the primary determinant of the age structure of a population and mortality has only a small effect: in such a case, estimates of the birthrate would be scarcely affected even if only an educated guess of mortality levels were used.[7]

To estimate the birthrate and level of fertility for Petrovskoe, we must assume that the mortality conditions in the village for the years between 1813 and 1827 approximated those that have been observed for 1850 to 1856. This assumption is necessary because the earlier lists, up to 1827, do not permit the calculation of mortality rates, and the age distribution of the population in the years 1850 and 1856 was too much affected by the crisis of 1848. Nevertheless, this assumption is not at all unreasonable. The evidence presented in the previous chapter reveals no major change in the standard of living of the Petrovskoe serfs between 1813 and 1856, and certainly no change in the size of their land allotments or the number of horses they owned. If life expectancy was lower earlier in the century, then the result would be an underestimation of the birthrate. But, as I will show, this possibility is very unlikely. In any case, with a stable population, a variation by as much as 2.5 years in the expectation of life would change the estimates of the birthrate by only 2 per 1,000. Thus, in spite of obvious difficulties, using the mortality levels of the 1850s to approximate those of the earlier period should not introduce a substantial error.

Table 14 shows the estimated birthrate for both sexes

---

7. Coale and Demeny, *Regional Model*, part 1, pp. 33–35; Hollingsworth, *Historical Demography*, 341; and L. Henry, *Manuel de démographie historique*, 2d ed. (Paris, 1970), 36–37.

TABLE 14

Estimates of the Birthrate from the Cumulative Age Distribution of
the Village of Petrovskoe

Age Group	1813	1814	1818	1821	1824	1826	1827
0–4	54.2	55.7	53.1	(45.9)	(36.4)	(45.7)	(45.6)
5–9	54.6	55.1	57.3	53.6	(44.0)	(45.7)	(42.8)
10–14	54.0	53.7	55.7	58.0	51.5	51.0	(47.4)
15–19	54.0	54.5	53.4	55.8	55.1	54.3	51.8
20–24	56.5	52.1	54.1	56.2	54.7	52.7	51.0
25–29	52.5	52.6	50.3	54.1	53.4	54.1	52.1
30–34	52.7	52.3	52.0	53.9	53.1	52.6	52.4
35–39	52.8	53.3	53.2	51.6	52.4	52.5	50.9
40–44	55.7	56.4	51.3	53.7	52.4	50.4	49.6
45–49	51.2	54.1	55.6	51.7	52.4	52.5	53.0
50–54	52.4	51.7	51.3	58.4	55.7	50.7	50.9
55–59	60.1	59.4	49.3	49.2	52.1	59.4	56.6
Median	54.0	53.9	53.1	53.8	52.4	52.5	50.9
Mean	54.2	54.2	53.1	53.5	51.1	51.8	50.3

Source: TsGADA, f. 1262, op. 1, ch. 1, ed. khr. 1495; op. 4, ch. 1, ed. khr. 41, 59,
121, 186, 344, 357; ch. 2, ed. khr. 822.
Note: Males e_0^o = 29.8; females e_0^o = 24.8. Estimates in parentheses are low; see text.

combined, based upon the age structure of the village population between 1813 and 1827. The results by sex expressed lon-
gitudinally are presented in tables 15 and 16. For females,
mortality level 3 from the Princeton "West" model stable population was used; for males, mortality level 6.[8] These levels
approximate the mean of the estimates for the expectation of
life determined previously.

It is clear that the method employed entails some uncertainty. The discrepancy between the sexes is sometimes very
large, though on a village level such differences are not uncommon.[9] Those estimates of the birthrate that rely upon data from

8. Coale and Demeny, Regional Model, part 2, pp. 78, 180.
9. R. D. Lee, "Methods and Models for Analyzing Historical Series of
Births, Marriages, and Deaths," in Population Patterns in the Past (New York,
1977), 343.

the age groups most affected by the crisis of 1821 are necessarily low and therefore have been placed in parentheses.

The seven nominative lists compiled between 1813 and 1827 reveal an exceptionally high but stable birthrate. The median of all eighty-four estimates covering persons born between 1754 and 1827 is 52.9; the mean is 52.6. Because these rates are among the highest ever recorded, underenumeration of the village population can be discounted, further attesting to the

TABLE 15

Estimates of the Female Birthrate from the Cumulative Age
Distribution of the Village of Petrovskoe

Years	Estimate 1	Estimate 2	Years	Estimate 1	Estimate 2
1754–58	54.8	—	1790–94	44.9	49.9
1755–59	61.0	—	1792–96	51.5	50.1
1759–63	55.8	54.8	1793–97	50.3	—
1760–64	58.3	—	1794–98	48.0	51.0
1762–66	54.0	—	1795–99	48.5	51.6
1764–68	57.7	57.8	1797–1801	54.5	54.3
1765–69	59.6	56.2	1798–1802	52.3	—
1767–71	64.0	61.0	1799–1803	49.2	52.7
1768–72	55.5	—	1800–1804	48.1	55.0
1769–73	59.9	58.8	1802–6	56.0	53.4
1770–74	58.4	56.8	1803–7	51.2	—
1772–76	54.1	50.1	1804–8	48.7	55.1
1773–77	50.9	—	1805–9	48.1	55.5
1774–78	52.6	53.0	1807–11	58.4	55.0
1775–79	52.6	54.8	1808–12	51.0	—
1777–81	55.8	52.5	1809–13	42.6	56.1
1778–82	51.9	—	1810–14	44.0	51.8
1779–83	54.3	55.0	1812–16	56.1	52.7
1780–84	53.9	52.3	1813–17	(48.8)	—
1782–86	53.2	51.0	1814–18	61.2	—
1783–87	49.7	—	1815–19	(50.3)	—
1784–88	51.6	54.3	1817–21	(51.4)	—
1785–89	52.9	53.0	1818–22	(43.2)	—
1787–91	52.6	49.9	1820–24	(35.4)	—
1788–92	48.5	—	1822–26	(45.7)	—
1789–93	45.7	46.7	1823–27	(43.3)	—

Source: See table 14.
Note: e_0^o = 24.8. Estimates in parentheses are low; see text.

accuracy of the original data.[10] In addition, the likelihood that the expectation of life at birth underlying these estimates should be lower, forcing an upward revision of the figures, is very small.

With a life expectancy at birth for females of 24.8 years, their age distribution between 1813 and 1827 reflects a gross reproduction rate (GRR) of 3.46, a very high level of fertility. In other words, the average woman living through the child-bearing period would give birth to almost seven children. The net reproduction rate (NRR), however, was only 1.36, implying a high death rate. On the basis of observed mortality levels, the overall death rate would be 38 per 1,000—34 for males and 41 for females. The rate for females may be closer to reality, however, because of the problems in estimating male life expectancy that result from recruitment. But estimating death rates and the NRR involves a substantial margin of error. Small changes in the expectation of life produce great differences in death rates, and the figures just given must be considered in this light.

The subsistence crisis of 1848–49 had a significantly greater effect on Petrovskoe than did the crisis of 1821, destabilizing the population to such an extent that almost any attempt to estimate the birthrate based upon the age structure from the 1850 and 1856 lists would be fruitless. The age interval 0–4, from the 1856 list, however, was obviously not affected by the crisis and may be used to estimate very roughly the birthrate for the years 1852–56. Surprisingly, although a rise in the birthrate might be expected as part of the recovery process following such a crisis, the figures suggest a birthrate of only 40.6 per 1,000. In all likelihood, fertility was lower as a result of Crimean War recruitment levies. Also, neither the illegitimate children of soldatkas nor their legitimate children born within nine months of their husbands' recruitment were included in these lists, and these omissions will push the estimate downward.

---

10. Wrigley, *Population*, 62. See D. M. Heer, "The Demographic Transition in the Russian Empire and the Soviet Union," *Journal of Social History* 1 (1968):205, for a similar comment on demographic data for the empire in the postemancipation period.

This last estimate can be compared with the monthly summary data of all registered births found in the archives for the same time period. Again, illegitimate children were not mentioned, and it is doubtful if stillborn children or those who died before baptism were included. From 15 October 1850 to 31 October 1854, the bailiff recorded 121 births in Petrovskoe, for an average annual birthrate of 40.2 per 1,000. During the following twelve months the birthrate fell to 27.2, and between

TABLE 16

Estimates of the Male Birthrate from the Cumulative Age Distribution of the Village of Petrovskoe

Years	Estimate 1	Estimate 2	Years	Estimate 1	Estimate 2
1754–58	65.4	—	1790–94	59.4	56.4
1755–59	57.8	—	1792–96	56.7	55.1
1759–63	49.1	43.9	1793–97	54.5	—
1760–64	45.2	—	1794–98	60.0	57.3
1762–66	44.4	—	1795–99	60.6	55.2
1764–68	44.8	44.9	1797–1801	58.0	53.9
1765–69	48.7	48.1	1798–1802	51.9	—
1767–71	52.8	57.8	1799–1803	58.8	54.1
1768–72	57.8	—	1800–1804	59.4	54.4
1769–73	51.5	52.5	1802–6	55.6	52.0
1770–74	54.5	54.7	1803–7	50.9	—
1772–76	49.4	52.3	1804–8	60.6	56.3
1773–77	50.9	—	1805–9	62.2	54.8
1774–78	53.0	49.6	1807–11	57.6	53.7
1775–79	54.1	50.1	1808–12	52.7	—
1777–81	51.7	52.5	1809–13	65.8	58.6
1778–82	54.2	—	1810–14	67.5	51.3
1779–83	51.2	51.5	1812–16	51.2	49.4
1780–84	50.7	52.6	1813–17	(46.0)	—
1782–86	50.1	49.8	1814–18	45.0	—
1783–87	49.6	—	1815–19	(37.7)	—
1784–88	52.9	49.7	1817–21	(40.4)	—
1785–89	52.4	51.9	1818–22	(42.5)	—
1787–91	55.3	55.1	1820–24	(37.5)	—
1788–92	53.3	—	1822–26	(45.7)	—
1789–93	58.4	53.9	1823–27	(48.0)	—

Source: See table 14.
Note: e_0^o = 29.8. Estimates in parentheses are low; see text.

1 November 1855 and 31 October 1857 the birthrate dropped to a very low 19.4. Allowing for a nine-month time lag, the decline in the birthrate coincides precisely with the pattern of recruitment. Of the twenty-two males who entered the military between 1850 and 1858, sixteen were drafted in 1854 and 1855. By 1858, however, two years after the last levy, the birthrate had recovered considerably and stood at 32.9 per 1,000.[11]

Any short-lived system of registration is likely to result in an underestimation of the true rate. The one-time effort required to compile a nominative list, which has as its sole criterion who is alive and present in the village, is much simpler than an ongoing process of vital registration, which involves the more complex, but statistically important, problem of infant births and deaths. Nevertheless, the pattern revealed by the data is intriguing, and the results, if low, may be considered minimum estimates.

It is not surprising that the birthrate at Petrovskoe was stable for at least seventy years, from 1750 to 1820, and if more data were available they would probably indicate that it remained stable over a much longer period, because population stability was a feature of many preindustrial societies. What is surprising is that the birthrate was stable at an unusually high level, a fact that had serious social and economic implications. First, the population of the village was quite young. The average age of all persons (on the basis of the nine lists) was 23.4 years, with 51.2 percent of the total population below age 20. Consequently, the dependency ratio for both sexes (the number of persons younger than 15 or 60 and over relative to those aged 15 to 59) was high, averaging 0.84 between 1813 and 1827. In other words, there was a very large number of non-working-age persons relative to workers. Between these same years, the percentage under age 20 fluctuated only slightly, from a high of 53.9 in 1821 to a low of 51.0 in 1827. Second, the mean age at first marriage for females must have been low, and there can be no question of family limitation at Petrovskoe, though much of the very high fertility was frustrated by death. Finally, it is likely that an annual growth rate of 0.5 to 1.5

11. TsGADA, f. 1262, op. 4, ch. 2, ed. khr. 652, 800, 823, 842.

percent persisted in the village for over one hundred years, from at least as early as the mid-eighteenth century, interrupted but not offset by periodic demographic crises. The uncertainty in the natural growth rate is a reflection of the problems involved in ascertaining the death rate.

From the nominative lists it is clear that the serfs of Petrovskoe did not follow the so-called European marriage pattern of waiting until their midtwenties to wed, which left as many as 40 to 60 percent of the women of childbearing age unmarried. Rather, the mean age at first marriage at Petrovskoe was 18.9 for females and 19.3 for males (see table 17). Usually, 30 percent of all females aged 15 to 19 and well over 90 percent of those from 20 to 24 were married. Even when the crisis of 1848–49 forced the postponement of many weddings, by 1850 only 29 percent of all females aged 20 to 24 were still single.

As one nineteenth-century ethnographer put it in discussing the high incidence of marriage among the peasants of Elatma district, Tambov province, two hundred miles directly north of Petrovskoe, "only freaks and the morally depraved do

TABLE 17

Average Age at First Marriage, Village of Petrovskoe

Years	Males		Females	
	N	Average	N	Average
1813–27	68	18.8	67	18.4
1831	—	—	5	19.1
1850–56	38	20.1	61	19.5

Source: Besides the nine nominative lists, TsGADA, f. 1262, op. 4, ch. 1, ed. khr. 754.
Note: It is possible that a few remarriages have been included in the data, since a serf listed as single on one list and married on the following could have married more than once during the interval. For the period 1813–27, the maximum interval was 3.75 years; between 1850 and 1856 a six-year interval is involved, since there are no intervening lists. The discrepancy between the number of marriages observed for males and females between 1850 and 1856 is a result of recruitment. Single women in 1850 who were soldatkas in 1856 obviously married during the intervening years. However, recruited serfs who married after 1850, but before entering the army or navy, cannot be distinguished from single males who were conscripted.

not marry."[12] In fact, women 20 to 40, the most fertile group, were rarely without husbands, and permanent celibacy was virtually unknown (see table 18). Thus it is likely that family and social pressures favoring early and universal marriage were compelling. The data suggest few deviations from this pattern. Table 17 does seem to suggest a slight rise in the mean age at first marriage between 1813 and 1856, an increase Peter Czap has also observed.[13] This was probably not so, though more evidence is required. The higher ages recorded between 1850 and 1856 are more likely the result of temporary delays in marriage owing first to the subsistence crisis and cholera epidemic of 1848–49 and then to recruitment levies during the Crimean War. There is certainly not adequate evidence to conclude that there was a gradual long-term increase in the age at first marriage during the nineteenth century.

High fertility made large, structurally complex three-generation households possible; they existed in large part because of prohibitions against household fission and, to a lesser extent, because of patterns of child adoption and household or family mergers. The household (*dvor*) is taken here to mean all persons living under one roof, sharing a residential unit that combined production and consumption functions in which virtually all property was held in common. The nominative lists clearly distinguished between the members of a household and those within it who were related by blood, so there is no confusion of household and family in the sources to complicate the analysis. But in actuality extremely few households had nonfamily members. The practice of taking in domestic servants, apprentices, or lodgers simply did not exist. As for orphans, given the household structures at Petrovskoe, in spite of the high mor-

---

12. A. P. Zvonkov, "Sovremennye brak i svad'ba sredi krest'ian Tambovskoi gubernii, Elatomskago uezda," in *Izvestiia Imperatorskago obshchestva liubitelei estestvoznaniia, antropologii i etnografii, Trudy etnograficheskago otdela,* 61 (Moscow, 1889), 9:30–31.
13. J. Hanjal, "European Marriage Patterns in Perspective," in *Population in History,* ed. D. V. Glass and D. E. C. Eversley (London and Chicago, 1965), 101–43; F. Lebrun, *La vie conjugale sous l'Ancien Régime* (Paris, 1975), 31–33; P. Czap, "Marriage and the Peasant Joint Family in the Era of Serfdom," in *The Family in Imperial Russia,* ed. David L. Ransel (Urbana, Ill., 1978), 110–13.

TABLE 18

Percentages of Females of Childbearing Age Single, Widowed, or with Husbands in Military Service

Year	Single					Widowed					Soldatkas					Totals				
	15–19	20–24	25–29	30–39	40–49	15–19	20–24	25–29	30–39	40–49	15–19	20–24	25–29	30–39	40–49	15–19	20–24	25–29	30–39	40–49
1813	68.0	5.0	0.0	2.9	0.0	0.0	0.0	0.0	11.4	35.7	0.0	10.0	29.0	8.6	0.0	68.0	15.0	29.0	22.9	35.7
1814	71.4	5.6	0.0	2.9	0.0	0.0	0.0	2.8	5.9	36.7	0.0	5.6	27.8	5.9	3.3	71.4	11.2	30.6	14.7	40.0
1818	77.8	4.2	0.0	2.0	0.0	0.0	0.0	0.0	0.0	31.0	0.0	0.0	10.5	18.4	6.9	77.8	4.2	10.5	20.4	37.9
1821	74.1	8.3	0.0	0.0	0.0	0.0	0.0	0.0	12.5	25.9	0.0	0.0	0.0	15.0	11.1	74.1	8.3	0.0	27.5	37.0
1824	55.3	3.7	0.0	0.0	0.0	0.0	0.0	0.0	14.6	24.1	0.0	0.0	5.6	9.8	13.8	55.3	3.7	5.6	24.4	37.9
1826	62.2	0.0	0.0	0.0	0.0	0.0	0.0	0.0	3.0	24.2	0.0	0.0	4.0	9.1	9.1	62.2	0.0	4.0	12.1	33.3
1827	77.8	3.4	3.7	0.0	0.0	0.0	6.9	0.0	0.0	14.7	0.0	0.0	3.7	8.8	8.8	77.8	10.3	7.4	8.8	23.5
1850	91.3	28.6	6.5	5.6	2.0	0.0	2.4	3.2	9.9	34.0	—	—	—	—	—	91.3	31.0	9.7	15.5	36.6
1856	57.1	12.0	10.3	8.5	0.0	0.0	4.0	0.1	8.5	14.8	—	—	—	—	—	57.1	16.0	10.4	17.0	14.8

Source: See table 14.

tality, the likelihood that a minor would be left with no related adult workers in the household was small. If a child's parents died, there was generally no need for adoption. Orphans, in almost all cases, continued to live with grandparents, aunts, or uncles, and these children posed no problems regarding either marriage or their access to land. There were very few instances when the commune or the bailiff had to be concerned with resettling orphans into other households. Presumably in such cases they were placed wherever there was room.

Tables 19, 20, and 21 show, respectively, households by structure, number of conjugal family units per household, and households by generational depth. For comparative purposes, the classification of households in table 19 is a slightly modified version of Laslett's system in which a family (or more properly a conjugal family unit) "consists of a married couple, or a married couple with offspring, or of a widowed person with offspring."[14]

Between 1813 and 1834, mean household size (MHS) at Petrovskoe varied from a high of 9.0 in 1818 to a low of 7.7 in 1824, the latter figure being the first observation after the 1821–22 crop failure. Given the observed life expectancy, age at marriage, household structure, and gross reproduction rate, a mean household size of 8 to 9 persons comes close to the biological maximum. In other words, the demographics of the village were the primary determinants of household size, and household fission was of secondary importance, though still critical. Households could not have been considerably larger unless the predominant structure of blood relations within them was altered by allowing multiple family households to exist that had members more distantly related than first cousins. But such households were rare.[15]

14. P. Laslett, "Introduction: The History of the Family," in *Household and Family in Past Time*, ed. P. Laslett (Cambridge, 1972), 29–31.
15. With an e_0^0 (life expectancy at birth) of 40, a GRR of 4.0, and an age at marriage of 20, MHS with an extended family structure with foster mothers would be 12.4 persons, while with an e_0^0 of 20, a GRR of 3.0, and the same age at marriage and household structure, the MHS would be 6.0. Petrovskoe comes very close to the midpoint of these parameters. T. K. Burch, "Some Demographic Determinants of Average Household Size: An Analytic Approach," in *Household and Family in Past Time*, ed. P. Laslett (Cambridge, 1972), 94–96.

TABLE 19

Households by Structure, Village of Petrovskoe

Household Structure	1813 N	1813 %	1814 N	1814 %	1818 N	1818 %	1821 N	1821 %	1824 N	1824 %	1826 N	1826 %	1827 N	1827 %	1850 N	1850 %	1856 N	1856 %
Solitaries																		
Widowed	2		1		0		3		2		2		1		5		8	
Single, or of unknown marital status	0		0		0		0		0		0		0		2		3	
Total	2	3	1	2	0	0	3	4	2	3	2	3	1	1	7	7	11	9
No family																		
Coresident siblings	0		0		0		0		0		0		0		1		0	
Coresident relatives of other kinds	0		0		0		0		0		0		0		1		1	
Persons not evidently related	0		0		1		1		1		1		1		1		0	
Total	0	0	0	0	1	2	1	1	1	1	1	1	1	1	3	3	1	1
Simple family households																		
Married couples alone	0		0		0		0		1		1		1		0		3	
Married couples with child(ren)	6		7		3		4		10		12		9		7		18	
Widowers with child(ren)	0		0		0		0		0		0		0		0		1	

The following is a complex statistical table printed sideways (rotated) on the page. The column headers are not present on this page (cut off), so only the row labels and numeric data can be transcribed. Values represent household counts and percentages for several estates/periods.

Widows with child(ren)	2	2	2	3	2	2	3	1	2	10	8
Soldatkas with child(ren)	1	1	0	2	0	0	2	1	0	0	0
Total	9	14	10	15	9	13	12	17	14	16	30 (24)
Extended family households											
Extended upward	2	1	1	5	2	4	3	6	4	5	11
Extended downward	0	0	2	2	2	1	2	3	1	4	5
Extended laterally	3	2	1	0	3	2	3	0	2	3	3
Combinations of above	0	0	5	1	5	3	5	3	3	2	6
Extension unknown	0	0	0	0	0	0	0	0	0	1	2
Total	5	8	3	5	10	10	13	17	14	15	27 (22)
Multiple family households											
Secondary unit(s) up	15	14	13	6	11	9	12	11	13		
Secondary unit(s) down	9	13	14	13	3	5	5	4	12		
Units all on one level	2	2	5	6	10	9	9	6	7		
Frérèches	5	6	5	5	6	4	4	9	6		
Other multiple families	17	16	13	14	17	20	19	32	18		
Total	48	75	51	78	47	49	64	64	62	56	45
Totals	64	100	65	100	50	78	69	99	47	125	101

Source: TsGADA, f. 1262, op. 1, ch. 1, ed. khr. 1495; op. 4, ch. 1, ed. khr. 41, 59, 121, 186, 344, 357; ch. 2, ed. khr. 822.

TABLE 20

Conjugal Family Units per Household, Village of Petrovskoe

Conjugal Family Units	1813		1814		1818		1821		1824		1826		1827		1850		1856	
	N	%	N	%	N	%	N	%	N	%	N	%	N	%	N	%	N	%
0	2	3	1	2	1	2	4	6	3	4	3	4	2	3	10	10	12	10
1	14	22	13	20	13	20	21	30	24	32	25	33	25	33	32	31	57	46
2	32	50	36	55	32	50	28	41	30	41	27	36	31	41	29	28	34	27
3	11	17	10	15	11	17	12	17	8	11	13	17	12	16	20	19	16	13
4	5	8	5	8	7	11	3	4	8	11	6	8	6	8	11	11	4	3
5							1	1	1	1	0	0			2	2	2	2
6											1	1						
Totals	64	100	65	100	64	100	69	99	74	100	75	99	76	101	104	101	125	101

Source: See table 14.

Table 21

Households by Generational Depth, Village of Petrovskoe

Number of Households

Number of Generations	1813		1814		1818		1821		1824		1826		1827		1850		1856	
	N	%	N	%	N	%	N	%	N	%	N	%	N	%	N	%	N	%
1	3	5	2	3	0	0	3	4	3	4	3	4	2	3	11	11	17	14
2	25	39	25	38	16	25	28	41	31	42	30	40	31	41	53	51	63	50
3	29	45	32	49	39	61	33	48	36	49	38	51	38	50	37	36	41	33
4	4	6	3	5	3	5	1	1	1	1	2	3	3	4	1	1	1	1
Unknown	3	5	3	5	6	9	4	6	3	4	2	3	2	3	2	2	3	2
Total households	64	100	65	100	64	100	69	100	74	100	75	101	76	101	104	101	125	100

Source: See table 14.

That MHS approached the biological limit is supported by evidence of the relative infrequency of household fission. Between 1813 and 1827 there were sixty-eight first marriages and fourteen remarriages in Petrovskoe, but the number of households increased only from sixty-four to seventy-six, or just one new household for every 5.7 first marriages. All of these new couples, however, remained in the village, and in almost every case the bride entered the household to which her husband belonged. Neither marriage nor even the death of a head of household precipitated the formation of a new household.[16]

Of the twelve households that undertook division between 1813 and 1827, in only two instances did the original household then have a new head. In contrast, thirty-two heads of household died during these fourteen years. The mean age at which a male serf became the head of a household by the death of the former head (assuming female ascendants could serve in this capacity) was 38.5 years. For those males becoming household heads owing to the division of one household into two or more, the mean age was 40.8 years. Thus a 19-year-old male serf, recently married, who had a life expectancy at this age of thirty to thirty-five more years, could anticipate becoming the absolute head of his own household only after waiting twenty years.

In the life cycle of a peasant household, it was at precisely the time when a male serf could first expect to become a grandfather (between age 35 and 45) that he established sole authority in his own household. Expressed in terms of probability, using the model life tables, fully 74 percent of all 20-year-old males would survive to age 40 to become heads of household. This suggests that the anxiety of never getting out from under an elder's authority would have been limited. If these same serfs were fortunate enough to live an additional twenty years, the cycle would repeat itself. The mean age of a male head of household undertaking the division of his own dvor was 58.7 years.

The rate at which households divided was a key factor

16. See also F. Barykov, "Obychai nasledovaniia u gosudarstvennykh krest'ian," *ZhMGI* 91 part 2 (1862):8–9.

regulating village life and one of the most critical aspects of social control. Maintenance of the life cycle just described permitted the continuous realization of a three-generation, multiple-family household ideal. An absolute prohibition of household fission, however, would have resulted in inordinately large, agnatically structured households similar to certain variants of the South Slav *zadruga*. But as table 22 shows, the pattern of division is evidence of a clear intent to prevent households from becoming extremely large, with members more distantly related than first cousins.

Males at age 40 ready to establish their own household by division represented, so to speak, a completed cycle, which if left unending threatened to undermine the patriarchal/matriarchal base of a dvor, converting it into a larger, loosely related household. Equally important, between 1813 and 1827, when the number of households kept pace with net population growth (see table 12), there was no separation of fathers and sons as households divided. The same holds true for

TABLE 22

Pattern of Household Divisions

Old Head/New Head	1813–27	1850–56
Same generation		
Brother/brother	4	7
Brother-in-law/sister-in-law	2	7
Cousin/cousin	1	3
Total	7	17
Different generations		
Uncle/nephew	2	5
Aunt/nephew	—	3
Father-in-law/daughter-in-law	2	1
Father/son	—	1
Father/stepson	—	1
Mother/stepson	1	—
Total	5	11

Source: See table 14.
Note: Between 1850 and 1856 only twenty-two households divided, but they formed a total of fifty households, twenty-two old and twenty-eight new; that is, some households split into three or four separate households.

the later period, 1850 to 1856, even though the number of households grew much faster than the village population for a short time.[17] In part the absence of father/son splits is attributable to the demographics of the village, for only a small percentage of 40-year-old serfs would have had fathers still alive. But these few sons clearly did not separate from their fathers.

Thus, since the average age of a new head of household was 40 and sons rarely lived apart from their fathers, fission must have occurred between two more distantly related and competing foci of three-generation authority in the household, thereby avoiding tensions created by the unfulfilled desires for patriarchal and matriarchal rights. For most male serfs, the years between the ages of 35 and 45 involved becoming head of a household, a new patriarch, and a new grandfather. Their wives enjoyed a similar change in status. As table 23 shows, there was little deviation in this mean age.

The most intriguing question that emerges from the study of household division relates not to the demographic factors favoring large agnatic households but to the pressures that prevented serfs from dividing before the potential head of household attained the age of 40. The evils of indiscriminate or unregulated household division in the regions where the repartitional land commune existed were well known to landlords

17. Between 1850 and 1856, households divided at a rate three times higher than during 1813–27, when the number of households grew by 1 percent annually. Estate records indicate that this high frequency of household division was both unusual and short-lived, beginning in the 1850s and ending by 1858. TsGADA, f. 1262, op. 4, ch. 2, ed. khr. 866, 7 November 1858. This is corroborated by the data from the nominative lists. The essential characteristics of the households of Petrovskoe were only slightly affected by the crisis of 1848–49, meaning that the household life cycle observed during 1813–27 persisted up to 1850. Nevertheless, the formation of many new households in the 1850s sharply reduced MHS and the number of multiple-family households. The age at which a male became the sole head of his household, however, was only slightly lower than previously noted, attesting to the recent nature of increased household fission. Had it existed for more than three or four years, the drop in age would have been dramatic. As to the cause, recruitment levies during the Crimean War are most suspect. Because larger households could more readily afford the loss of an adult male worker, in times of heavy recruitment they were more susceptible to the draft. To avoid this many large households divided into smaller units, which for some unclear reason the bailiff permitted, though it eventually resulted in the termination of his services.

TABLE 23

Percentage of Males by Age Never Having Been Heads of
Household, Village of Petrovskoe (Female Heads Allowed)

Age	1813	1814	1818	1821	1824	1826	1827	1850	1856	Average
25–29	91.7	100.0	93.8	100.0	81.8	88.5	91.7	84.6	87.5	91.1
30–34	66.7	73.3	91.7	80.0	68.4	70.0	73.9	92.6	75.5	76.9
35–39	56.3	52.6	61.1	100.0	66.7	53.3	71.4	77.4	45.5	64.9
40–49	33.3	29.4	33.3	31.8	42.7	35.0	29.2	40.0	32.7	34.2
50–59	21.7	11.1	10.0	8.3	7.1	0.0	6.7	9.5	16.7	10.1

Sources: See table 14.

and bailiffs in prereform Russia.[18] In Petrovskoe it was felt
necessary to force the serfs to live in "artifically" large and
complex households. The failure to maintain the delicately balanced life cycle underlying the three-generation patriarchal
household would result, it was believed, in the economic ruin
of the peasants and the rise of social disorder on the estate.

When a new bailiff took over the operation of Petrovskoe
in 1834, he noted in a weekly report to his supervisors in
Moscow:

> Division among the peasants was permitted by the pre-
> vious management. Everyone fulfilled his whims, which
> were carried to excess; nephew divided from uncle, broth-
> er from brother. And at the present time a family with
> only one working-age couple cannot carry out either its
> estate labor obligations or own field work, and such
> households will always be poverty-stricken. Because of
> this, it is strictly forbidden for the village elders to divide

18. Dmitriukov, "Nravy," 267; Rudnev, "Selo Golun'," 107–8;
ZLOSKh za 1853, ch. 1, pp. 358–59; Ia. P. Rudnev, "Zametki po raznym
khoziaistvennym predmetam," *ZLOSKh za 1854*, ch. 2, pp. 300–301;
ZLOSKh za 1855, ch. 2, pp. 117–19; Kishkin, "Dannye i predpolozheniia,"
227–28; Nasonov, "Iz istorii," 506–7; N. K. Brzheskii, *Ocherki iuridicheskago byta krest'ian* (Saint Petersburg, 1902), 62, 103–4, 112–15; Aleksandrov, *Sel'skaia obshchina*, 300–301; A. Efimenko, "Semeinye razdely," in
Izsledovaniia narodnoi zhizni (Moscow, 1884), 1:133; and V. P. Mukhin,
Obychnyi poriadok nasledovaniia u krest'ian (Saint Petersburg, 1888), 41–43.

households at will without the permission of the estate management.[19]

Identical sentiments were expressed by another new steward when he arrived at Petrovskoe in 1858:

> From the lack of attention [given by the previous bailiff] to the way of life of the peasants, many of them have divided into the very smallest of families, with poverty the consequence of such division, and with poverty comes theft, drunkenness, and many other vices. . . . For the future, the division of peasants is prohibited.[20]

That some adult males on the Petrovskoe estate were prevented from living in the smaller, less complex households they preferred is supported by evidence from the manuals of discipline kept by the various bailiffs. In 1818 there were 418 households on the entire estate. Over the next twenty-five years approximately 125 new households were established by division, or five per year, with an average annual increase of slightly over 1 percent. More households wanted to divide. Between 1821 and 1840 at least thirty-seven households split without appropriate approval, resulting in corporal punishment for the adult male attempting to set up his dvor and the reestablishment of a single household. The punishment records are complete for only nine of these nineteen years, so it is probable that even more serfs divided their households without permission, seeking to accelerate the rate of household formation.

What the bailiffs felt to be the optimum size and structure of serf households did not coincide with the desire of many adult males to avoid the authority of an uncle, aunt, elder brother, or cousin. Nevertheless, the dangers of permanent subordination were both appreciated and avoided. The pattern of household division reveals that the diligent steward carefully regulated peasant households so as to balance the demographic pressures that would quickly dilute kinship relations within them with the desire for the independent smaller, but feared poorer, units that many younger adult serfs plainly wanted.

19. TsGADA, f. 1262, op. 4, ch. 1, ed. khr. 496, 12 April 1834.
20. TsGADA, f. 1262, op. 4, ch. 2, ed. khr. 866, 7 November 1858.

The bailiffs, therefore, believed they were forcing on these serfs a way of life that sacrificed interpersonal relations among household members for a higher standard of living in the dvor and greater harmony in the village as a whole. The fact of being a serf in Petrovskoe stripped individuals of the right to resolve these matters for themselves and so to decide their own appropriate equilibrium level.

Presumably small households had truncated developmental cycles, most frequently owing to death, recruitment, or a sex imbalance in one generation. Household extinction or mergers, however, were unusual. Of the sixty-four households in Petrovskoe in 1813, fifty-seven (89 percent) were still present fourteen years later. Some of these, of course, had divided to form new households. There was only one merger, when a 65-year-old widow living alone went to live in a seemingly unrelated household, though she may have been a distant relative. Six households' fate is unknown. Some may have moved to another estate village or more probably were transferred to another Gagarin estate. Some may have become extinct. Whatever the actual number, it is small. Thus it is the stability and longevity of households, in spite of their many passing internal changes, that is noteworthy.

In summary, estimates of life expectancy at birth in Petrovskoe show that the overall standard of living must have been similar to that of many parts of preindustrial Europe. Yet life in Petrovskoe took place in a framework of stable and very high fertility, early and universal marriage, and large, closely related, structurally complex three-generation households. These circumstances, though by no means unique to Petrovskoe, varied considerably from much of central and western Europe, where later marriage and lower fertility made smaller, simpler households more common, if not the norm. Individual households in much of Europe were more fluid, and they had more varied structures. They experienced comparatively high rates of extinction and consequently lacked continuity over time.[21]

21. Wrigley, *Population*, 131–34, 192; Lebrun, *Vie conjugale*, 57–63; E. Shorter, *The Making of the Modern Family* (New York, 1975), 29–39; William J. Goode, *World Revolution and Family Patterns* (New York, 1963),

The peasant household in Petrovskoe thus stood between the stem family, common throughout much of central and western Europe, and the very large Serbian *zadruga* or Baltic *Gesind*, which usually had from ten to thirty members.[22] With roughly three-quarters of all village residents living at any one time in households with two or more conjugal family units, and with two-thirds of all inhabitants similarly in households of three or more generations, virtually every serf would have experienced these circumstances for a number of years. Many spent their whole lives in households of this type.

A male serf rarely left the paternal household as long as his father was alive. Even excessive division did not result in a son's separating from his father, according to the bailiff's comment in 1834. Upon the death of the head of a household, the economic consequences were minimal. Although a brother or son might inherit the rights and privileges of the patriarch, nephews and other brothers were not dispossessed. Rather, they remained within the household until they could establish their own multiple-family, three-generation unit, thereby maintaining the ideal. With household life cycles compressed into twenty years, the essential characteristics of any individual household varied only slightly over time. As a result, and of great importance, fluctuations in a household's productive strength were minimized, and vulnerability to cyclical extremes of poverty and wealth owing to changes in household composition were reduced. Households as units of production and consumption persisted as if economically immune to the births, marriages, and deaths occurring within them. This stability was the real goal of the bailiff, for the smooth transition of every household through life's demographic rewards and traumas greatly facilitated the servile system of labor.

7–17; Laslett, *Household and Family*, passim; Louise Tilly and Joan Scott, *Women, Work, and Family* (New York, 1978), 24–27.

22. Shorter, *Making of the Modern Family*, 35–37.

3

BAILIFFS AND PATRIARCHS:
A CONJUNCTION OF INTERESTS

MARRIAGE PATTERNS, HOUSEHOLD STRUCTURES, AND FERTIL-
ity levels, of course, were not simply mandated by the bailiff.
For the historian it is necessary to distinguish among the
ecological, cultural, and seigneurial influences affecting the
structures of serf life—in particular the development of serf
domestic groups. This chapter seeks to interrelate the material
base of society and its demographic framework with the social structures of Russian serfdom erected on them. It seeks
to analyze the effects of the physical and human constraints on
the institution of serfdom and to describe the structure of
social control that existed for the purposes of economic exploitation. This requires a discussion of status, of the distribution of wealth and power, and of the exercise of authority on
the estate.

In an agricultural society with a very low level of technology and more than adequate amounts of arable land, as in
Petrovskoe and much of the central agricultural region in imperial Russia, labor was of the utmost value and the primary determinant of output. Other than draft animals, additional
capital inputs were extremely limited. But in Russia the climate
uniquely affected the structure of field labor organization. As a
consequence of the extremely short growing season—five and a
half to six months instead of the eight to nine months in western Europe—under the three-field system the harvesting of
winter and spring cereals and the plowing and sowing of the
winter field all came in quick succession within the span of six
weeks. From mid-July to the end of August was the harvest
season, the *stradnaia pora* as the Russians called it, literally the
time of suffering. It was an agonizing period of exertion de-
manding that numerous tasks be accomplished simultaneously.
A work team, or tiaglo, of husband and wife together proved
the best allocation of labor resources. A single male simply
could not complete all the necessary field work if he were to

allow the cereals to mature fully yet avoid the danger of an early frost.[1]

There thus emerged in Russia a clear differentiation of field labor by sex. During the harvest season, women used sickles to cut rye, winter wheat, if any, and sometimes oats, while the men reaped the other spring cereals with scythes. Winter crops could not be cut with a scythe because it knocked too many seeds off the stock, but this was not a problem with less ripe spring cereals. The women then tied the grain into sheaves for drying, and the men began plowing the winter field. While they sowed the next year's rye crop, the women started to cart the sheaves from the fields, assisted by their husbands if time permitted. In general, plowing, harrowing, cutting hay, and harvesting with a scythe were men's field work; tending the kitchen garden and hemp field, raking hay, cutting stalks with a sickle, tying them, and transporting them to the threshing floor were women's field work.[2]

A partnership was essential. Single or widowed females were never part of a work team, and rarely did males carry a full tiaglo alone. Of all males aged 15–19, the interval during which they first assumed some estate field labor obligations, receiving in return a land allotment, 38 percent carried no tiaglo, and none of these were married; 32 percent carried a

---

1. In the Far North and in Finland, for example, an even shorter growing season did not impose the same constraints. This was due either to low population density, abundant forests, and the use of slash-and-burn techniques of farming or to the possibility for substantial nonagricultural subsistence alternatives—hunting and especially fishing. N. Kalachov, "Iuridicheskie obychai krest'ian v nekotorykh mestnostiakh," in *Arkhiv istoricheskikh i prakticheskikh svedenii, otnosiashchikhsia do Rossii* (Saint Petersburg, 1859), 2:25; Kishkin, "Dannye i predpolozheniia," 226; A. G. Smirnov, *Ocherki semeinykh otnoshenii po obychnomu pravu russkago naroda* (Moscow, 1878), 76–81; and Nasonov, "Iz istorii," 518. See also Olga Crisp, "The Pattern of Industrialization in Russia, 1700–1914," in *Studies in the Russian Economy before 1914* (London, 1976), 21.

2. The weekly reports of the bailiff of Petrovskoe to Moscow usually noted the tasks assigned to men and women during the previous seven days, and these documents reveal the division of labor. See also Mashkin, "Byt," 95–96, 101; Preobrazhenskii, "Volost' Pokrovsko-Sitskaia," 79–80; and D. I., "Zametki o krest'ianskoi sem'e v Novgorodskoi gubernii," in *Sbornik narodnykh iuridicheskikh obychaev, Zapiski Imperatorskago russkago geograficheskago obshchestva po otdeleniiu etnografii,* 2 (Saint Petersburg, 1900), 18:266.

half-tiaglo, only 4 percent being married; and 29 percent carried a full tiaglo, at least three-quarters being married.[3]

To maximize output on the Petrovskoe estate the bailiff had to maximize the number of work teams. In practice this meant that the distribution of corvée obligations had to be synchronized with internal changes in household composition resulting from marriage and death so as to avoid the underutilization of labor. When a young couple married it immediately formed a new tiaglo or work team, further increasing the productive capacity of the estate. The earlier serfs married, the sooner this economic benefit to the estate would be realized.[4]

But if young couples had had to establish their own households, early marriage would have necessarily confronted both the problem of capital accumulation and parental concerns regarding the premature loss of an adult laborer. In contrast, had the serfs of Petrovskoe found it necessary to delay marriage seven to eight years, until the mid- or late twenties as in western Europe, then the productive capacity of the estate and all serf households would have been reduced by anywhere from 17 percent (assuming all single males over 19 carried a half-tiaglo) to 35 percent (if males had no corvée obligations until marriage).[5] Roughly speaking, a figure of 20 percent

---

3. TsGADA, f. 1262, op. 1, ch. 1, ed. khr. 1495; op. 4, ed. khr. 41, 59, 121, 186, 344, 357; ch. 2, ed. khr. 822. Of this last group, in all likelihood, more than 75 percent were married, because the nominative lists often failed to distinguish between single males and those who had been widowed shortly after their first marriage. A recently widowed male aged 15–19 would have formed a full tiaglo upon marriage and was formally obligated to fulfill his responsibilities until the next redistribution of land and corvée duties. Nevertheless, young single males from families with no other working-age males did on occasion carry a full tiaglo, with a mother, sisters, or younger brothers assisting in the field work. See also I. Tiutriumov, "Krest'ianskaia sem'ia: Ocherk obychnago prava," *Russkaia rech'* no. 7 (1879):135–37.

4. D. I., "Zametki," 262–63; Kalachov, "Iuridicheskie obychai," 25; Kishkin, "Dannye i predpolozheniia," 226; Nasonov, "Iz istorii," 518; A. Gerschenkron, "Agrarian Policies and Industrialization: Russia, 1861–1917," in *The Cambridge Economic History of Europe*, 6, part 2 (Cambridge, 1965), 749; and Czap, "Marriage and the Peasant Joint Family," 115.

5. These figures are based upon the total number of working person-years lived for all males between 19 and 54, the latter being the mean age of retirement for surviving males, assuming the estimate of expectation of life at birth determined above. Coale and Demeny, *Regional Model Life Tables*, part 2, p. 7.

seems reasonable as the amount of gross grain production that would have been lost had marriages followed the "European" pattern. Gross income would have suffered comparably.

Overcoming these problems was accomplished, first, by tying the execution of estate labor obligations to the right to use an allotment of peasant arable land, a practice common throughout all of the central agricultural region and much of Great Russia as well. This provided a new couple with immediate access to a plot of land, the most crucial capital input for its maintenance. Arable land was thus constantly being redistributed to reflect marriages, retirements, and deaths (see table 24). This is what is meant by a repartitional land com-

TABLE 24

Peasants with Tiaglos Imposed or Removed, 1824–25

Household Number	Name	Age	Tiaglo	Age	Tiaglo	
					Imposed	Relieved
1	Prokhar Matveev	44	1	45	—	$\frac{1}{2}$
2	Iakov Ivanov	16	—	17	$\frac{1}{2}$	—
—	Ivan Petrov	43	1	44	—	$\frac{1}{2}$
11	Miron Ivanov	17	$\frac{1}{2}$	17	1	—
13	Nikolai Polikarpov	16	$\frac{1}{2}$	17	1	—
17	Evtei Timofeev	16	$\frac{1}{2}$	17	1	—
22	Iakov Fadeev	15	—	16	$\frac{1}{2}$	—
23	Prokhar Matveev	15	—	16	$\frac{1}{2}$	—
—	Matvei Mikheev	46	1	47	—	$\frac{1}{2}$
24	Efim Egorov	15	$\frac{1}{2}$	16	1	—
25	Terentei Leonov	16	$\frac{1}{2}$	16	1	—
35	Minai Ivanov	17	$\frac{1}{2}$	18	1	—
—	Savelii Federov	50	1	51	—	$\frac{1}{2}$
38	Timofei Nikolaev	14	—	15	$\frac{1}{2}$	—
47	Taras Vasilov	15	—	16	$\frac{1}{2}$	—
51	Sergei Andreev	18	$\frac{1}{2}$	19	1	—
61	Vasili Stepanov	15	$\frac{1}{2}$	16	1	—
62	Ivan Savel'ev	17	$\frac{1}{2}$	18	1	—
69	Evtei Maksimov	49	$\frac{1}{2}$	50	—	$\frac{1}{2}$

Source: TsGADA, f. 1262, op. 4, ch. 1, ed. khr. 291, l. 52–53: "An excerpt from the household lists of peasants, of who precisely will be relieved of tiaglos for senility, old age, or the inability to work, and in place of the above on who will be imposed."

mune, a village with a periodic and either partial or total redistribution of the arable land. Second, virilocal postmarital residence not only obviated the need for much additional capital accumulation but constituted a windfall for the bridegroom's household. Often the mere addition of a daughter-in-law increased the number of tiaglos in a household from one to two or two to three, thereby increasing its total arable land by 50 to 100 percent. Of course, with a tiaglo also came burdens, as the word itself implies, both taxes and corvée, and a need for livestock to support these obligations. But the benefits were still great, and parents thus had a strong economic incentive to see that their sons married young. "Get married at 18 in order to settle on a tiaglo" (*V vosemnadtsat' let zhenit'sia, chtob na tiaglo sadit'sia*) was common advice given to young males.[6] Third, the payment of a substantial bride-price (or bridewealth) known as *kladka,* given by the groom's head of household to the bride's, enticed households to part with their unmarried mature female laborers. Kladka, in effect, redistributed wealth among households without upsetting patriarchal authority within them.

Kladka had both characteristics of bride-price, the permanent movement of resources from the groom's household in exchange for rights to the bride, and indirect dowry, defined by Goody as gifts of "money indirectly contributed by the groom

6. P. Efimenko, "Sem'ia Arkhangel'skago krest'ianina po obychnomu pravu," *Sudebnyi zhurnal,* July–August 1873, 97–98. Efimenko is referring here to customary practices in central Russia, not in the Far North. V. Dal', *Poslovitsy russkago naroda* (Moscow, 1862), 362. Tiaglo in this case means the unit of allotted land associated with the formation of a work team and the assumption of corvée. On the benefits of early marriage for peasant elders, see Brzheskii, *Ocherki iuridicheskago byta,* 180–81; Zvonkov, "Sovremennye brak," 30–31; Efimenko, "Sem'ia," 97; P. Efimenko, *Pridanoe po obychnomu pravu krest'ian Arkhangel'skoi gubernii* (Saint Petersburg, 1872), 39–41; A. Zaloskin, "Khoziaistvennye statisticheskie zamechaniia po selu Abakumovo, Riazanskoi gubernii, Pronskago uezda, pomeshchika G . . . na," *Zhurnal zemlevladel'tsev* 2, no. 6 (1858):41; N. Lebedev, "Byt krest'ian Tverskoi gubernii, Tverskago uezda," *ES* 1 (1853):186; K. Myl'nikova and V. Tsintsius, "Severno-velikorusskaia svad'ba," in *Materialy po svad'be i semeino-rodovomu stroiu narodov SSSR* (Leningrad, 1926), 1:24–27; N. Otto, "Iz narodnago byta: Novgorodskaia svad'ba," *Severnaia Pchela,* no. 137 (1862):545; Pr. V. E-iu, "Opisanie sel'skoi svad'by v Sengileevskom uezde, Simbirskoi gubernii," *Etnograficheskoe obozrenie* 42, no. 3 (1899):108–9; and F. G. Terner, "Tri publichnyia lektsii po statistike Rossii," *Ekonomist* 3, no. 1 (1860):68.

to the endowment of the bride."[7] The distinction is important, even if blurred within the custom of kladka itself, for bride-price is a "circulating societal fund," a redistribution of resources limiting socioeconomic differentiation among households, while indirect dowry does not necessarily entail the permanent alienation of any property from either household. Indirect dowry with virilocal residence results in all wealth remaining in place. Gifts bought by the groom for the bride accompany her to her new household. Thus with indirect dowry the groom's family would not experience any loss of wealth.[8]

Marriage almost everywhere involves the transmission of property, but in most of Great Russia supplying a newly married couple with a conjugal fund by direct or indirect dowry was not important. At Petrovskoe the estate provided arable land through the repartitional land structure, and the groom's family provided an established household. Little else was needed except clothing. In fact the custom of direct dowry (*pridanoe,* which also means trousseau), "a type of pre-mortem inheritance to the bride"[9] from her family, was of little or no consequence where the repartitional land commune existed.

Between 1871 and 1874 a special government commission concerned with the reorganization of the township courts (*volostnye sudy*) investigated peasant customary practices in fifteen provinces of European Russia, including all twelve districts of Tambov province. In Borisoglebsk district where Petrovskoe was situated, ten of the twenty-nine townships were studied, though the Petrovskoe estate, a township by itself, was not one of them. Nevertheless, in two of the townships adjacent to Petrovskoe the commission noted that "a dowry [pridanoe] is not given, but the bridegroom pays a kladka for the bride." Of the eight remaining townships, in seven dowries were "never given" and in the eighth, closest to the district seat of Borisoglebsk, they were given "very rarely."[10]

7. J. Goody, "Bridewealth and Dowry in Africa and Eurasia," in *Bridewealth and Dowry,* ed. J. Goody and S. J. Tambian (Cambridge, 1973), 1–5.
8. Ibid., 2, 46.
9. Ibid., 1.
10. *Trudy komissii po preobrazovaniiu volostnykh sudov* (Saint Petersburg, 1873), 1:389–486.

Many nineteenth-century ethnographers were surprised to discover that peasants did not give their daughters direct dowries, but the evidence was overwhelming. Observers for the Imperial Russian Geographic Society found the practice of kladka widespread in regions where the repartitional land commune existed. Zelenin's annotated index to the society's archives gives literally dozens of references to kladka. Soviet ethnographers conducting fieldwork in the village of Viriatino in northern Tambov in the early 1950s were told by informers that marriage rituals in the past had involved "a sum of money, which the groom gives." They concluded that "the presence of kladka, while at the same time no terms were set for a dowry, was characteristic of Tambov wedding rituals."[11] Direct dowries were common only in the far north and in Little Russia, where lands were held in perpetuity. In fact, after the introduction of the repartitional commune in Arkhangel' province direct dowries declined in importance.[12] To quote the nineteenth-century ethnographer V. P. Mukhin: "the custom of giving a kladka for the bride is very strictly observed in those areas where it is not usual to give a dowry; thus kladka in this case is like a surrogate dowry, coming from the side of the groom."[13] In 1874 Aleksandra Efimenko, another student of peasant life, noted that where kladka was part of the marriage contract, no conditions were set for a bride's dowry.[14] Nothing, however,

11. D. K. Zelenin, *Opisanie rukopisei uchenago arkhiva Imperatorskago russkago geograficheskago obshchestva*, 3 vols. (Petrograd, 1914–16), passim; Akademii Nauk SSSR, Institut etnografii im. N. N. Miklukho-Maklaia, *Trudy*, n.s., *Selo Viriatino v proshlom i nastoiashchem* (Moscow, 1958), 41:85; V. P. Mukhin, *Obychnyi poriadok nasledovaniia u krest'ian* (Saint Petersburg, 1888), 88–90, 132–36; Tiutriumov, "Krest'ianskaia sem'ia," 155–56; A. Efimenko, "Narodnye iuridicheskie vozzreniia na brak," *Znanie*, no. 1 (1874):15; Smirnov, *Ocherki semeinykh otnoshenii*, 182–83; "Sloboda Trekhizbianskaia," *ES* 2 (1854):7.

12. P. Chubinskii, "Ocherk narodnykh iuridicheskikh obychaev i poniatii v Malorossii," *Zapiski Imperatorskago russkago geograficheskago obshchestva po otdeleniiu etnografii* 2 (1869):690–91; Efimenko, *Pridanoe*, 8–17.

13. Mukhin, *Obychnyi poriadok*, 135–36.

14. Efimenko, "Narodnye iuridicheskie vozzreniia," 15. See also S. V. Pakhman, *Obychnoe grazhdanskoe pravo v Rossii*, 2 vols. (Saint Petersburg, 1877), 2:68; and A. Afansas'ev, "Kritika: Etnograficheskii sbornik," *Otechestvennye zapiski* 90, nos. 9–10, part 4 (1853):25.

TABLE 25

Customary Amount of Kladka

Province	Uezd	Year	Amount of Kladka (rubles assignats)
Arkhangel'	Shenkurskii	1854	20–35
Vladimir	Muromskii	1849	17–35
Voronezh	Pavlovskii	1850	Not more than 20
	Korotoianskii	1850	50–100
Viatka	Elabuzhskii	1849	35–105
Kazan'	Zakamskii krai	1850	25–45
Kaluga	Medzynskii	1856	40–140
	Zhizdrinskii	1849	9
Kursk[a]	Oboianskii	1862	3–24 and more
Nizhegorod	Sergachskii	1850s	up to 50
	Sergachskii	1850s	7–14
	Not specified	1849	15–50
	Vasil'skii	1849	40–100
	Kniagininskii	1849	20–40
	Kniagininskii	1849	10–60
	Arzamaskii	1850	15–30
	Alizhegorodskii	1848	up to 100
	Likoianovskii	1850	5–80
Novgorod	Cherepovskii	1850	up to 50
Penza	Not specified	1850	15–20
	Kerenskii	1857	up to 50
	Saranskii	1853–54	35–85
Perm	Verkhoturskii	1848	20–30
	Shadrinskii	1849	10–210
Riazan'	Zaraiskii	1867	20–35
	Mikhailovskii	1876	5–50
	Spasskii	1854	7–50
Iaroslavl'[b]	Molozhskii	1853	20–40
Simbirsk[c]		1840	Rarely more than 150
Simbirsk[d]		1862	3–105
Vladimir and Nizhegorod[e]		1853	50–100
Iaroslavl'[e]		1853	20–40
Kaluga, Kursk, Tambov[e]		1853	70–245
Great Russia[f]		Second half of the eighteenth century	15–150

(continued)

TABLE 25 *(Continued)*

Sources: Unless noted, D. K. Zelenin, *Opisanie rukopisei uchenago arkhiva Imperatorskago russkago geograficheskago obshchestva,* 3 vols. (Petrograd, 1914–16), passim.

[a]Mashkin, "Byt krest'ian Kurskoi gubernii, Oboianskago uezda," *Etnograficheskii sbornik* 5 (1862): 23.

[b]A. Preobrazhenskii, "Prikhod Stanilovskii na Siti, Iaroslavskoi gubernii, Molozhskago uezda, *Etnograficheskii sbornik* 1 (1853): 141–45.

[c]V. B., "Simbirskie obychai pokupat' nevest," *Otechestvennye zapiski* 9, no. 7 (1840): 28–29.

[d]N. Aristov, "Ocherk krest'ianskoi svad'by," *Volga,* no. 13 (1862): 49–50.

[e]A. Afanas'ev, "Kritika: Etnograficheskii sbornik," *Otechestvennye zapiski* nos. 9–10, part 4 (1853): 25.

[f]V. I. Semevskii, "Domashnii byt i nravy krest'ian vo vtoroi polovine XVIII v.," *Ustoi,* no. 2 (1882): 76.

prohibited the bride's household from giving their daughter or new in-laws small gifts or from contributing directly to the wedding feast, and this was sometimes done.

Kladka was essentially a payment of money from the groom's household to the bride's, the amount being set at the time of betrothal. Often a fur coat or other clothes for the bride were also specified in the marriage agreement. Neither livestock nor, of course, land was ever exchanged as kladka, though these were common endowments where direct dowries existed. Some, and occasionally all, of the kladka money went to cover the cost of the bride's trousseau, wedding expenses (*stolovye den'gi*), and gifts, usually clothes, to the future husband and in-laws. This is what is meant by the indirect dowry aspect or portion of kladka, for no redistribution of wealth was involved, since it all returned to the groom's household with the bride—minus, of course, the expenses of the actual festivities.[15] But kladka payments were usually substantial, frequently far exceeding the expenditures required of the bride's family.

15. Zelenin, *Opisanie,* passim; Mukhin, *Obychnyi poriadok,* 113–16, 132–34; Rudnev, "Selo Golun'," 107–8; Efimenko, "Narodnye iuridicheskie vozzreniia," 14; Efimenko, *Pridanoe,* 7; Semenova, *Zhizn' "Ivana.,"* 3; Troitskii, "Selo Lipitsy," 89; Tiutriumov, "Krest'ianskaia sem'ia," 155; M. E. Mikheev, "Opisanie svadebnykh obychaev i obriadov v Buzulukskom uezde, Samarskoi gubernii," *Etnograficheskoe obozrenie* 42, no. 3 (1899):146–47; N. Aristov, "Ocherk krest'ianskoi svad'by," *Volga,* no. 13 (1862):49–50; N. Vinogradov, "Narodnaia svad'ba v Kostromskom uezde," *Trudy Komstromskago nauchnago obshchestva po izucheniiu mestnago kraia* 8 (1917):74–79; and N. Kostrov, "Svadebnye obriady Minusinskikh krest'ian," *Illiustratsiia,* no. 176 (1861):10.

Table 25 presents information on the customary amount of kladka paid in the middle of the nineteenth century for regions where it was common. Most of the figures come from responses to a questionnaire sent out by the Imperial Russian Geographic Society in 1848 on the investigation of the "ordinary Russian person." Contributors were primarily village priests, local landlords, doctors, statisticians, teachers, and seminary students—"the wide mass of the rural intelligentsia," as one archivist describes them.[16] Abstracts were published of many of the responses from thirty-six provinces, Arkhangel' through Saratov.[17] For fourteen provinces of European Russia this was not done. In addition, from some of the thirty-six provinces there were only a few responses, and frequently authors did not specify the amount of kladka. Not many figures were available from other sources. Thus, the absence of a province from table 25 should not necessarily be interpreted as signifying absence of the custom.

It is not clear how much of the kladka the bride's family was required to spend on gifts, but her household generally kept a sizable portion for itself, this being the bride-price or wealth-equalizing aspect of the exchange. Simply put, because the repartitional land commune immediately provided the bridegroom's household with a unit of peasant arable land upon the formation of a new work team, the bride's household required compensation for the loss of a laborer and any decline in its economic and social status resulting from her departure. Kalachov, a nineteenth-century student of peasant customary law, noted that a girl's parents concerned about the loss of a worker would stipulate in the marriage agreement either that she spend the harvest season at home or "that the family of the bridegroom pay a redemption for her, known as kladka."[18] Pakhman, who also wrote on peasant customs in the nineteenth century, saw the dual nature of kladka, a payment both to re-

16. Akademiia Nauk SSSR, Geograficheskoe obshchestvo, *Russkie geografy i puteshestvenniki: Fondy arkhiva geograficheskogo obshchestva* (Leningrad, 1971), 9.

17. Zelenin, *Opisanie*, vols. 1–3, passim.

18. Kalachov, "Iuridicheskie obychai," 24. See also Tiutriumov, "Krest'ianskaia sem'ia," 137, for a virtually identical statement.

duce wedding costs and to compensate for the person of "the bride herself, as a laborer the family is losing by the girl's marrying out."[19] According to Efimenko, a well-known nineteenth-century Russian ethnographer, "in some southwestern steppe provinces the payment for the bride is determined by simple competition," the highest bidder getting the girl.[20] Mukhin, in studying peasant inheritance practices, found that the amount of kladka was greater in regions where a female's labor was more highly valued. In Nizhegorod province women involved in bast production could do exactly the same work as men, and thus a bride's family could demand a high bridewealth for her.[21] Bridewealth or bride-price also had its counterpart, "groomwealth." On the rare occasion when the male became part of the bride's household, usually because it had no other working-age males, his parents required compensation for the loss of his labor.[22] In sum, to quote another nineteenth-century ethnographer: "Dowries do not play a large role in peasant life; frequently the bridegroom not only does not receive a dowry, but even further he has to compensate the parents of the bride for their loss of her free labor."[23]

Young unmarried females were in a very ambiguous position in their natal households. Although their labor was valued, they were viewed as temporary members of the household. They had no claim to land where agriculture was the primary pursuit, but their departure would bring in a kladka, which would allow a brother or male cousin to marry. Daughters, granddaughters, and nieces of marriage age were both consumers and laborers, yielding small, short-run gains but having no prospects for substantial long-run benefits for their elders as did unmarried males. Thus peasants were constantly balancing the mean age at marriage—in other words, how long a daughter should work for them—with the customary size of kladka,

19. Pakhman, *Obychnoe grazhdanskoe pravo*, 2:60–62.
20. A. Efimenko, "Krest'ianskaia zhenshchina," *Delo*, no. 2 (1873):194–98.
21. Mukhin, *Obychnyi poriadok*, 17–19.
22. Semevskii, "Domashnii byt," 77.
23. Tiutriumov, "Krest'ianskaia sem'ia," 155–56. See also Afanas'ev, "Kritika," 25, and Smirnov, *Ocherki semeinykh otnoshenii*, 122.

the wealth she could attract. This balance could vary with changing economic circumstances.

The acquisition of a daughter-in-law was a major expenditure, and the bridegroom's household had to be sure it got a good worker in order to recoup its investment. A bad choice could ruin a household, for the additional allotment of peasant arable land and the extra worker had to offset the costs not only of the kladka but of an extra mouth to feed, higher taxes, and increased estate labor obligations. Marriage was too important for the household seeking either to minimize its losses or recoup its investment, too important for the commune having to pay taxes, and too important for the estate trying to maximize production to permit the young persons involved to play any significant role in mate selection. Marriage rituals included the mutual inspection of households by the parents (*smotrina* or *osmotr*) and differed little from property transactions. The matchmaker, often a relative, having been sent by the young man's parents, would usually greet the father of the potential bride by saying, "we have a buyer, and you have the goods" (*U nas est' kupets, a u vas tovarets*) to signify the reason for the visit. Love was not a factor in marriage and was even thought to be harmful, since it could interfere with more important concerns. The groom's family gave consideration solely to the woman's health, skills, and ability to work; the bride's, to being sure it would receive a fair kladka. Terms were set orally by a marital agreement (*brachnyi sgovor*) and were made binding by a *rukobit'e*, a ritual clapping of hands by the two fathers or heads of household. In addition, these agreements were occasionally sanctified by a priest and were always celebrated by a bout of heavy drinking (*zapoi* or *propoi*).[24]

Economic motives were clearly in the minds of the Pe-

---

24. Descriptions of marriage and wedding rituals are numerous. See Efimenko, "Krest'ianskaia zhenshchina," 77, 197–98; Smirnov, *Ocherki semeinykh otnoshnii,* 228–42; Efimenko, *Pridanoe,* 39–41; Efimenko, "Narodnye iuridicheskie vozzreniia," 1–22; Efimenko, "Sem'ia," 32; Aristov, "Ocherk," 49; Pr. V. E-iu, "Opisanie sel'skoi svad'by," 110–11; Tiutriumov, "Krest'ianskaia sem'ia," 123–29; Otto, "Iz narodnago byta," 545; Mikheev, "Opisanie svadebnykh obychaev," 144–46; Vinogradov, "Narodnaia svad'ba," 74–79; Myl'nikova and Tsintsius, "Severno-velikorusskaia svad'ba," 35–36; A. Nikolaev, "Krest'ianskaia svad'ba v Zvenigorodskom uezde,

trovskoe serfs when they arranged marriages. Household serfs required the permission of the central estate office in Moscow to marry, and the archives of the estate hold many of the parents' petitions. The language was formal, undoubtedly composed by a scribe, but the reasons were plain. Karneia Abramova, a widow with four daughters, sought to marry off her eldest, Praskov'ia, 18 years old, "in order to avoid my having to support [her]."[25] Arkhip Aglovin, the father of six children including a 22-year-old daughter, Elena, with an illegitimate infant, requested permission for her to marry a free man for exactly the same reason.[26]

Parents were also often desperate for their sons to marry and bring a daughter-in-law into the household, as the following petition reveals:

I have two sons, Savelii in Moscow on a passport and Fedot who lives with me, and both have come of age, [but] are not married. And since my wife and I have gotten old and fallen into decrepitude, and with all this, moreover, I have at home a daughter who is constantly in need of bedclothes and other domestic items, so I dare to trouble the main office with my most humble request to be favorably disposed to pay merciful attention to our extreme situation to allow our son Fedot to enter into marriage. For this we should pray to God for the health of Your Excellency and the director of the main office.

IVAN SMETANIN[27]

Moskovskoi gubernii," *Severnaia pchela*, nos. 209–210 (1863):921–25; N. F. Sumtsov, *O svadebnykh obriadakh, preimushchestvenno russkikh* (Kharkov, 1881), 22–34; E. G. Kagarov, "Sostav i proiskhozhdenie svadebnoi obriadnosti," in *Sbornik Muzeia antropologii i etnografii AN SSSR* (Leningrad, 1929), 160–63; V. A. Aleksandrov, "Vologodskaia svad'ba," *Biblioteka dlia chteniia*, no. 5 (1863):6–13; N. R-v, "Svadebnye obychai v Ostashkovskom uezde v polovine XIX veke," *Tverskaia starina*, no. 2 (1913):39; and V. B., "Simbirskie obychai pokupat' nevest," *Otechestvennyia zapiski* 9, no. 7 (1840):28–29.
    25. TsGADA, f. 1262, op. 4, ch. 1, ed. khr. 649, l. 25 (22 December 1854).
    26. Ibid., l. 150 (18 October 1854).
    27. TsGADA, f. 1262, op. 4, ch. 2, ed. khr. 866, l. 24 (12 January 1859).

Economic concerns even affected the seasonal pattern of marriages. The limited evidence available suggests that most first marriages took place in the fall, between September and November, somewhat less often in January and February following the prohibition of Advent, much less frequently in the spring, and almost never in the summer. Peasant sentiments were summed up by the saying "A betrothed girl in the household—a corpse at the table" (*Nevesta na dvore—mertvets na stole*) or the reverse, "All winter I fed her, so let her work for me this summer" (*Zimu, Ia ee prokormil, tak pust' mne eto letom zarabotaet*).[28] Thus the very timing of a wedding was a mechanism for redistributing wealth.

But it was primarily the abundance of land, its constant redistribution, and the bride-price aspect of kladka that prevented socioeconomic differentiation from developing in much of Great Russian peasant society, as in Petrovskoe. As Goody writes, bridewealth provided for a double dispersal of property. Money passed in one direction, the bride and land in the other. Moreover, the bride's new household was where the children would be, and they would further disperse the wealth resulting from the added unit of arable land.[29] Kladka was a circulating pool of resources in the sense that "what goes out for a bride has to come in for a sister." Thus it served essentially to regulate marriage rather than to increase the father's wealth.[30] In contrast, the intent behind a bride's dowry is to endow a woman with enough property so she can attract a husband of her own rank. Dowries exist in societies with substantial socioeconomic differentiation, for their purpose is to preserve the status of the family into the next generation. A daughter with a dowry would not have to marry down, and this reinforces stratification in the society. "Dowry differentiates," Goody says, "just as bridewealth tends to homogenize."[31]

---

28. Czap, "Marriage and the Peasant Joint Family," 107–8; Mashkin, "Byt," 23; Mukhin, *Obychnyi poriadok,* 121–22; N. Lebedev, "Byt krest'ian Tverskoi gubernii, Tverskago uezda," *ES* 1 (1853):186; N. Galentorn, "Svad'ba v Saltykovskoi volosti, Morshanskago uezda, Tambovskoi gubernii," in *Materialy po svad'be i semeino-rodovomu stroiu narodov SSSR* (Leningrad, 1926), 1:171–73; and N. Shternberg, "Novye materialy po svad'be," in ibid., 10.
29. Goody, "Bridewealth," 13.
30. Ibid., 5.
31. Ibid., 17–25, 47.

In Russia, bride-price or bridewealth was not concerned with the future status of the household. Rather, it merely facilitated marriage, greatly easing economic constraints. The distribution of wives was closely related to the distribution of sisters. In effect, kladka constantly moved toward creating an economic equilibrium. As long as villages had adequate amounts of arable land "to satisfy the needs of *net* additional numbers of married couples" or the peasants had other ready means of earning a living, wealth would flow in both directions.[32] In addition, the custom of kladka and the availability of land served to overcome any sex imbalance in the offspring of individual households. If a father with three daughters and no sons had to give three dowries, it might well have been impossible for them all to marry, and definitive celibacy would have adversely affected estate and peasant production levels. Furthermore, because of high bride-price payments, children were very dependent upon the head of household or their father to arrange marriages and to negotiate properly regarding the kladka. A bad deal—accepting too low a kladka, for example—might leave the household with too little money to find brides for its own unmarried males. Bride-price, therefore, directly affected the social and material well-being of the present generation, while the necessity for correct patriarchal management of marriage enhanced the authority of the elders in the household.[33]

Boserup has argued that bride-price is common in rural societies where very primitive systems of field cultivation are used and where most agricultural work is done by women. In contrast, "where plough cultivation predominates and where women do less agricultural work than men . . . a dowry is usually paid by the girl's family."[34] Goody has suggested that bride-price and dowry are "related less directly to women's contribution to agriculture and more to the problem of 'status placement' in societies with varying degrees of socio-economic

32. Ibid., 18; and Gerschenkron, "Agrarian Policies," 749; emphasis in Gerschenkron's original.
33. Goody, "Bridewealth," 5.
34. E. Boserup, *Women's Role in Economic Development* (London, 1970), 50.

differentiation." Goody does note, however, that more advanced plow cultivation allows for much greater stratification than the primitive slash-and-burn, digging stick, and hoe techniques that were practiced where population densities were low and land was not usually scarce.[35]

According to these interpretations, the presence of brideprice in much of Great Russia would be rather difficult to explain. Although population density was lower than in the rest of Europe, the three-field system of plow agriculture was firmly in place in Great Russia by the early nineteenth century, and more primitive tillage systems existed only on the periphery.[36] Nevertheless, the theses of Boserup and Goody have something to contribute to the understanding of life in Petrovskoe and much of Great Russia.

But first, what was the extent of socioeconomic differentiation at Petrovskoe? Certainly some serf households were better off than others. "The majority of the field peasants are in good economic condition; among them there is a part middling and poor," the bailiff noted in the spring of 1844.[37] Soviet historians have seen stratification almost everywhere in Russian serf society throughout the first half of the nineteenth century, with the development of greater differentiation particularly in evidence from the 1830s onward, deepening the crisis of the feudal system until its collapse in 1861. This viewpoint is virtually a cliché in Soviet historical literature. Koval'chenko, examining data from Petrovskoe, has concluded that between 1813 and 1856 "the characteristic feature of the stratification of the peasantry at the Petrovskoe estate was the rapid growth of the stratum of the poorest peasants," that is, households having fewer than three horses.[38]

35. Goody, "Bridewealth," 23, 46.

36. M. Confino, *Systèmes agraires et progrès agricole* (Paris, 1969), 26–55.

37. TsGADA, f. 1262, op. 4, ch. 1, ed. khr. 615, l. 11 (December 1843–April 1844).

38. Koval'chenko, *Krest'iane*, 205–8. For other scholarship echoing the same interpretation regarding stratification, see Koval'chenko, *Russkoe krepostnoe khoziaistvo*, passim; Federov, *Pomeshchich'i krest'iane*, 251–53; Grekov, "Tambovskoe imenie," 489–91; and P. A. Zaionchkovskii, *Otmena krepostnogo prava v Rossii* (Moscow, 1968), 21–24.

To examine stratification in a peasant society requires a dynamic analysis of household mobility. Socioeconomic stratification is not the uneven distribution of wealth and status at a single point in time, the definition both Litvak and Koval'chenko assumed, but is differentiation over time giving rise to separate strata with distinct members, each stratum having its own economic interests, social orientation, strategies for survival, and means for maintaining or improving its status. It is simply not adequate to state that in any given year some households were wealthier than others. In addition, an analysis of stratification cannot be done solely on the level of the household, ignoring possible changes in its size and structure, another error of Koval'chenko's. Often per capita measures are more useful and accurate, as Litvak himself has pointed out in sharp criticism of Koval'chenko's analysis of the Gagarin estates.[39]

At Petrovskoe, until 1825 partial redistributions of peasant allotments, demesne obligations, and tax burdens, all of which were apportioned by tiaglos, took place annually in the spring; thereafter this occurred once every two years. There was never a need for a general repartition, since the ongoing process of readjustment took care of all serf marriages, recruitment levies, flight, migration, retirements, and deaths. With the repartitional system, the total area of a household's arable land depended upon the number of tiaglos, which was essentially a function of household size (see figure 3). Litvak's own recalculation of Koval'chenko's original figures shows this equitable distribution of land, though Litvak himself fails to mention it. Larger households thus had more land, but as figure 4 shows, landholdings per capita were nearly equal regardless of the number of tiaglos or members in a household. Of the population in the village of Petrovskoe, 82 percent lived in households of six to fourteen persons. In these households the average holding by household size fluctuated from 1.46 to 1.70 desiatinas per capita, a range of only 16 percent. Very large households, those with more than fourteen members and with 8 percent of the village population, had just slightly lower aver-

---

39. T. Shanin, *The Awkward Class* (Oxford, 1972), 45–80; Koval'chenko, *Krest'iane*, 64; and Litvak, *Ocherki istochnikovedeniia*, 90–92.

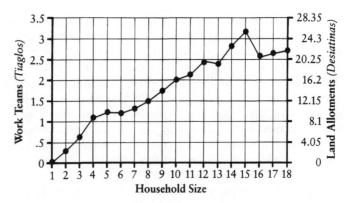

FIGURE 3: Work teams (tiaglos) and land allotments (statutory desiatinas) by household size, village of Petrovskoe (1813–27). *Source:* TsGADA, f. 1262, op. 1, ed. khr. 1495; op. 4, ch. 1, ed. khr. 41, 59, 121, 186, 344, 357.

age per capita holdings, varying from 1.22 to 1.70 desiatinas. Finally, households of fewer than six persons were subject to wide statistical variance, but they were neither uniformly richer nor poorer than larger households. In any case, the data for both very large and very small households are too limited to permit any conclusions. Where the body of data is adequate (for households of six to fourteen persons), it shows that the communal process of annual or biennial partial repartitions was extremely effective in providing equal access to arable land based upon labor capabilities and consumption needs.

There were few additional sources of revenue at Petrovskoe that could have given rise to substantial economic differentiation. Cereal cultivation was the primary pursuit of the peasants, while wealth in livestock derived from the land. Handicrafts and cottage industries were poorly developed in this region, and the Petrovskoe peasants did not engage in such pursuits. The serfs had very limited access to extra land, the estate renting out only ninety desiatinas of reserve to both its own and nonstate peasants. The bailiffs preferred to let these lands lie fallow. During the winter, the peasants spent much of their time threshing grain and transporting it to market, though they were able to undertake some private cartage. Distribution of this work, however, depended in large part on the distribution of horses, which was rather equitable (see fig. 4). Estate records do indicate that four serfs rented the fishing rights to the lake on estate property, presumably providing them with some additional income, but there are no references to other such arrangements.[40] Although opportunities for outside work were limited in much of the central agricultural region, this was less true elsewhere in Russia. Consequently some economic differentiation, even though still constrained by the custom of kladka, may have been present in other regions.

Studies of many preindustrial societies have found a positive correlation between household size and wealth per capita. According to a number of empirical investigations, larger households tend to have higher capital/worker ratios and seem to benefit from more efficient use of productive factors because of economies of scale.[41] Nevertheless, the data from Petrovskoe show that if there was any accumulation of advantages by larger households that might have functioned collectively as a societal centrifuge separating the peasants into distinct economic layers, these advantages were confronted with strong egalitarian and leveling mechanisms.[42] Table 26 suggests that as households increased in size they tended to have a higher ratio of nonworkers to workers, generally because they had a greater proportion of children. This offset some of the advantages of larger size. Figure 4 shows the rather even distribution of wealth by household size at Petrovskoe, especially for households of from six to fourteen persons, which encompassed over 80 percent of the village population. Again, no conclusions can be drawn for the too few very large or very small households.

This does not imply that there were not substantial differences among individual households in wealth per capita. Compare the following two households in the village of Pe-

40. TsGADA, f. 1262, op. 4, ch. 1, ed. khr. 615, l. 10–11; ed. khr. 649, l. 93; and ch. 2, ed. khr. 862, l. 6–7.
41. Shanin, *Awkward Class,* 63–68.
42. Ibid., 63–121.

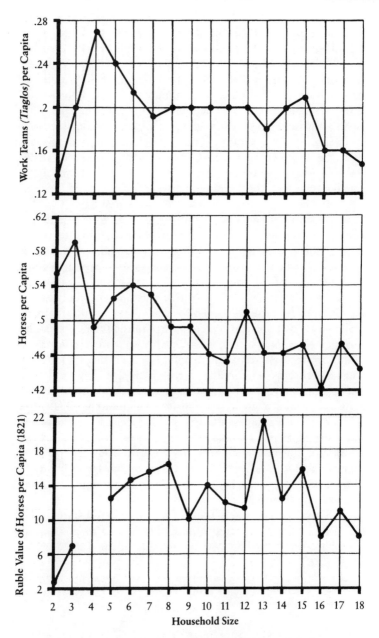

FIGURE 4: Per capita distribution of land and livestock by
household size, village of Petrovskoe (1813–27). *Source:* TsGADA,

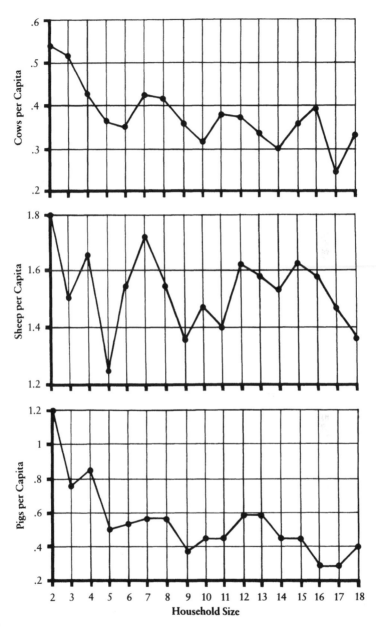

f. 1262, op. 1, ed. khr. 1495; op. 4, ch. 1, ed. khr. 41, 59, 121, 186, 344, 357.

TABLE 26

Age Structure by Household Size, Village of Petrovskoe (1813–21)

Age	Household Size																	
	1	2	3	4	5	6	7	8	9	10	11	12	13	14	15	16	17	18
0–19	0.0	30.0	43.8	39.6	43.7	46.2	53.0	54.6	53.2	55.6	55.5	54.6	53.8	59.5	56.2	60.4	64.7	55.6
20–59	16.7	60.0	52.1	58.3	54.9	52.2	42.9	42.5	41.5	41.2	42.6	41.3	41.9	36.3	41.1	35.4	32.4	33.3
60+	83.3	10.1	4.2	2.1	1.4	1.6	4.1	2.9	5.4	3.2	1.9	4.2	4.3	4.2	2.7	4.2	2.9	11.1

Sources: TsGADA, f. 1262, op. 4, ch. 1, ed. khr. 41, 59, 121, 186.
Note: Figures are percentages.

trovskoe in 1813: the first, household number 20 in the inventory, was headed by Fedor Ivanov, age 45, and his wife Afim'ia Egorova. They had three children: Ivan, whose wife Afim'ia Nazarova lived with them; Andrei, age 12 and retarded; and Alena, age 3. In all there were six persons, with two tiaglos, three horses, two cows, fifteen sheep, and five pigs. Household number 25, headed by Peter Nazarov and his wife Arina Federova, was much worse off. Peter had three unmarried sisters, one of whom was crippled, three daughters of his own, a widowed sister-in-law, and her three unmarried children living with him. Peter and his wife composed the only tiaglo and had to support twelve persons with half the land and virtually the same livestock holdings as Fedor Ivanov.[43]

But such differences were not the result of customary, legal, or institutional factors favoring economic differentiation. At Petrovskoe, wealth did not depend upon inheritance, family status, or the ability to command a disproportionate amount of productive resources. The biological life cycle of households and luck determined much of the differentiation. For Peter Nazarov it was unfortunate that his parents died leaving him with three unmarried sisters, unfortunate that his brother died leaving him with four dependents, and unfortunate that all his own children were as yet unmarried. In contrast, fate was generous to Fedor Ivanov by giving him four adult workers in his household of six persons. "Far from being extraordinary occurrences, crises and strokes of luck formed an integral part of peasant life," Shanin writes, and they "must, therefore, have caused marked socio-economic mobility among peasant households."[44]

Fate could indeed be generous, but only temporarily. At Petrovskoe, whether owing to biological or random factors, the rich got poorer and the poor richer. A dynamic analysis of peasant households, excluding those that underwent partitioning, merger, or extinction (these substantive changes being inherently leveling mechanisms),[45] reveals very strong equalizing tendencies in the village. Table 27 traces the fate of the forty

43. TsGADA, f. 1262, op. 4, ch. 1, ed. khr. 41.
44. Shanin, *Awkward Class,* 115.
45. Ibid., 81–94.

households in the village of Petrovskoe that did not experience either partition or merger between 1813 and 1827. They make up 63 percent of all households. The table shows that the more tiaglos (and allotted arable land) a household had in 1813, the greater the likelihood that it had fewer in 1827. Of the fourteen households with two or more tiaglos in 1813, eight (57 percent) had fewer work teams by 1827, three (21 percent) had the same number, and three had more. Conversely, of the twenty-

TABLE 27

Dynamic Study of Peasant Mobility, Village of Petrovskoe
(1813–27)

Number of Tiaglos	Number of Households in 1813	Number of Households in 1827		
		Fewer Tiaglos	Same Number of Tiaglos	More Tiaglos
0.0	2	—	—	2
1.0	22	3	9	10
1.5	2	—	—	2
2.0	10	5	2	3
2.5	4	3	1	—
Total	40	11	12	17

Number of Horses	Number of Households in 1813	Number of Households in 1827		
		Fewer Horses	Same Number of Horses	More Horses
0	1	—	—	1
1	2	—	—	2
2	11	1	3	7
3	9	3	2	4
4	9	3	1	5
5	7	2	1	4
6	1	1	—	—
Total	40	10	7	23

Source: TsGADA, f. 1262, op. 1, ed. khr. 1495; op. 4, ch. 1, ed. khr. 41, 59, 121, 186, 344, 357.

six households with fewer than two tiaglos, fourteen (54 percent) had more, nine (35 percent) had the same, and only three (12 percent) had fewer in 1827. The distribution of horses is the measure most frequently used by Soviet historians for analyzing economic differentiation. The results for Petrovskoe are somewhat masked by an aggregate shift upward, an increase of forty in the total number of horses owned by the households, the consequence of an estate program assisting the peasants in their purchase. Nevertheless, the pattern was the same. Households with fewer horses (zero to two) in 1813 were on the whole in a better position in 1827. Those with many horses (five to six) in 1813 were poorer, relatively speaking, fourteen years later. Finally, it should be noted that mobility for households not experiencing merger or division has a built-in upward bias caused by population growth.

It was impossible to carry the analysis beyond 1827, since the gap between subsequent household inventories was too great. With long intervals between compilations and corresponding changes in household membership and composition, given that most peasants did not have last names, individual households could not be followed with any certainty. Litvak does note that of the forty-two poor households (by his measure) on the entire Petrovskoe estate in 1813, only two were in this category in 1856. But he rightly suggests that many were lost from observation. Nevertheless, he recognizes the potential usefulness of a dynamic analysis and sharply criticizes Koval'chenko for failing to undertake one, though Litvak refrains from making one himself, calling it a difficult methodological problem.[46]

At Petrovskoe, all indexes suggest that wealth was distributed on an extremely equitable basis, limited only by biological and random fluctuations over which the serfs, the commune, and the estate had little or no control. Moreover, there was no permanent or definitive economic differentiation, no *kulaks* (rich peasants) or *bedniaks* (poor peasants) in the Soviet sense, only households that were in a constant state of

---

46. Litvak, *Ocherki istochnikovedeniia*, 103.

flux. Household mobility was endemic, stratification nonexistent. Social status, were it to exist at Petrovskoe, could not have been defined by land, the most valuable asset in the society, because it was out of the serfs' hands, regularly redistributed, and allotted according to the ability to work it. Livestock, though a potential source of status, depended upon cereal cultivation and communal pastures and consequently mirrored their distribution. Beyond land and livestock, there was little of value.

Thus Goody's argument that bride-price reinforces economic equality and is practiced in societies that are "relatively homogeneous," with little socioeconomic differentiation and little concern for status placement, holds true for Petrovskoe. Bride-price, however, does not require a primitive level of agricultural technology, for elaborate mechanisms such as the repartitional land commune, biological life cycles, the pattern of household division, merger, and extinction, and random multidirectional mobility may provide the same egalitarian socioeconomic structure. Furthermore, Boserup's suggestion that bride-price is common in rural societies where women make a substantial contribution to field labor is also valid, though ecological and not solely technological reasons may explain the high value placed on female agricultural labor.

Kladka complemented other leveling practices and tendencies at Petrovskoe by limiting the economic differentiation that otherwise would necessarily have resulted from marriage and the addition of a new work team, through evenly distributing daughters and daughters-in-law and exchanging one for the other. The economic costs of not participating in the process, of having an unmarried daughter instead of a kladka either to keep or to use to attract a daughter-in-law, were extremely high. "In Russia the organization of the repartitional commune is such that there are always more married male peasants than unmarried; indeed, it is seldom possible to meet an unmarried man. And this striving to marry for economic motives has led in some places to monstrous consequences."[47] According to the

47. Quoted in Efimenko, "Sem'ia," 107–13. See also Semevskii, "Domashnii byt," 74.

author of this statement, written in the nineteenth century, these consequences were ludicrously early ages for boys at marriage, sometimes as young as 6 or 7 years old, and *snokhachestvo,* sexual relations between fathers-in-law and daughters-in-law, one of the major prices paid by new female members of the household. Neither of these seem to have been problems at Petrovskoe. But given the availability of arable land, both kladka and the repartitional system are linked with early marriage because they promoted the creation of new wealth, increased production capacity, broadened the commune's tax base, and most important, implied the sharing of this new wealth between the bride's and bridegroom's households. These benefits were obviously desired as early as possible, as soon as the young couple could assume the necessary responsibilities.

This egalitarian distribution of wealth among households according to their size or number of tiaglos, the balance of land, labor, and livestock, was also the optimal use of productive resources given the level of agricultural technology and the other constraints at work in the society. Any imbalance would have lowered total production, for too many horses in one household given its land and labor and too few in another meant that the estate and both households would have suffered. Consequently, bailiffs and landlords were very conscious of the need for equitable distribution of wealth. Sir Donald Mackenzie Wallace, on his travels through Russia in the 1870s, noted that serfowners, "for evident reasons of self-interest, as well as from benevolent motives" previously had prevented the development of economic differentiation. With the emancipation in 1861, however, "the Communal equality thus artificially maintained" by serfowners was weakened as enterprising individuals sought to better their status. Early in 1861 the editors of the journal of the Imperial Moscow Agricultural Society similarly informed its readers, few though they may have been, to expect much greater economic stratification among peasant households following the emancipation. Whereas up to now both poor and well-to-do peasants had the tools and draft animals to work the land—a consequence of "landlord tutelage"—following the first crop failure "artificial households," those that had been the beneficiaries of estate financial assistance, would no longer be able to farm.[48]

Nasonov found that on the estates of the Iusupov family, poor management resulted in economic differentiation among the serfs. In other words, a good bailiff had to intervene directly in peasant affairs to prevent stratification, even that caused by luck or the biological life cycle of households. Enforcing the periodic redistribution of the plowlands and ensuring equal access to communal pastures and meadows for all households were of the utmost importance. But the bailiff on the Nasonov estate was also instructed to prevent the serfs from renting out their allotments to one another, to restrict their sale of grain and livestock, and to assist poorer households in acquiring draft animals.[49]

Serf estate managers thus had a number of ways to optimize production: (1) maximize the size of the demesne; (2) maximize the number of tiaglos, that is, regulate first marriage, the remarriage of widows and widowers, and the age at retirement; and (3) equalize wealth. During the course of the nineteenth century, estate managers came to realize that merely increasing the number of tiaglos or the size of the demesne did not necessarily increase revenues. In fact, such policies could ruin an estate by undermining the peasants' well-being and exhausting their livestock. Rather, high revenues rested on the ability of estate administrators to make each tiaglo equally capable of cultivating the land without exhausting the peasants or their draft animals.[50] Of course, optimizing the number of tiaglos and the size of the demesne were still important, but simply increasing the peasants' obligations could be carried to excess. The vigorous pursuit of the equalization of production capacity had no inherent economic dangers.

The size of the demesne was largely fixed by the serfs'

---

48. Donald Mackenzie Wallace, *Russia on the Eve of War and Revolution*, ed. Cyril E. Black (New York, 1961), 342; "Neskol'ko slov o zemledel'cheskikh orudiiakh," *Sel'skoe khoziaistvo*, part 2 (February 1861):35.

49. A. N. Nasonov, "Iusupovskie votchiny v XIX–om veke," *Doklady. Akademiia Nauk SSSR*, ser. B (January–February 1926):1–3.

50. A. N. Shishkov, "Mysli o khoziaistve i otchetnosti," *ZLOSKh za 1855*, part 2 (1856):142–46; Nasonov, "Khoziaistvo krupnoi votchiny," 345.

ability to work the land properly. At Petrovskoe the serfs were responsible for cultivating 13.5 acres of arable land and 2.7 to 3.5 acres of hayfield per tiaglo, the latter being used to support the estate's considerable horse-breeding activities.[51] This was the customary size of demesne obligations in the region, and it is likely that simply assigning the peasants more land to work would have resulted in less efficient land usage and no necessary increase in production.[52]

The regulation of marriage, which obviously affected the number of tiaglos, has already been discussed. The benefits to serf elders, who took care that all the descendants in their households married young, meant that the bailiff himself did not have to intervene directly and force serfs into a first marriage. Rather, the conjunction of interests between heads of household and the estate management favoring early and universal marriage caused parents, grandparents, or aunts and uncles to assume the initiative and responsibility. At Petrovskoe there is no evidence at all that the bailiffs ever had to arrange first marriages for the field serfs.

In contrast, Governor Sievers of Novgorod wrote that in the late eighteenth century "landlords in Russia usually compel young people to marry, and they do this in order to have another couple, that is, a new tiaglo, on which it is possible to impose work or a quitrent."[53] Certainly it is possible to cite a number of instances when serfowners arranged all the marriages for their peasants,[54] but little is known about the circumstances in which even the parents of the couple had no say. It does seem logical, however, that in villages with substantial socioeconomic differentiation resulting from infrequent repartitions of land or other factors, especially the availability of nonagricultural work, the incentives for heads of household to arrange early marriages would be absent, status placement would be a more important consideration, and landlords

51. Koval'chenko, *Krest'iane*, 271; and TsGADA, f. 1262, op. 1, ch. 1, ed. khr. 256, 2830a, 2833; op. 4, ch. 1, ed. khr. 615; and ch. 2, ed. khr. 902.
52. See chap. 1, pp. 21–24, nn. 10–16.
53. Cited in V. I. Semevskii, *Krest'iane v tsarstvovanie Imperatritsy Ekateriny II*, 2 vols. (Saint Petersburg, 1881–1901), 1:276.
54. See ibid., 276–81.

would have to intervene directly to increase the number of tiaglos. There is evidence to support this argument. In a small village in Podol'sk district, Moscow province, a number of males of poor families found it impossible to marry, since the parents of single females for economic reasons refused to let their daughters wed, preferring to have an extra worker at home. When the village was sold to a new serfowner, the fathers of the single males requested that the lord force the girls to marry. The landlord, upon noting that single women on neighboring estates were not accustomed to continuous work, were a burden on their relatives, and were good only for increasing sexual depravity and contributing to the decay of public morality, ordered them to be married off within three years. "How . . . could well-intentioned serfowners not interfere in peasant marriages?" the owner of this village asked.[55] According to Kalachov, economic stratification among serf households was the main reason landlords interfered in marriage. And if the serfowner did not intervene, then the commune or village elders took matters into their own hands, arranging marriages at village assemblies. Such interference was recognized as a necessary evil, but peasant communes and serfowners felt that an additional tiaglo was more important than household status placement or the social costs of compelling a marriage.[56]

In the absence of socioeconomic differentiation, the mutual benefits to heads of household and the estate assured early and universal first marriage and higher production. It also meant that the bailiff need not interfere in the marital process. When remarriage was at issue, however, the whole social and economic structure, the collusion of authorities and interests, collapsed. The high mortality rates at Petrovskoe and consequently the high incidence of widowhood had very serious implications, since they significantly reduced the number of tiaglos. Between 1813 and 1856, based upon ten years of ob-

55. A. P., "Opisanie uluchsheniia byta krest'ian Moskovskoi gubernii, Podol'skago uezda, v imenii AVP," *Zhurnal zemlevladel'tsev*, no. 13, part 5 (1858):5–6.
56. Kalachov, "Iuridicheskie obychai," 25–27.

servation, an average of 7.3 percent of all women aged 30–39 were widows; of women aged 40–49, almost 27 percent were. None of these women were part of a tiaglo or carried any estate corvée responsibilities, and it seems they like their situation.

> Field peasant widow Avdot'ia Kashtanova has been given a *vyvodnoe pis'mo* [a receipt for payment to the lord for granting personal freedom] in order to marry a nonestate peasant. In addition to this, the estate administration begs to report that at the Petrovskoe estate very many widows, having been spoiled by the customary procedure of giving them land, the so-called widow's allotment, absolutely refuse to marry your own peasants in order to avoid tiaglo obligations.[57]

The bailiff suggested at least stopping the policy of allowing widows to purchase their freedom if they married outside the estate, since this only encouraged them to do so. Fifty-two and one-half rubles assignats (fifteen silver rubles) was the required payment for manumission in one instance in 1854, and presumably there was a fairly standard price.[58] The bailiff at Petrovskoe would have preferred an extra tiaglo, but the central office in Moscow was willing to settle for the money.

A widow with unmarried children, unless she was head of the household, was in a difficult position in her deceased husband's dvor. Her children, whom the household had supported and raised, were valued for their future role in attracting a kladka or obtaining an allotment. Thus the household was reluctant to part with them. Were a widow to remarry into another household, the departure of her children would result in a substantial loss. Demographics significantly intensified the problem, for as a woman's likelihood of becoming a widow increased with age, so her children came closer to maturity. Thus a widow with sons and daughters approaching marriage age was an attractive acquisition for another household. But

---

57. TsGADA, f. 1262, op. 4, ch. 1, ed. khr. 649, l. 43–44 (19 April 1855).

58. Ibid., l. 152 (4 November 1854).

the younger a widow and her children, the less desirable they were both to their own household and to any into which she might marry. Moreover, if a widow remarried, she would form a tiaglo and have to work, and of course her not working not only was a problem for the bailiff and the commune but was a source of considerable tension in her deceased husband's household. The widow's allotment, no more than three acres of arable land, might cover her immediate family's cereal needs, but it made no contribution toward the maintenance of livestock or the farmstead and yielded no surplus for other expenses.

The complex of factors affecting the status of widows only increased the ambiguity of their position and produced a variety of alternatives for resolving their uncertain role in their marital household and on the estate. At Petrovskoe, the bailiff and undoubtedly the commune as well preferred that widows remarry. The widows did not. Widowers, who were assigned a half-tiaglo upon the loss of their wives, generally desired to remarry in order to obtain a full tiaglo, and thus more land, and a wife to meet their domestic needs, but when possible they sought single women. Military recruitment usually ensured a surplus of single females. Forcing widows to marry estate peasants, leaving these women alone and allowing them to avoid work, and getting rid of them by permitting marriage outside the estate and receiving money for their manumission were all policies available to estate managers, and at one time or another all were used by the bailiffs at Petrovskoe.

The problem with widows was an inevitable consequence of the incentives favoring early and universal first marriage. Heads of household were often in conflict with each other and the estate over the remarriage of a widow. As a result, the reluctance of widows to remarry and the absence of benefits to both the households involved meant that a high incidence of widowhood was frequently one of the social, economic, and cultural consequences of serf life. Clearly, the power of the bailiff, the will of the commune, and the interests of some patriarchs were being compromised.

The age of retirement also obviously affected the number of tiaglos and, consequently, the level of production. But the age at which the serfs stopped working was in large part deter-

TABLE 28

Male Age at Retirement, Village of Petrovskoe (1813–27)

Age	Percentage Not Working	Percentage with Half Tiaglo	Percentage with Full Tiaglo
40–44	2	3	95
45–49	10	27	63
50–54	39	30	31
55–59	85	15	0

Source: See table 27.

mined by their physical capabilities. Thus the bailiffs had only limited flexibility. Manuals of instruction written for estate managers often suggested that males be required to carry a tiaglo until age 60 or 65, but this was wishful thinking.[59] In practice most serfs, it seems, were relieved of their corvée responsibilities and allotments during their fifties.[60] The mean age when males were freed of their tiaglos at Petrovskoe was 54 years. The household inventories indicate that males in their forties not carrying a full share of obligations were not able to do so, either for reasons of health or because they were widowers. Ninety percent of all males aged 45–49 worked, but thereafter the proportions dropped quickly. Sixty-one percent aged 50–54 worked, while only 15 percent of all males aged 55–59 still cultivated the demesne, none with a full tiaglo (see table 28). There is no indication of how the age of retirement was determined for specific individuals, but overall it should be noted that serfs in their mid-fifties were very likely to have grandsons and grandnephews close to marriage age. In all likelihood the ability of a household to maintain its economic viability, consumer/labor ratio, or *tiaglosposobnost'* (tiaglo capability), as it was called, was a major factor in permitting individuals to be relieved of corvée obligations.

Finally, to optimize production, the bailiffs at Petrovskoe, like those elsewhere, sought to ensure the equitable distribution

59. Confino, *Domaines et seigneurs,* 111–12.
60. Blum, *Lord and Peasant,* 513.

of wealth and even to reduce inequalities caused by random or biological fluctuations. This was essential to maintain early and universal marriage and to avoid the inefficient use of resources. At Petrovskoe the bailiff's efforts included overseeing the repartitions of the demesne and peasants' land, arranging for land surveys of the estate, helping households without enough horses acquire draft animals, preventing serfs from renting out their allotments or dealing in their corvée responsibilities, and releasing individuals from work obligations for a year or two to help them out of economic difficulties. All these had the effect of reducing economic stratification.

Allocating land according to the labor capabilities of a household was fairly simple, requiring little intervention by the bailiffs. At the communal assemblies held in the spring, often the only meeting of the village communes during the course of a year, tiaglos were redistributed. There was little room for dispute, since obligations in most instances were clear. When necessary, individual strips of land were awarded by drawing lots. The only potential problems were when to assign half-tiaglos to young, unmarried males and when to reduce the responsibilities of older men. Conflicts were either resolved by the commune or routinely decided by the bailiffs, for they never reported any such problems to their superiors in Moscow.

Constant expansion of the demesne and the peasants' fields, the establishment of two new settlements on the estate during the nineteenth century, and the varying rates of net population growth for the eight villages of the estate necessitated periodic resurveying. The need to distinguish peasants' arable land from the demesne, the need to see that the increase in tiaglos did not create inequities in the land area assigned to each work team, and the need to provide each settlement with communal lands in proportion to its number of tiaglos required the hiring of a surveyor to realign and, where possible, consolidate the fields and to redistribute pasturelands. At Petrovskoe this was done approximately every twenty years.

In contrast to overseeing the repartition and hiring a surveyor, the bailiffs' other attempts to limit economic differentiation among households involved more careful scrutiny of the peasants' lives. Efforts were directed primarily at providing poorer households with assistance to make them more productive. In particular, the bailiffs at Petrovskoe kept very detailed records of households with too few horses to carry out their labor obligations and to support their family members. Following the subsistence crisis and shortage of feed during the winter of 1833–34, which presumably caused considerable economic mobility resulting from changes in consumer/worker ratios and livestock holdings for many households, approximately 20 percent of all work teams had too few horses, according to the bailiff after he examined every household on the estate. Almost 4 percent of all work teams had no horses whatever.[61] Over the next few years, the estate spent 2,500 rubles to buy horses for these tiaglos, in effect significantly reducing the economic consequences of the crisis and leveling much of the economic stratification it created. By 1839 only 11.3 percent of all work teams had too few horses to work the demesne and allotted arable land, almost half the number of five years earlier. Only 2 percent completely lacked draft animals.[62]

Crises required a considerable infusion of capital by the estate if land, labor, and livestock were to be kept in balance, peasant well-being assured, and production of cereal maximized. One of the reasons household lists were compiled was to monitor the status of individual households and see that each had the requisite amount of livestock, especially draft animals, given its number of tiaglos or work teams. From these documents the bailiffs drew up lists of households in need of horses and forwarded their recommendations to the central office in Moscow. The character of the head of household and the reputation of its members—whether the family was hardworking or lazy, whether it managed its domestic affairs with care or neglect—were noted. These comments influenced the decision of the estate management to lend these serfs money to buy horses, the debts to be paid back usually within two years.[63] Again the result was to reduce stratification and the risk that poorer households would go under.

61. TsGADA, f. 1262, op. 4, ch. 1, ed, khr. 521, 541.
62. TsGADA, f. 1262, op. 4, ch. 1, ed. khr. 396, l. 27, and ed. khr. 558, l. 189.
63. TsGADA, f. 1262, op. 4, ch. 1, ed. khr. 135, l. 2–7; ed. khr. 101 (June 1818); ed. khr. 137 (September 1819); ed. khr. 190 (October 1821). See also "Neskol'ko slov," 35.

Being remiss toward household responsibilities, cultivating the allotted arable land poorly or renting it out, sowing the fallow field, or selling grain or other items without permission all contributed to economic differentiation by undermining a household's well-being. Moreover, in some of these instances certain households benefited at the expense of others. The bailiffs at Petrovskoe tried to prevent all such acts. The manuals of discipline for the estate cite seventy-three instances of punishment involving these five offenses during the thirteen years for which the records are complete. They constitute only 2.2 percent of all punishments administered, suggesting their relative infrequency, though selling grain or livestock without permission might easily have gone undetected. The nature of the other offenses, however, makes it highly unlikely that they would have gone unnoticed, and even if no disciplinary action were taken, such incidents would have been recorded.[64] Consequently, the bailiffs were effective in preventing the serfs from engaging in activities that would have resulted in greater economic differentiation, though more probably the peasants themselves, or more correctly the heads of household, refrained from doing so.

There was good reason for the peasant commune to share the estate's concern and to have a strong commitment to economic equality. Although state and local taxes and other money dues were assessed per male soul according to the tax censuses, it was common in many parts of Russia to reapportion the taxes by tiaglo, with the commune as a whole responsible for the total sum. This was done at Petrovskoe. If a work team defaulted on its payment, the others had to make good the loss. Thus the peasant commune had some interest in seeing that each tiaglo was capable of meeting its money obligations. But this concern only implied the assurance of a minimum level of well-being, not the radically egalitarian distribution of wealth that existed at Petrovskoe.

Many anthropologists and sociologists have noted that the constant fear of subsistence crises in precapitalist peasant societies has given rise to what James Scott has termed a "subsistence ethic." This moral outlook, it has been suggested, was shared by the French, Russian, and Italian peasants in the nineteenth century and is present in many developing countries today.[65] The subsistence ethic meant that, economically, peasants were risk avoiders, while socially they sought relationships that would provide assistance in times of crisis. But more important, Scott says, it entailed the right to a "subsistence niche" and in normal times ensured the "survival of the weakest."[66] Communal lands, open fields divided into strips, and even periodic redistribution of plowlands were all techniques of the subsistence ethic. Essentially, a community shared the risks of an uncertain environment.

There is no reason to suspect that this attitude was not present at Petrovskoe. But again, as with communal tax concerns, this moral outlook required only a limited reallocation of wealth to provide "a minimal subsistence insurance," not the greatest possible limitation of socioeconomic differentiation.[67] At Petrovskoe, more than simply a subsistence ethic was involved. The remarkably egalitarian distribution of wealth was a vital part of the social and political order on the estate. The forces leveling economic differences, along with early and universal marriage, high fertility, large patriarchal households, and stable forms of domestic groupings, served to structure and distribute power among the serfs and to realize the central purpose of the institution of serfdom—income for the landlord. All these characteristics of serf life were fundamental supports in a system of control that rested on the collusion and cooperation of the bailiff and patriarchs, the heads of household.

Investigations into social stratification within peasant communities have usually centered on the differentiation of households by wealth and status. Small landholders, tenant

65. James C. Scott, *The Moral Economy of the Peasant: Rebellion and Subsistence in Southeast Asia* (New Haven, 1976), 2.

66. Ibid., 3, 41, 43. See also Jere R. Behrman, "Supply Responses and the Modernization of Peasant Agriculture: A Study of Major Annual Crops in Thailand," in *Subsistence Agriculture and Economic Development*, ed. C. R. Wharton, Jr. (Chicago, 1969), 236; J. W. Mellor, "The Subsistence Farmer in Traditional Economies," in ibid., 214; H. Myint, "The Peasant Economies of Today's Underdeveloped Areas," in ibid., 103; and K. Polanyi, *The Great Transformation* (Boston, 1957), 163–64.

67. Scott, *Moral Economy*, 5.

farmers, and landless laborers are generally contrasted, or peasants with a similar relationship to the productive process are distinguished on the basis of land and livestock holdings per capita. Certainly this method of analysis would be fruitless for Petrovskoe, for there were no such differences. But a patriarchal society is also highly stratified. There exists a sharp intergenerational division that cuts across all households and provides a foundation for interhousehold or communal control.

A patriarchal society at its foundation entails nothing more than the movement of wealth and power away from the young and toward the old. With the patriarchal structure in Petrovskoe, the household was more than anything else the unit of exploitation used not only by the noble landlord as a member of the political elite, but by serf patriarchs as well. A patriarch sought to better his status not by claiming a disproportionate share of wealth or productive resources in the village, not by competing with other households, but by exploiting more effectively the members of his own household. Status was defined by position within the household, the ability to control economic and fertility decisions, and the power to maintain advantage over other household members.

The egalitarian distribution of land, labor, and livestock not only optimized estate and peasant production of cereal at Petrovskoe, raising the standard of living for all, it minimized conflicts between households, limiting disputes over wealth and power within the political leadership of the village. What emerged was a ruling stratum of peasants in which membership was primarily a function of age. This ruling elite, the heads of household, shared with the estate management a number of concerns, and together they functioned in a social system that advanced and protected their common interests. In upholding the large patriarchal family either by directly controlling household fission or by granting village elders the right to regulate household size, the bailiffs supported the very foundation of patriarchal authority. And this authority assured the estate of a strong ally in the battle to get the remainder of the serf population to work productively and behave properly.

The immediate economic advantages of early and universal marriage to both patriarchs and the estate have already been discussed. In essence, for the male's household, a marriage never worsened and almost always improved its consumer/labor ratio and its allotment size per capita, to the benefit of all family members but the new couple. Equally important, the high fertility that resulted from this marriage pattern was the only means by which a patriarch and his wife could avoid destitution in their old age, given the high level of mortality. Moreover, high fertility made it possible for serf elders to be freed from their field work responsibilities by their mid-fifties, thereby avoiding some of the drudgery of peasant life. After age 55, most patriarchs were simply managers, while others in the household worked. But even before this it is likely that heads of household enjoyed a privileged position in the nature and amount of work they performed. Stable high fertility and large households considerably enhanced the managerial functions of the patriarchs. They were called the *bol'shak*, the big one, the boss, the one who gives orders; their wives, the *bol'shitsa* or *bol'shukha*. Nineteenth-century Russian ethnographers frequently commented on the strict, almost despotic control that patriarchs exercised in their households.[68] At Petrovskoe, households worked an average of forty-two acres of arable land, including the demesne, all in scattered strips. The bol'shak was responsible for allocating and overseeing his household's labor and livestock to get the most out of the land. Larger households also permitted some specialization of labor. This was especially true for women: some cooked year round, others tended the livestock and watched the children and in the spring and summer worked the fields and took care of the kitchen garden. It was for the bol'shitsa to see that the household benefited as much as possible from the proper division of these tasks.

In other peasant societies with stable high fertility, the advantages for patriarchs have included not only the kind of work done, but better food and clothing, precedence in feeding,

---

68. Zvonkov, "Sovremennye brak," 24–27; Tiutriumov, "Krest'ian-skaia sem'ia," part 1, p. 285; Kalachov, "Iuridicheskie obychai," 19–20; A. M., "Narodnye iuridicheskie obychai i deistvuiushchee zakonodatel'stvo," *Delo*, no. 8 (1870):32; Semevskii, "Domashnii byt," part 2, pp. 71–72; and Mukhin, *Obychnyi poriadok*, 62–69.

and privileged use of house space and facilities.[69] In Russia the bol'shak clearly had preferential use of space in the hut. In winter the bol'shak and his wife slept on the *polati* (sleeping platforms) directly over the stove, the warmest place in the hut. In summer it was the other married couples who had to move out and into various outbuildings and storerooms. The "beautiful" or "red" holy icon corner (*krasnyi, sviatoi, obraznoi ugol*) was also the elder's (*starshii*) corner. Here was the table where the family ate meals, with the place beneath the icon reserved for the head of household. He relinquished his place only on a son's wedding day, when the newly married couple sat under the icon during the celebration feast.[70]

The spiritual owner of a peasant household and a symbolic idealization of the patriarch, the embodiment of his authority and privileges, was the *dedushka-domovoi*, the grandfather house spirit, thought by peasants throughout Great Russia to share the economic fate of his household. While belief in house spirits was common in many parts of Europe, their characters were often quite different. In Russia every household had its own domovoi, who lived behind the hearth below the bol'shak's bed and was often addressed as *khoziain*, head of household. If the domovoi looked favorably upon the family, its horses were strong and healthy; if he became angry, the animals grew thin and died. The domovoi saw to all trifles in the household. He liked fertile domestic fowl and livestock and was intolerant of needless expenditures. In a word, the domovoi was hardworking, thrifty, economical, and painstaking, and the peasants took great care not to offend him in any way.

The domovoi was thought to be a good-natured elderly being with a gray beard and stooped posture. Most important, he would communicate only with the eldest member of the household if he wished to inform the family of some good or evil to come. If a family moved into a new hut, the patriarch

69. J. C. Caldwell, "A Theory of Fertility: From High Plateau to Destabilization," *Population and Development Review*, no. 4 (1978):555–57, 560–61.

70. Sumtsov, *O svadebnykh obriadakh*, 186–87; Malykhin, "Byt," 210–11; Semevskii, "Domashnii byt," part 1, pp. 110–12; and Troitskii, "Selo Lipitsy," 83–84.

would ask the domovoi to accompany it and bring his favor to the new home. As an invitation, a few hot ashes were taken from the stove of the old hut and buried in the corner of the new one under the icon, where the head of household normally sat. The domovoi always accepted. Fights between domovoi of different households were seen as one house spirit trying to better his dvor at the expense of the other. A domovoi could not live with another house spirit, and if two households merged the domovois struggled for control of the house. The power of the domovoi was so great that often these families found it impossible to stay together.[71]

Whether peasant patriarchs at Petrovskoe were better fed and clothed than other members of their households is unknown, but stable high fertility brought them considerable power and benefits. Lower fertility and smaller households would have undermined the position of the patriarchs. In essence the reproductive pattern supported the economic pattern and perpetuated the gradations of material advantage within the family.[72] Stable high fertility at Petrovskoe was also one of the key factors that stabilized household structure, greatly compressing the duration of household life cycles and providing for the constancy of the three-generation, multiple-family unit. This, coupled with the egalitarian distribution of wealth, meant that patriarchal power within a household varied little over time, since the bol'shak did not have to adapt to greatly different family patterns, labor and livestock resources, or levels of well-being.[73] In sum, the power of the patriarchs, supported by the entire economic and social structure of life, was unequaled and unchanging.

Stable households and maximum production benefited not only the estate and the heads of household but every serf at Petrovskoe. Nevertheless, the estate and the patriarchs derived the greatest share of wealth and power, based upon a conjunc-

71. Bondarenko, "Pover'ia krest'ian Tambovskoi gubernii," 116–20; A. Afanas'ev, "Dedushka domovoi," in *Arkhiv Istoriko-iuridicheskikh svedenii otnosiashchikhsia do Rossii*, part 6 (Moscow, 1850), 16–22; and I. Dobrozrakov, "Selo Ul'ianovka, Nizhegorodskoi gubernii, Lukoianovskago uezda," *ES* 2 (1853):57–59.
72. Caldwell, "Theory of Fertility," 566.
73. Ibid., 565.

tion of interests. As a result, intergenerational antagonism was structurally endemic at Petrovskoe, with the patriarch and his wife on one side and the exploited members on the other. But the battlefield for this conflict was not restricted to the household. The peasant commune and the bailiff were also responsible for maintaining social and economic order.

4

COMMUNAL FUNCTIONS
AND CONTROL

THAT THE COMMUNE (MIR) SHOULD BE VIEWED AS AN INSTITU-
tion reflecting intergenerational conflict in Russian peasant
society would certainly come as a shock to Herzen, Hax-
thausen, and those Slavophiles and others who saw it as an
indigenous form of socialism. But the commune played a central role in maintaining patriarchal authority. Yet this was far
from its only function. The commune was also one of the key
forces holding this little society together. In most instances the
patriarchs tried to represent the interests of all the serfs, and
obviously not all conflicts were between generations. In addition, the commune addressed the estate management and especially local government authorities with a collective voice
and organization, and this gave the peasants substantial autonomy. In fact the commune provided a social cohesiveness that
the household could not give. Patriarchy within the family may
well have been inimicable to the young, but patriarchy within
the commune often served the common good. While these elders did support individual heads of household in dealing with
recalcitrant family members, the patriarchs, who embodied
communal wisdom, experience, interests, and action, did much
to bind the peasants together.

Although the mir has been the subject of intense ideological controversy, little work has been done in studying the records of communes themselves. There are some good reasons
for this. The most detailed information about the Petrovskoe
commune concerns its relations with government officials. The
estate office kept the financial records of the commune, noting
all its expenditures. Since sending a serf on communal business
to the district seat in Borisoglebsk or the provincial capital in
Tambov always involved travel costs, all such trips were recorded and the reasons for them specified. These documents,
which reveal decisions of the patriarchs, are therefore an excel-
lent source for seeing how the bureaucracy at its lowest levels

interacted with the basic unit of peasant society in Russia, the commune. But aside from these records, the commune figured only incidentally in the bailiffs' papers. Communal festivals and village celebrations received no mention at all. Most likely much was handled orally, and other communal concerns were of little interest to estate managers. This was probably the case on many other serf estates as well.

The archives of the Petrovskoe estate give no indication of how often village or estate assemblies met, though it seems clear that meetings were not very frequent. Each village had its own *obshchestvo* (village organization), and for general estate matters it seems that representatives from each were summoned, these being the *pervostateinye stariki,* elders of consequence. This avoided communal assemblies of four hundred to five hundred persons, which would have been unwieldly. It is not known how long these and other peasant functionaries served, but the bailiff could remove them from their positions at will.

The functions and powers of the Petrovskoe commune were extensive. Besides distributing tiaglo obligations and peasant allotments, it assessed, collected, and paid taxes and other money dues, determined many communal expenditures, and petitioned the central estate office in Moscow with its grievances and concerns. The commune also administered justice by adjudicating disputes, conducting investigations, disciplining its members, and providing internal police supervision as required by law. In addition, it elected peasant functionaries, oversaw household divisions, determined who would be recruited into military service, maintained work discipline, fixed the order of field labor (though much was well established by custom) and natural dues, cultivated the communal arable land to provide emergency grain reserves, gave some assistance to the needy, and saw to many of the needs of the parish church and clergy. The commune dealt with numerous local officials, bribing them when necessary and providing them or military troops with transport, food, and billeting.

Before beginning an in-depth discussion of the commune's functions, it would be useful to describe in broad quantitative terms the major age-specific status or generational differences at Petrovskoe to see how they relate to the mir and its role in serf society. First, almost half of the estate population consisted of children under 17. Rarely did serfs marry or carry estate labor obligations before this age. Children worked from a very early age, and they lived in their natal household, unless it underwent division, even if orphaned. All matters of upbringing were handled within each peasant household. There is little evidence that either the estate or the commune interfered in head-of-household or parent/child relationships until the assuming of corvée obligations became a concern or unless it was necessary to find orphans a foster home and establish their property rights. The only exception was for household serfs, especially boys, who usually began learning a skill or craft between ages 10 and 12, the estate seeing to their training.

At the other end of the age spectrum were the heads of household. They and their spouses constituted approximately 17 to 19 percent of the total population and, for males, roughly one-quarter of all tiaglos. It is to this group that many of the advantages in this little society accrued. All heads of household participated in village assemblies directly and in estate assemblies indirectly through their representatives. Approximately 40 percent of the male heads of household were no longer assigned full corvée obligations by virtue of their age. Moreover, from the remaining group came all the serf functionaries on the estate, the *burmistr* (serf manager), *starostas* (village heads), *smotritels* (overseers), *nariadchiks* (drivers), and possibly *sotskiis* (serf police agents). In 1837, in the only archival listing of these persons, there were forty such serfs on the Petrovskoe estate, slightly more than one-fifth of all working heads of household, and these peasant functionaries enjoyed a variety of work privileges.[1]

About one-third of the estate population fell between the children and the elders. This middle group carried three-quarters of all field-work obligations. From the time of their arranged marriage until their ascension to head of household, a period of rarely less than ten years and of fifteen to twenty-five years for most, these serfs worked but were accorded no priv-

1. TsGADA, f. 1262, op. 4, ch. 1, ed. khr. 558, l. 190.

ileges on the estate, in the commune, or within their own household. Males who failed to conform to required norms were sent into the army or, in extreme cases, exiled to Siberia. For young adults, flight was the only refuge from submission and exploitation, an alternative that rarely succeeded.

Recruitment, household division, and the maintenance of work discipline gave rise to intergenerational conflict in the exercise of communal authority. And in all matters, those who worked but were not heads of household were excluded from decision making. Yet the generational split in the commune was not so clear as in the household. While this gathering of old men sought to preserve its interests, its fate was tied to that of the young. Moreover, the problems of poverty and social deviance were not simply generational. Therefore a more subtle view of authority is needed for the commune, and its more complex purposes require appreciation.

This chapter will first examine communal concerns with general welfare, in particular assistance to the needy, and then turn to the commune's attempt to protect itself from bureaucratic interference by local government authorities, to its relations with the parish church, to the administration of justice, and finally to the establishment of recruitment priorities.

The commune at Petrovskoe did not establish or maintain any economic institutions or charitable organizations to minister to the needs of its members. In 1858, in anticipation of the emancipation, the government sent out a questionnaire to all estates with over one hundred male serfs. One series of questions read:

> Are there not on the estate some sort of economic or charitable institutions such as a mir cooperative, village bank, emergency grain stores, almshouse, hospital, orphanage, and the like? By what means are they maintained, and how were they established? At the present time, what measures are taken to guarantee the subsistence of widows, orphans, and impoverished and elderly persons?

To this the bailiff of the Petrovskoe estate responded:

> There is no mir cooperative or village bank. The communal granary, in which is stored the statutory amount of

grain per soul, is full. There is also a hospital, which is maintained at the expense of the lord; for subsistence, widows, the elderly, and orphans are given land under grain crops [sowed, but not harvested by the mir]; the impoverished are given exemptions on their work days for the lord.[2]

A hospital was set up at Petrovskoe in the early 1820s, at considerable cost to the estate. The peasant commune never contributed any funds for its upkeep, though before its establishment the mir did spend some money on medicines for the ill. For two or possibly three years a doctor was hired by the estate, with an annual salary of two thousand rubles, to train two household serfs to be *podlekars,* doctor's assistants. In addition, between 1821 and 1824 the estate spent over 1,200 rubles for various medicines and equipment.[3]

The success of the hospital in improving the health of the peasants is difficult to determine. As Wrigley writes, "In Europe it was not until the last years of the nineteenth century that the medical contribution to the reduction in mortality became clearly important."[4] The observed life expectancy at birth at Petrovskoe for the years 1850–56 hardly suggests any substantial effect of estate medical care on peasant health. When a hospital was set up in 1821 on the Gagarin estate of Pokrovskoe, also in Tambov province, the doctor there wrote to the prince: "Your peasants flee from the hospital like a Jew from the cross."[5] Though the doctor bitterly attacked peasant superstitions, given contemporary medical practices the serfs pursued the prudent course.

Maintaining grain reserves in case of crop failure was required by law. In 1820 a document on land usage at Petrovskoe notes that each tiaglo worked an additional half desiatina of land in the spring fields beyond the normal peasant allotment

2. TsGADA, f. 1262, op. 4, ch. 2, ed. khr. 862, l. 7–8.
3. TsGADA, f. 1262, op. 4, ch. 1, ed. khr. 115, 190, 210, 233.
4. Wrigley, *Population,* 176.
5. TsGADA, f. 1262, op. 1, ch. 1, ed. khr. 1196 (25 January 1821). See also Mashkin, "Byt," 86; and Malykhin, "Byt," 215.

and demesne obligation. It is likely that the grain from this land went for the communal reserves. Similar documents for 1834 and 1849, years after major crop failures, show clearly that the serfs worked a total of 320 extra statutory desiatinas (864 acres) to replenish the emergency stores. Moreover, each year the commune was required to report to the local authorities in Borisoglebsk on the size of the harvest and the status of the reserves.[6]

Assistance to individuals came primarily as land that had been plowed and sowed by the commune. Harvesting, carting, drying, winnowing, and sifting the grain, however, were the responsibility of the needy themselves. It was extremely rare for the estate to relieve adults capable of working from tiaglo responsibilities. In 1837, the only year for which there is such detailed information, out of 715.5 tiaglos on the Petrovskoe estate, 25.5 were exempted from corvée entirely. Most of these, however, had been freed from their labor obligations because their homesteads had burned down in May. Fewer than 1 percent of all tiaglos were exempted that year for reasons of poverty.[7] Similarly, more than thirty years of financial records for the Petrovskoe commune reveal only a handful of exemptions from taxes and money dues approved by the village assemblies because of poverty.

The mir did have to make allowances for those who were unable to pay on time. Generally, after three years the commune gave up trying to collect the tax arrears owed it, in effect freeing the poor from some of their obligations. Between 1819 and 1843, an average of 4.4 percent of all annual taxes and money owed eventually turned out uncollectible, with 7.4 percent the highest figure for any one year. All those who paid taxes underwrote the cost of these defaults, for the commune was collectively responsible for the total sum due.[8]

---

6. TsGADA, f. 1262, op. 4, ch. 1, ed. khr. 161, l. 2; ed. khr. 615, l. 5–6; op. 1, ch. 1, ed. khr. 2833, l. 38–39.

7. TsGADA, f. 1262, op. 4, ch. 1, ed. khr. 558, l. 182, 190.

8. TsGADA, f. 1262, op. 4, ch. 1, ed. khr. 75, 115, 139, 168, 189, 214, 236, 275, 313, 384, 414, 433, 452, 483, 507, 527, 546, 564, 584, 593, 601, 608, 656; ch. 2, ed. khr. 722, 750, 782, 805, 828, 848, 868, 887. Although these rates for annual arrears seem low, in part testifying to the skills of the professional managers of Petrovskoe, figures for other serf estates often appear

TABLE 29

Allotment of Arable Land

Use	Acres	Percentage of Total
Peasants' allotments (690.5 tiaglos)	14,915	94.6
Church servitors	238	1.5
The elderly, boys, and orphans	425	2.7
Nontiaglo households	119	0.8
Excess for the needy	65	0.4

Previously, I mentioned that households with at least one working couple, but unable to produce enough food to survive, rarely exceeded 4.5 percent of the village population, virtually identical with the size of annual tax defaults. An even more sensitive group was those households with no tiaglos at all. With this group included, all together approximately 8 percent of the population was incapable of meeting its subsistence needs, and it is to these peasants that the commune and the estate provided help. An 1820 land survey gives the amounts of arable land the estate turned over to the commune to plow and sow for the impoverished (see table 29).[9] The 8 percent of the estate population presumably in need of economic assistance meant that the approximately 260 persons in the three bottom groups were supported by the 609 acres of arable land the commune plowed and sowed for them in the spring. With an average yield this would surely have guaranteed their subsistence.

The commune spent most of its funds to pay soul, road, bridge, postal, and local taxes and dues and to cover the costs of recruitment. All together these averaged 88 percent of total revenues, leaving the commune little to spend for other purposes (see table 30). Moreover, because the commune paid in assignats—paper money—it had to pay a premium, a *lazh,*

to be higher than they actually are. It was not unusual for landlords to cite as arrears not the annual amount in default, but all accumulated back taxes and dues dating from whenever they first began keeping records. These arrears were in fact no more than bookkeeping entries, for the serfowners had long given up trying to collect them.

9. TsGADA, f. 1262, op. 4, ch. 1, ed. khr. 161.

TABLE 30

Communal Taxes and Major Expenditures at Petrovskoe

Years	Taxes and Dues per Tiaglo (rubles)	Percentage of Total Anticipated Revenues Never Collected	Percentage of Actual Annual Revenues Expended for Poll, Road, Bridge, and Postal Taxes and for the Commutation of Obligatory State Services	Percentage of Actual Annual Revenues Expended for Recruitment Costs
1819–20	8.50	6.9		
1820–21	13.00	6.7	62	17
1821–22	10.00	7.4	88	0
1822–23	9.00	5.3	94	0
1823–24	9.00	5.0	92	0
1824–25	15.50	5.0	54	8
1825–26	9.00	4.7	92	0
1826–27	9.40	5.6	94	0
1827–28	12.00	1.6	72	20
1828–29	13.00	2.3	63	17
1829–30	12.00	1.4	70	9
1830–31	10.00	2.5	84	20
1831–32	12.25	3.5	68	14
1832–33	—	—	—	—
1833–34	12.00	—	—	—
1834–35	14.00	2.8	71	9
1835–36	13.00	4.4	79	0
1836–37	15.40	5.1	81	7
1837–38	—	—	—	—
1838–39	15.50	3.9	77	0
1839–40	—	—	—	—
1840–41	3.45	3.3	96	6
1841–42	3.45	7.2	—	—
1842–43	3.71	1.6	87	0
1854–55	6.58	—	85	11
1855–56	7.00	—	67	12
1856–57	5.00	—	94	0
1857–58	5.00	—	93	0
1858–59	6.00	—	83	0
1859–60	—	—	—	—
1860–61	6.00	—	94	0

Note: After 1839, ruble values are expressed in terms of silver, not assignats. For the years 1854–61 the amount of taxes in arrears is unknown, and percentages are based upon anticipated, not actual, revenues.

on the money it owed the state. Until the monetary situation was stabilized with the reforms of the late 1830s, the premium fluctuated from eight to eighteen kopeks per ruble, in effect increasing taxes by that percentage.[10] In addition, contact with government officials frequently meant additional payments. Paying taxes in Borisoglebsk always involved gifts of money to the *kaznachei* (treasurer), *povytchik* (clerk), *prikaznyis* (petty officials), and *prisiazhnii* (notary). If the district *zasedatel'* (assessor) happened to be in the office, he too did not depart empty-handed. In 1820–21 the Petrovskoe commune gave a total of forty-five rubles to officials for accepting its two annual tax payments; by 1838–39 the amount had risen to over one hundred rubles, these bureaucrats not losing in the decline in the value of paper money. During the intervening years, no tax payment was ever made without being accompanied by such gifts.

These "surcharges" upon the payment of taxes, along with similar gifts accompanying other transactions of government business, can be considered unofficial supplements to the salaries of officials for performing specific legal functions. The commune and the bailiff, who also approved of such practices, were merely trying to keep the favor of these officials and have their affairs handled promptly and correctly in order to avoid any confusion in their dealings with the government. For example, in the fall of 1822, for writing rough and final drafts of a report that was required by law on the sowing and harvesting of cereals that year, the commune gave to the clerk and his assistants 5.20 rubles in cash, spent 1.36 rubles buying food and other refreshments for them, and presented another clerk, the *protokolist*, with an additional 10 rubles besides having to pay the appropriate legal fees for such a document.[11] Similarly, when Arkhip Mikheev, the elected police agent in the village of Petrovskoe, was sent to the district court in Borisoglebsk to file a complaint about the behavior of a retired soldier living in the village, he spent 2.10 rubles for a clerk to take the report and

---

10. TsGADA, f. 1262, op. 4, ch. 1, ed. khr. 75, 115, 139, 168, 189, 214, 236, 275, 313, 384, 414, 433, 452, 483, 507, 546, 564, 584, 593, 601, 608, 656; ch. 2, ed. khr. 722, 750, 782, 805, 828, 848, 868, 887.
11. TsGADA, f. 1262, op. 4, ch. 1, ed. khr. 214 (November 1822).

88 kopeks for a scribe to copy it on stamped paper, which itself cost another 66 kopeks.[12] There are hundreds of similar examples in the financial records of the Petrovskoe commune. Peasant flight, the theft of horses, and accidental death had to be reported to the *zemskii sud,* that is, the district court and local police authority. Moreover, paying taxes, handing over recruits and criminals, filing various reports and notices, and obtaining information on state corvée obligations brought the commune in contact with government officials. In many though far from all instances, the conduct of regular government business involved the routine payment of gratuities.

Quite distinct from these were bribes. The most common were attempts to prevent inquests into sudden or accidental deaths. In some instances the commune and the estate hoped to cover up the facts of the case, but more often they simply wished to avoid costly and prolonged legal proceedings, which would take up valuable work time. The documents of the Petrovskoe commune are candid. On occasion it bribed the parish priests, who were legally required to report all incidents in which a person had died before receiving the sacrament. In April 1829 the following expenditure of twenty-five rubles was noted: "Given to the priest Onisim Alekseev and the junior deacons of the village of Kanin for the burial of a field peasant from the village of Kanin who drowned in the Vorona River, in order not to bother the district court and cause an inquiry costing a great expenditure of money."[13] During the subsistence crisis of 1834, forty-two rubles were "given to Petrovskoe church servitors by the peasant commune on the sudden deaths of persons without receiving the sacrament, in order not to cause further troubles on account of the burials."[14] Between 1823 and 1840 there were six similar instances when the parish priests were paid "not to cause further inquiries" or "not to make a report to the authorities."[15]

It was cheaper to bribe village priests than local govern-

12. TsGADA, f. 1262, op. 4, ch. 1, ed. khr. 546 (October 1835).
13. TsGADA, f. 1262, op. 4, ch. 1, ed. khr. 414.
14. TsGADA, f. 1262, op. 4, ch. 1, ed. khr. 507.
15. TsGADA, f. 1262, op. 4, ch. 1, ed. khr. 214 (July 1823); ed. khr. 236 (March 1824); ed. khr. 564 (November and December 1835); and ed. khr. 584 (March and August 1840).

ment authorities, but nevertheless most accidental deaths were not covered up. Some included peasants outside the estate as victims or witnesses and could not easily be concealed. Also, local officials derived a considerable portion of their income from conducting inquests, and presumably they would have been suspicious of any village or estate that did not report what was considered to be a normal number of cases.

Upon the discovery of a corpse or the occurrence of a death from other than natural cases, the elected police agent of the appropriate village of the estate would inform the district court and have a report sent to the nobility's court assessor requesting an investigation. This petition usually cost no more than two rubles, though it could reach as high as thirteen. The court assessor generally came to the estate promptly, often within a few days, accompanied by a clerk or two, two soldiers, and on occasion the district doctor. Rarely would a second visit to the estate be needed, and it was unusual for witnesses to be summoned subsequently to Borisoglebsk to give further testimony. This was because at every inquest the commune paid the assessor and his assistants to avoid such developments. Sixty-three rubles were "given as a gift to Borisoglebsk district court assessor Sotsyperov in the examination of a dead body . . . , in order to prevent any further troubles."[16] When assessor Spitsyn came to Petrovskoe to investigate both a drowning and the death of a serf in the apiary, wine, fruit liquor, and food were provided at communal expense. In addition, Spitsyn was given over twenty-eight rubles "so as not to conduct any further investigation."[17] In all, between 1820 and 1840 the records of the commune cite twenty-three bribes to district assessors investigating accidental deaths—three or four times that many if their assistants are included—"to refrain from delaying the peasants further," "not to carry the inquest further," or "to avoid further consequences." On the average, it cost the Petrovskoe commune sixty rubles to influence the outcome of such inquests.[18]

16. TsGADA, f. 1262, op. 4, ch. 1, ed. khr. 414 (October 1828).
17. TsGADA, f. 1262, op. 4, ch. 1, ed. khr. 507 (May 1834).
18. TsGADA, f. 1262, op. 4, ch. 1, ed. khr. 139 (April 1820); ed. khr. 160 (December 1820); ed. khr. 189 (February 1822); ed. khr. 214 (October

In Russia, peasants were required to fulfill state corvée obligations, essentially repairing roads and bridges. At times the commune of Petrovskoe was able to convert this into a money payment, but often it had to supply the laborers demanded. The officials who assigned the sections of the road to be repaired, as well as the overseers of the work itself, were readily bribed. In fact some of these officials were in such powerful positions that their dealings with the Petrovskoe commune appear to be little short of extortionate. "By order of the Borisoglebsk district chief of police, 407 male workers should be sent to level the steep slope of a mountain on the Kirsanov road near the ravine called 'Bare,' but at the request of bailiff Ivan Ivanov indulgences were made in this, for which forty-two rubles is given to him, Gospodin chief of police, as a gift."[19] Such indulgences included getting assigned "on the designated mountain a more advantageous section to work" and, quite probably, a reduction in the number of workers required, since 407 men represented almost 60 percent of the estate's male work force.[20] Threatening other estates and communes with having to level the same slope of the mountain probably provided the district chief with a considerable income. Payments were also made to district officials for assigning tracts of road that were close to the estate and for extending the deadline when the work was to be completed. Finally, the overseers of the actual labor were often bribed to allow the commune to send fewer than the mandated number of men.[21]

There were numerous other instances of extortion or bribery. Twenty rubles were paid to the rural assessor so that troops would not be quartered on the estate, and it is hard to

1822 and March 1823); ed. khr. 275 (November and December 1824); ed. khr. 414 (March 1829); ed. khr. 507 (April 1834); ed. khr. 527 (March and June 1835); ed. khr. 546 (August 1836); ed. khr. 564 (January, March, and April 1837); ed. khr. 584 (October 1839 and March 1840); ch. 2, ed. khr. 722 (August 1827); and ed. khr. 782 (October 1838 and February and April 1839).

19. TsGADA, f. 1262, op. 4, ch. 1, ed. khr. 414 (June 1829). See also ed. khr. 433 (October 1829).

20. Ibid.

21. TsGADA, f. 1262, op. 4, ch. 1, ed. khr. 189 (June 1822); ed. khr. 275 (October 1824 and June 1825); ed. khr. 384 (May 1828); ed. khr. 414 (October 1828 and January 1829); ed. khr. 433 (May 1830); and ed. khr. 750 (June 1832).

believe this official did not make the rounds of neighboring villages.[22] When two counterfeit notes were discovered among those paid as taxes in March 1816, fifty rubles were given to the treasurer "so that this would not lead to further trouble."[23] Forty-two rubles were given to the court assessor when an undocumented person was found residing in Kanin, "for releasing the managers of the estate and other residents of the village of Kanin from major responsibility and judicial investigation."[24] The following year, to cite again from the records of the commune:

> During the conduct of an investigation in the village of Petrovskoe by Borisoglebsk *dvorianskii zasedatel'* Sotsyperov about a peasant of Shatsk district belonging to landlord Frolova, who had personal evidence that he [the serf] was known to be living as a fugitive in the village of Petrovskoe with peasant Fedor Kuznetsov and others, so that the investigation will be resolved in our favor sixty-three rubles was given to him and his assistants in gratitude.[25]

With the outbreak of cholera in 1830 substantial areas of Tambov province were placed under quarantine, disrupting trade. The Petrovskoe commune paid the colonel in charge of maintaining the cordon ten rubles for various "indulgences and favors," presumably to allow some movement of people and goods.[26] Upon noticing errors in the sixth tax census of 1811, the commune spent over 300 rubles "so the matter will not be discovered" by provincial officials.[27] Finally, in the winter of

---

22. TsGADA, f. 1262, op. 4, ch. 1, ed. khr. 189 (March 1822).
23. TsGADA, f. 1262, op. 4, ch. 1, ed. khr. 75.
24. TsGADA, f. 1262, op. 4, ch. 1, ed. khr. 414 (January 1829).
25. TsGADA, f. 1262, op. 4, ch. 1, ed. khr. 452 (September 1830).
26. TsGADA, f. 1262, op. 4, ch. 1, ed. khr. 452 (December 1830). See also I. Dubasov, "Kholernyi god v Tambove, 1830," *Russkaia starina*, no. 12 (1875):742–47; I. Dubasov, "Tambovskaia kholernaia smuta v 1830–1831 godakh," *Istoricheskii vestnik* 29 (1887):620–28; and I. Iakunin, "Kholera v Tambove v 1830–om godu: Po razskazam ochevidtsev," *Vestnik Evropy* 55, book 10 (1875):204–23.
27. TsGADA, f. 1262, op. 4, ch. 2, ed. khr. 750 (June 1832); ch. 1, ed. khr. 507 (May 1834).

1840, following a bad harvest the previous fall, upon receiving the approval of the Moscow estate office the commune paid the district marshall of the nobility 150 rubles "for granting permission to give the peasants grain from the reserves," presumably for not waiting for official authorization.[28]

All these examples of gratuities and bribes paid by the Petrovskoe commune date from the years 1815 to 1843, and they certainly provide ample evidence of the institutionalized government corruption and bureaucratic mismanagement so often described in Russian literature. Earlier records of the commune as well as those for 1844–54 were not found in the archives, and documents on expenditures between 1854 and 1861 present a quite different story. Although small gifts of money still accompanied the payment of taxes, no other gratuities or bribes were recorded. It is possible, of course, that the commune simply decided it unwise to note such expenditures, or the estate may have taken over the commune's functions, paying off officials itself. But it is also possible that the introduction of the *stanovoi pristav* in 1837, a local judicial and police officer with responsibility and jurisdiction for only a part of a district, reduced bribery and corruption by placing an intermediary between local bureaucrats and the commune or the estate. This office was salaried, and each commune contributed as part of its money dues.[29]

The only other items of significance in the commune's budget went to cover some of the expenses of the two parish churches at Petrovskoe. As was required by law, the estate provided the clergy with a total of sixty-three agricultural desiatinas (227 acres) of arable land, which the church servitors and their families worked themselves. There is no evidence that the bailiff, the central estate office, or even Prince Gagarin himself was at all concerned with the peasants' spiritual well-being, participation in religious rites, or church attendance. This again may suggest substantial communal autonomy, though it more likely testifies to the weakness of Russian Orthodoxy as a religion without content or theology. The serfs themselves did

28. TsGADA, f. 1262, op. 4, ch. 1, ed. khr. 584 (March 1840).
29. TsGADA, f. 1262, op. 4, ch. 1, ed. khr. 656; ch. 2, ed. khr. 805, 828, 848, 868.

not even care a great deal about maintaining the church. In the village of Petrovskoe, the iconostasis in the church had long since become faded and discolored. There was a bell tower but no bells. The fence around the churchyard had fallen down. The priest and other clerics lived over a mile away from the church, and their household structures were "very dilapidated." In Kanin the church lacked a bell tower altogether, though the iconostasis was in somewhat better shape.[30] In January 1832, senior priest Ivan Dmitriev, the superintendent of several local parishes, on a routine inspection ordered the church at Petrovskoe sealed up because it was in such a state of disrepair, "but at the request of the parishioners and church servitors this was revoked, for which ten rubles were given to him in thanks by the elected police agent with communal consent."[31] The following year both churches were given new roofs, but nothing else was done. Ten years later, local church authorities demanded that the necessary repairs finally be made.[32]

To His Honor, Manager of the Estates of His Excellency Prince Nikolai Sergeevich Gagarin, Pavel Antonovich Zubov

From Village of Kanin Priest Stefan Vasil'ev Smirnov

I have the honor to report to Your Excellency that in our village of Kanin, the wooden church has great defects, which absolutely must be repaired, namely: it does not have a bell tower, which must be built new; the faded iconostasis, restored; the walls, both interior and exterior, painted with a decorous paint; the wooden roof, which leaks in many places, redone, and for greater durability it would be better to roof with tin plate and paint copper [?]; to have the broken twenty-pud bell recast [?] into a new one of the same weight; and to build a fence around

30. TsGADA, f. 1262, op. 4, ch. 1, ed. khr. 121 (1 January 1818); ed. khr. 150 (1 September 1819).
31. TsGADA, f. 1262, op. 4, ch. 1, ed. khr. 750.
32. TsGADA, f. 1262, op. 4, ch. 1, ed. khr. 598, l. 4.

the church, which will all cost by our estimate not more than five thousand rubles; such above defects, which our superiors have repeatedly pressed, now they compel us to fix; the peasants belonging to the parish of this church are in no position to do this because of crop failures in recent years; thus, by reporting this to Your Excellency, I most humbly ask you to . . . give a fitting and proper appearance to a church of God.

23 FEBRUARY 1842

Neither the estate nor the commune had particularly good relations with the parish clergy. The estate was often unwilling to supply the materials and labor needed to keep the churches and the clergy's household structures in repair, and the commune felt quite free to complain to clerical authorities about excessive requisitions and fees asked by the parish priests. For almost five years, from August 1821 until May 1826, the Petrovskoe commune was involved in legal proceedings against one of its priests, Aleksei Polikarpov, who according to the parishioners charged too much for performing occasional religious rites. What began as an argument between Polikarpov and the church elder concluded with the commune's filing a sixty-six-page list of grievances against the priest in the Borisoglebsk clerical board and the Tambov clerical consistory. Eventually a new priest was assigned. In 1838 the peasants of the parish of Kanin began similar proceedings against their priest "for various offenses committed by him."[33]

Finally, it is not completely clear from the commune's financial records precisely how much control the mir had over its funds. Large expenditures often required approval from Moscow. Moreover, although taxes were fixed, bribes to government officials were in the commune's interest, and expenditures on the church were totally at the commune's discretion, the estate management on occasion ordered the commune to

33. TsGADA, f. 1262, op. 4, ch. 1, ed. khr. 160 (August 1821); ed. khr. 189 (May and June 1822); ed. khr. 214 (October 1822); ed. khr. 275 (July 1825); ed. khr. 313 (October 1825 and May 1826); ed. khr. 558 (11 October 1836), l. 49; ed. khr. 649 (30 November 1854 and 26 July 1855), l. 54–56, 149; ed. khr. 782 (September 1838).

cover certain costs. In June 1841 there was an uprising on the estate. Little is known about the revolt, though it may have resulted from a decision of the Moscow office to sell to Siberian factories drunkards, thieves, and serfs derelict in meeting their household obligations, along with their entire households. The estate forced the commune to pay the costs of notifying local authorities of the uprising, feeding the soldiers who came to restore order, transporting those arrested to Tambov, and exiling others. In all, total costs to the commune were almost a thousand rubles.[34]

There is little information about the administration of justice and the resolution of disputes among the serfs by the commune. The elders had the right to punish an individual by flogging, though the punishment was supposed to be supervised by the bailiff. A serf bringing a complaint to the elders generally had to accuse someone specifically. Only then would the commune investigate the matter, and only as related to the accused. Guilt was most often established by confession. Falsely accusing someone—that is, casting aspersions on a serf's character—and bothering the elders without sufficient cause were also punished by whipping.[35] The reputation of both parties in a conflict was an important consideration in the decisions taken by the elders and greatly influenced the compensation due the injured party or the punishment imposed on the guilty serf, as the following example reveals:

> On 31 March last year, 1828, near the end of Holy Week, various property disappeared from the storeroom of stableman Ivan Timofeev Akhriapkin and his wife Pelageia Vasileva, in the theft of which was suspected stableman Iakov Grigor'ev, but at that time he did not confess to it. Last 3 February the above-mentioned Pelageia recognized her lost shawl at the home of Fedos'ia Iunova, a soldier's wife from Kanin, and upon investigation it turned out that she had received this shawl from the above-men-

34. TsGADA, f. 1262, op. 4, ch. 1, ed. khr. 593, 605. There is no reference to this uprising in *Krest'ianskoe dvizhenie v Rossii v 1826–1849 gg.*, ed. N. M. Druzhinin (Moscow, 1961).

35. TsGADA, f. 1262, op. 4, ch. 1, ed. khr. 413 (March 1829).

tioned stableman Grigor'ev for weaving for him six yards
of cloth. The following had disappeared from Pelageia:

A new calico dress worth 9 rubles 20 kopeks; a
checked gingham dress, 7 rubles 20 kopeks; a French silk
shawl, 6 rubles; a large yellow cotton kerchief, 5 rubles; a
white calico shirt front, 50 kopeks; an old cotton print
three-cornered scarf or kerchief, which has a recognized
value of 50 kopeks, in all 28 rubles 40 kopeks—for which
Iakov Grigor'ev was beaten with a birch rod and had half
his head shaved, and to compensate Pelageia it was ordered to take from him livestock of equal value; and although Grigor'ev ought to pay for the stolen items with
livestock of twice the value, since the above-mentioned
Pelageia had fornicated with Grigor'ev, for her debauched
behavior only equal value was paid up in punishment.[36]

For some crimes the bailiff would assemble a special council of
elders:

Last August 1833 two horses having a purchase price of
140 rubles disappeared in the forest from village of Kanin
peasant Filip Nikiforov. By the testimony of Kanin peasant Patomol Semenov, the thief of these horses was peasant Il'ia Agapov of the same village. For such a trial the
elders of consequence [*pervostateinye stariki*] were
gathered from all villages, who decided to take from
Agapov the aforesaid sum in livestock.[37]

Agapov was also flogged and turned over to government authorities for criminal proceedings.

If stolen items could not be returned, it was common for
the commune to order the confiscation of other property from
the thief, often two or three times the value of the goods taken.
Nevertheless, the compensation to the injured party had to be
balanced with the capability of the thief's household to con-
tinue to fulfill its labor obligations to the estate, and on these

36. Ibid.
37. TsGADA, f. 1262, op. 4, ch. 1, ed. khr. 496 (19 October 1833). See
also ed. khr. 558 (June 1836).

grounds the bailiff and even the Moscow estate office would directly interfere in communal affairs, overturning the decisions of the elders.[38] Finally, though the commune hoped that peasants would resolve their own conflicts without bothering the elders, individuals were not permitted to inflict punishment on serfs who were not members of their own household. In 1827, upon discovering who had stolen a pane of glass, a dress, and a pair of shoes from his home, Galaktion Vorob'ev, rather than bringing the matter to the attention of the commune, forced the two guilty peasants "to walk naked and barefoot in the cold" around the village. For this Vorob'ev was whipped.[39]

Distributing land and tiaglos, collecting taxes, electing peasant functionaries, cultivating the arable land for the emergency stores and the needy, bribing officials, and determining the calendar of field labor seem to have been fairly routine matters for the commune to administer. Neither the bailiffs' weekly reports nor other documents relating to the commune cite any instances of serious disputes over these issues. Obviously the elders were governed by agricultural traditions and were committed to economic equality among households. In addition, they were in agreement that local bureaucrats should be kept both distant and content.

In contrast, determining who would be sent into the army to fill draft quotas was a highly divisive issue. For a household, the economic costs of losing an adult male laborer were considerable. A household not only lost a work team and an allotment of arable land, it still had a daughter-in-law and possibly infant children to support. Patriarchs saw their security in old age diminished, and if recruitment occurred within a year or two of marriage, they would not even have recovered the brideprice.

Young males viewed conscription as comparable to a sentence of death. At Petrovskoe, some cut off an index finger to avoid recruitment; others drank poison or acid hoping to damage their internal organs. Often those fearing they would be recruited simply took flight. Others tried to escape en route to induction centers. In response, communal assemblies were

38. TsGADA, f. 1262, op. 4, ch. 2, ed. khr. 846 (20 December 1857).
39. TsGADA, f. 1262, op. 4, ch. 1, ed. khr. 380 (October 1827).

held in secret, and once a serf was designated for conscription he was placed in leg irons and kept under constant guard. It usually took as many men to transport the recruits to Tambov as there were peasants to be inducted. The commune often bribed army doctors to declare serfs who maimed themselves fit for military service.[40]

Recruits had to be between the ages of 17 and 35, and their year of birth had to be certified by the village priest from parish registers before induction. It was therefore rather difficult to have a serf conscripted who was outside the legal age limits, and there was only one instance at Petrovskoe. Between 1834 and 1849, the mean age of recruits on the estate was 25.7 years; between 1850 and 1858, 23.5 years. Most were married, since fewer than 15 percent were below age 20. Recruitment rarely fell on heads of households, and though they had an economic stake in the outcome, the elders were primarily deciding the fate of those a generation younger. It is unclear why the mean age of recruits was so high, and why they most often were taken after marriage, thus leaving so many soldatkas, essentially widows. The documents fail to touch on this issue. One logical, though purely speculative answer, is that it gave the commune more time to sort out the troublemakers and loafers.

Recruitment priorities at Petrovskoe were first to rid the estate of undesirables and then for households to draw lots if draft quotas were still not filled. "Because of the proclamation of a recruit levy, it has been ordered to elect elders from each village to make according to form a priority list of suspected or known troublemakers," the bailiff wrote in his report of 22 October 1834.[41] In August 1837 the bailiff informed the Moscow office that persons "discovered stealing, remiss in domestic matters, and especially those lazy and without horses" would be given as recruits.[42] This was common practice on many estates.[43]

40. TsGADA, f. 1262, op. 4, ch. 1, ed. khr. 139 (January 1820); 160 (January 1821); 189 (February 1822); 275 (November 1825); 384 (July 1828); 452 (May 1831); 507 (October and December 1834); 750 (September 1831).
41. TsGADA, f. 1262, op. 4, ch. 1, ed. khr. 518, l. 22.
42. TsGADA, f. 1262, op. 4, ch. 1, ed. khr. 558, l. 219.
43. Aleksandrov, Sel'skaia obshchina, 76, 247–52, 267, 275–76.

The commune itself often took the initiative in maintaining order and ridding the estate of deviant individuals.

> From the village of Kanin, peasants Prokhar Medvedev, Egor Sedov, and blacksmith Egor Kamkov, originally a field peasant, have repeatedly been suspect in various thefts, but as their guilt was not established, they remained under suspicion. Now all three were convicted in the theft of a wheel from the stud farm and of property belonging to various persons, and so the peasant commune, having long recognized them as scoundrels, requests the estate to get rid of them, the commune taking on itself all obligations both corvée and dues, for which the Petrovskoe administration has the honor to report to the main office and humbly asks permission . . . to give them now against the next recruit levy, since they will be physically fit for this . . . and the peasants will be spared ruin, since they [the guilty serfs] have almost completely ruined a few families, and meanwhile this will deter others from similar crimes.[44]

Egor Sedov apparently was not accepted by the army, for in November 1860 the bailiff wrote to the Moscow office:

> As the entire commune has repeatedly applied to the estate administration with an earnest request to exile the aforesaid Sedov to Siberia for many evident thefts, . . . the estate humbly asks to obtain the agreement of His Excellency for resettling Sedov in Siberia, since [he is] worthless and harmful to the entire estate.[45]

These were not unusual examples. The commune and the estate were in agreement that serfs convicted in district criminal courts should be recruited or exiled, but such instances were uncommon, in part because most troublemakers were con-

---

44. TsGADA, f. 1262, op. 4, ch. 2, ed. khr. 846 (10 December 1857). See also ed. khr. 750 (November 1832) and ed. khr. 507 (December 1833).
45. TsGADA, f. 1262, op. 4, ch. 2, ed. khr. 884, l. 11.

scripted before they could commit offenses that required formal judicial proceedings. The bailiffs at Petrovskoe kept detailed manuals of discipline, recording all the offenses committed by serfs. One of the main purposes of these manuals was to assist in drawing up recruit lists.

From the recruit lists of 1831 and 1834 it is clear that many of those designated for conscription had committed more than one offense, and almost two-thirds had been involved in the theft of estate or peasant property (see table 31). It is understandable that the commune would have desired to get rid of those who stole from other serfs, and recruitment was one of the few ways the bailiffs could control the theft of estate prop-

TABLE 31

Reasons for Induction into the Army, Estate of Petrovskoe

	Frequency	
Reason	1831	1834
Theft of estate property	15	14
Theft of peasant property	14	9
Selected by lot	6	—
Lazy and remiss in household responsibilities	6	3
Lazy and remiss in household responsibilities, resulting in destitution	5	1
Committed various pranks	4	3
Not fulfilling corvée responsibilities	2	—
Poverty	1	2
Disobedient toward head of household	1	1
Flight	1	1
Father a thief	1	1
Convicted in criminal court	1	—
Widower and crippled	1	—
Without a home	1	—
Divided household without estate permission	—	4
Negligent with fire	—	2
Disobedient toward estate manager	—	1

Sources: TsGADA, f. 1262, op. 4, ch. 1, ed. khr. 518, l. 29–40; ch. 2, ed. khr. 753, 1. 1–8.
Note: Many serfs on the recruit lists had committed more than one of the offenses above. In 1831 there were thirty-nine names on the recruit list; in 1834, thirty-five names.

erty. Not only might the threat of conscription directly deter stealing, but it made an entire household and especially the heads of household responsible for the behavior of their younger adult males. If a family wished to safeguard its material well-being, and if a patriarch desired a labor supply to exploit so as to ensure his future, both would have to help restrain the theft of goods from the estate. In other words, what was good for the estate also benefited the bol'shak and his entire household. In addition, heads of household who themselves stole estate property ran the chance of having eligible males from their families conscripted.

It was important for patriarchs to be able to coerce younger males dissatisfied with their family situations to work. The heads of household, therefore, also used the threat of recruitment to control laziness, disobedience, and failure to fulfill household obligations. After theft, these were the most common reasons the patriarchs selected individuals for military service. A son or nephew disgruntled about his lack of authority, status, or economic position in the household faced conscription and with it the dispossession of property, disinheritance, and the loss of all future rights and benefits that came with age. Young male serfs were thus under great pressure to conform to the will of their ascendants and to adhere to the norms that patriarchy implied at Petrovskoe.

While the bailiffs and the commune were in essential accord that thieves should be conscripted, and while the estate supported patriarchal authority by giving village elders the right to have their disobedient or indolent sons and nephews recruited, the commune and the estate were often at odds about what to do with the poor—that is, those with too few tiaglos to support their households. At one point the estate's policy was to fill remaining draft quotas by selecting serfs by lot from only large households under the premise that they could best absorb the loss of a male laborer. Although households with three or four tiaglos would suffer a decline in their standard of living if they lost a male to military service, they would still be economically viable, able to feed their members and carry out their reduced labor obligations. Also, Prince Gagarin, the owner of Petrovskoe, allowed those peasants who had been selected for conscription by lot to purchase exemptions for 1,000 rubles, payable over three years. Between 1811 and 1812, during the Napoleonic Wars, at least nine households took up this offer. In 1855 two serfs who had been found unfit for active service in the regular army but suitable for induction into the militia were exempted when their families offered to pay the estate 350 rubles each. In 1833, in reporting a request to purchase a recruit exemption for 1,000 rubles, the bailiff wrote to Moscow that "although there aren't any suspicions against the family, yet being a large family, it ought already to assume recruit obligations."[46] Such payments for exemption from the draft, for removing a household from the lottery, were extraordinarily large, indicating the value a household placed on its male workers. It was also a reward for the hardworking. From the estate's perspective, by making the economically strong carry the burden of recruitment, whether by a son or by payment, the bailiffs avoided creating greater destitution and hardship, provided another mechanism for equalizing wealth, and increased revenues by selling exemptions.

A major problem, however, was that placing a disproportionate share of recruit obligations on larger households created an incentive for them to divide in order to be less likely to lose a worker to the draft. In times of war when recruitment levies were high and many serfs had to be selected by lot, even the heightened risk of impoverishment resulting from a smaller number of tiaglos and a reduced ability to cope with a retirement, accident, or death of a male worker did not deter households from partition. During the Crimean War (1853–56), the military demanded 36 recruits per 1,000 male souls (tax units), plus an additional 6 per 1,000 from many of the Great Russian provinces to make up for previous regional inequities. At Petrovskoe the number of households in the village shot up from 104 to 126 in the six years 1850 to 1856. It is unclear why the bailiff was not able to limit these household divisions, but possibly the patriarchs of larger households felt the potential dangers and economic losses of dividing were more than offset by the likelihood of losing a male worker and by the cost of having to support the recruit's wife and children for many years. Other

46. TsGADA, f. 1262, op. 4, ch. 1, ed. khr. 20 (September 1811); 29 (September 1812); 496 (October 1833); 649 (April 1855).

factors may also have been at work—pent-up demand for partition, domestic disputes, and possibly, if Soviet historians are to be believed, the imminent demise of serfdom. Regrettably, the documents from Petrovskoe offer no insight into this matter.

The commune saw in recruitment a way to rid itself of poorer and less productive households, especially those that were likely to default on taxes and dues. The target of the commune was primarily poorer, smaller households with only one tiaglo, called *odinokie*, especially those in which the head of household was young and inexperienced. Such households did not conform to the patriarchal three-generation, multiple-family ideal and had virtually no margin of safety against accident or illness. In these households any mismanagement of household affairs could easily result in destitution. In 1837 the bailiff wrote that frequently "the mir has to pay all the taxes and dues for one-tiaglo households and to fulfill their estate and state corvée obligations." Putting a greater share of military obligations on these households served the interests of the village elders in many ways. It reduced the number of males who would be conscripted from their households, and it reduced the number of young heads of household who might have been a source of envy for other serfs of the same age. Moreover, according to the bailiff, conscription from smaller households did not foster division that undermined patriarchal authority. If anything, at this level, the threat of recruitment induced mergers. For the commune, such a policy provided an alternative for dealing with the poor, reduced the number of households that required communal assistance, and was yet another means of limiting economic differentiation.[47]

In contrast to the commune, the estate was at times reluctant to have the sole male of a household recruited. Such households had often been the recipients of financial assistance from the estate, which would have no way of recovering its investment if these serfs were now conscripted. In 1837, however, after a three-year effort by the estate to reduce the number of households without horses, the bailiff concluded that those still

47. TsGADA, f. 1262, op. 4, ch. 1, ed. khr. 558 (10 August 1837).

lacking draft animals had only themselves to blame. He asserted that "from obvious laziness they have not come by a horse, regardless of being odinokie." He therefore decided that it would be "useful that the peasants be convinced that recruits will be taken from one-tiaglo households, and thus those without horses would make a greater effort to acquire a horse for themselves." Furthermore, the bailiff noted that by instituting this policy the pressure for larger households to divide would be reduced, and so in time would be the number of one-tiaglo households.[48] All these sentiments were identical to the interests of the serf patriarch.

The picture of the Petrovskoe commune presented here is far from complete, but the limitations of the documents preclude further analysis. Nevertheless, some aspects of communal activity emerge clearly. By providing tax relief or giving over cultivated lands to the needy, the commune did much to ensure the survival of all its members, including the economically weak. The basic approach of the commune, however, was to control access to productive resources. Communal repartitions of arable land and the assigning of labor obligations by tiaglo limited economic differentiation, and they seem to have aroused little controversy among the patriarchs, that is, between households. Institutional forms of assistance to the needy were not used, and direct grants or exemptions to the poor were limited to a very small percentage of the population.

While communal life was certainly not harmonious, in most instances the mir had the serfs' common well-being at heart. The commune served the general good and used its funds to attain freedom from internal deviants and bureaucratic interference, acts the estate found desirable as well. But this does not mean that the commune did not uphold exploitative relationships, only that exploitation did not imply competition between households to subsist or survive. The commune was the instrument of the elders, and they held the power to regulate household division and determine recruitment priorities, decisions that greatly affected the lives of those a generation younger. Even with conscription, where the interests of the estate and

48. Ibid.

the elders were somewhat at odds, the patriarchs at times were successful in getting the bailiff to rid the estate of smaller and economically less viable households. This policy not only reduced socioeconomic stratification but preserved the wealth of the patriarchs. Most often, however, communal actions were of benefit to the estate. But as successful as the patriarchs seem to have been in working with the bailiff for their common advantage, both were in fact confronted by an enormous amount of resistance and noncooperation, which reflect how deep generational status differences were at Petrovskoe.

5

PUNISHMENT, FEAR, AND CONTROL

AT PETROVSKOE THERE WAS NOT A SPIRIT OF COMMUNITY, BUT a conjunction of interests and a collusion of authority. Life was highly integrated, but not well integrated or harmonious. Dearth, demons, disease, and death stalked everyone, however their consequences might be minimized. Insolence, disorderly conduct, quarreling, and fighting were common serf behavior. Serfs stole from the estate and from each other. They willingly informed on other serfs to estate authorities and were beset by a constant and pervasive fear of corporal punishment, public ridicule, loss of status, recruitment, and exile. Serf functionaries and family heads responsible for overseeing field work found laziness, negligence, apathy, and absenteeism widespread among the younger workers they had to supervise, threatening their patriarchal authority and privileges, their level of material well-being, and the profitability of the estate. This behavior was the inevitable concomitant of serfdom. In the end, far outweighing the economic exploitation of the landlord was the social oppression of serf over serf.

Examining the aspects of authority at Petrovskoe—the household, the commune, and in this chapter the bailiff—reveals that getting the serfs to work and behave as desired was far from perfectly accomplished. The structures of control carried high social and economic costs. It is impossible to know what the serfs of Petrovskoe thought of their own behavior, but the manuals of discipline kept by the bailiffs record what to the modern observer seems an appalling level of tension, conflict, violence, and punishment. These records of manorial discipline not only included offenses committed against the estate such as theft or negligence at work, but also cited punishments for creating domestic disharmony, stealing from other serfs, breaking communal rules, or engaging in numerous other acts considered antisocial. For thirteen agricultural years, September through August, the records of the estate are complete, citing a total of 3,331 instances of disciplinary action, an average of

256 per year, almost all confined to adult males. For nine additional years the data for a number of months are lacking. In all, 4,187 punishments are recorded. But the documents note only punishment administered by the bailiff, though the records make clear that serf overseers and drivers did beat field peasants. There is no indication how common such beatings were. Also, on at least some occasions, individuals meted out punishment without the authorities' approval.[1]

Yet the level of conflict at Petrovskoe was considerably higher than the documents even indirectly indicate. The bailiffs were primarily interested in regulating the behavior of adult males without undermining patriarchal authority. In Russia, published manuals of instruction for estate managers rarely touched on internal family relations.[2] At Petrovskoe the bailiffs did not punish children. Fewer than 5 percent of those disciplined were women. Offenses committed against a member of the same household constituted only 1.1 percent of the total. But to think that the behavior of males revealed by the manuals of discipline did not at least partially reflect women's and children's patterns of interpersonal relations and attitudes toward work would be to suggest a society totally lacking integration, a process of socialization, and male role models. According to numerous observers, discord within peasant households was commonplace; wife beating was usual.[3] In August 1825 Timofei Vorob'ev, a field peasant from Petrovskoe, was flogged "with severity" for "impetuous behavior and inhuman fighting with his wife."[4] Widows on occasion asked the bailiff to discipline their sons for disobedience.[5] Manuals of discipline for

1. TsGADA, f. 1262, op. 1, ch. 1, ed. khr. 889, 1129, 2419; op. 4, ch. 1, ed. khr. 212, 248, 269, 308, 345 (347), 380 (381), 408 (413), 428 (429), 447, 463, 479, 503, 523, 542, 561; op. 4, ch. 2, ed. khr. 824, 843, 863. The files in parentheses are duplicates.
2. Aleksandrov, Sel'skaia obshchina, 94.
3. Kishkin, "Dannye i predpolozheniia," 227–28; Kalachov, "Iuridicheskie obychai," 17–18; Efimenko, "Krest'ianskaia zhenshchina," 60, 81; Semenova, Zhizn' "Ivana.," 85–87; A. M., "Narodnye iuridicheskie obychai," 34–36.
4. TsGADA, f. 1262, op. 4, ch. 1, ed. khr. 269, l. 20.
5. TsGADA, f. 1262, op. 4, ch. 1, ed. khr. 429, l. 17–18 (May 1830); ed. khr. 463, l. 16–18 (April 1832); ed. khr. 479, l. 21–22 (June 1833); ed. khr. 523, l. 2–3 (October 1834); l. 6–7 (December 1832).

other serf estates often cite instances of corporal punishment of family members at the request of the head of household.[6] The pressure for households at Petrovskoe to split up has already been discussed. Thus the evidence suggests that bailiffs were reluctant to interfere in most domestic matters, but women and children were hardly immune to the conflict and violence that so clearly pervaded the lives of the men as recorded in the manuals of discipline.

Punishment by the bailiff was spread throughout the adult male population at Petrovskoe. It was not a case of a few deviant individuals repeatedly being disciplined. During the two agricultural years September 1826 through August 1828, at least 79 percent of the adult males were flogged, 24 percent more than once. For a total adult work force, male and female, of 1,305 serfs, there were 714 incidents of whipping during this period, an average of 0.27 floggings per adult worker per year. By way of comparison, Fogel and Engerman in their study of American Negro slavery were able to find one plantation with reliable data on flogging, that of the Louisiana planter Bennet H. Barrow, "who believed that to spare the rod was to spoil the slave." The frequency of whipping there over the two-year period 1840–42 was almost two and a half times the level at Petrovskoe. Almost half of the slave hands, however, were not whipped at all during this period, not very different from Petrovskoe, where 56 percent of the working adult population was able to avoid the birch rod between 1826 and 1828. The main differences seem to be that at Petrovskoe females were rarely whipped and males were much less likely to be beaten more than once.[7] In the late 1850s, when the frequency of corporal punishment or other disciplinary action at Petrovskoe was considerably lower, over the two agricultural years 1856 and 1857 20 percent of all adult males were punished, but only 2 percent more than once. On average, based upon the thirteen years of complete data (September 1819–August 1821, September 1826–August 1834, September 1839–August 1840,

6. Aleksandrov, *Sel'skaia obshchina*, 295.
7. Robert W. Fogel and Stanley L. Engerman, *Time on the Cross: The Economics of American Negro Slavery* (Boston, 1974), 145.

and September 1856–August 1858), roughly one-quarter of all adult male serfs were disciplined at least once during the course of a year.

As I have stated, the bailiffs of Petrovskoe had two quite separate problems: to motivate the serfs to work and to prevent them from engaging in theft, domestic disputes, or other forms of social disorder. But punishment, as a method of control, was not equally successful in these endeavors. This was largely due to two interrelated factors. First, the estate was organized for productive purposes within the confines of a traditional agrarian economy, where production levels and profits depended heavily upon labor input. Thus the forms of punishment available to the bailiff were severely restricted. Second, the need to limit social disorder and theft took precedence over the maintenance of a strict work regime. It was more important for life to go on smoothly than for work rules to be rigidly adhered to.

Of the punishments the bailiffs employed, recruitment and exile, the most forceful forms of coercion from the serfs' perspective, could be used only in the most extreme cases. Considered by the serfs to be violent acts, these punishments often engendered great violence, whether in open rebellion as in 1841, when a number of households designated for transportation to Siberia rioted, or in the form of self-inflicted wounds, as was so often the case with recruitment. Equally, the bailiffs could not exile a whole village and still run a profitable estate. Moreover, for both these punishments there were legal restrictions of age, health, and, for recruitment, sex.

Putting serfs in confinement or forcing them to wear an iron collar around the neck (*sheinaia rogatka*), the latter being a punishment the government eventually prohibited as a form of torture, prevented the peasants from working. Given the purpose of the estate and the potential damage to an entire household's well-being, these were not very useful forms of discipline. Consequently, at Petrovskoe there were only five instances of jailing (0.1 percent of the total), usually to hold an individual for state authorities, and eleven (0.3 percent) involving the rogatka.

Essentially, the bailiffs had at their disposal four forms of punishment that they believed helped maintain the daily order and ensure the functioning of the estate. Whipping serfs with a *rozga,* a birch rod, was the most common form, used in 97.8 percent of the 4,187 instances of punishment. The exceptions were for men too old or ill to be whipped. For the agricultural years 1856–57 and 1857–58 the manuals record the exact number of lashes: the mean for the 159 cases was 37.4, the highest in any one instance was 80.

In approximately 10 percent of all punishments, for the most serious of offenses, a flogging was accompanied by shaving half a man's head and beard, levying a fine, or, if he were a peasant functionary, removing him from his position of responsibility. Shaving half a serf's head and beard seems to have been a particularly odious form of discipline. In 1844 the governor of Pskov, Major General Bartalov, requested from the minister of internal affairs, Count L. A. Perovskii, the authority to limit the landlords' right to impose on their serfs such a "visible mark of shame." Bartalov argued that this practice embittered serfs against their lord, noting that it violated popular sensibilities to cut hair in this manner. The minister refused to restrict the powers of the lords, stating that "although it would be desirable not to see the use of this measure on serf estates," it was not a form of torture in itself and was effective in disciplining serfs of poor behavior and preventing them from taking flight after being flogged.[8] At Petrovskoe, approximately 6 percent (258 cases) of all punishments included shaving half the head and beard along with whipping.

Fines were also considered severe punishment, and they involved not just the payment of money, but often the seizure of livestock. Generally, any loss of property is keenly felt in a peasant society, but in Russia, because most property was jointly owned by all the members of a household, levying a fine against an individual in effect punished an entire dvor. Consequently, fines were a form of collective punishment usually imposed when a whole household had benefited from an offense. Fines were levied in 146 instances, 3.5 percent of the total.

8. Correspondence of 12 and 22 July 1844 from the archives of the Ministry of Internal Affairs, Department of the Police Executive, delo 413, reported by A. B., "Brit'e pomeshchikami polgolovy krest'ianam dlia presecheniia samovol'nykh otluchek," in *Arkhiv istorii truda v Rossii* (Petrograd, 1921), 2:151–52.

Finally, serf functionaries, though the objects of considerable abuse both from the bailiff and from field peasants, enjoyed a number of privileges. Overseers and drivers were freed from the drudgery of estate field labor, which meant that both they and their horses were in considerably better condition to work their own fields.[9] Elsewhere their households were exempted from recruitment, though this was not the case at Petrovskoe.[10] For most other tasks, serf functionaries simply enjoyed the benefits of being the boss. To strip these serf elders of their authority and status was a form of discipline available to the bailiff. Peasant functionaries committed 13 percent of all the offenses recorded in the manuals of discipline. Generally these men were punished by flogging alone, but in 5 percent of the cases the offender also lost his privileged work status.

Punishable infractions fall into a number of different categories (see table 32). Theft brought the most severe form of punishment. Not only was the thief flogged, but 74 percent of all fines and 77 percent of all the incidents of shaving half the head and beard were for stealing. Theft, as has been shown, was also the primary reason the estate or commune designated a serf for recruitment. The punishment varied with the items stolen and their intended use. Stealing goods to sell them, approximately 15 percent of all thefts, was more severely punished than stealing for the thief's own use. Thieves caught selling their goods were three times more likely to have their heads shaved or to be fined. American slaveholders were also less tolerant when goods were stolen for sale.[11]

It was comparatively easy for serfs to steal from the estate. Sowing, harvesting, processing, and transporting cereals afforded numerous opportunities to steal grain. Also, rarely did a week pass in summer when a peasant was not beaten for turning his livestock out into estate fields to graze. In winter, pilfering timber from estate woodlands was virtually a daily occurrence even though the bailiff had ten to fifteen men con-

9. TsGADA, f. 1262, op. 4, ch. 1, ed. khr. 488, l. 190 (May 1834).
10. Aleksandrov, *Sel'skaia obshchina*, 62.
11. Eugene D. Genovese, *Roll, Jordan, Roll: The World the Slaves Made* (New York, 1974), 600.

CHAPTER FIVE

TABLE 32

Major Reasons for Punishment (Complete Data Years Only)

Offense	Frequency	Percentage of Total Offenses
Work-related offenses	1,410	39.8
Theft	1,008	28.5
Intentionally allowing livestock in grainfields	331	9.4
Violent or disorderly behavior	213	6.0
Negligence during watch	189	5.3
Domestic offenses	97	2.7
Acting without permission	49	1.4
Absence from village	34	1.0
Drunkenness	34	1.0
Other	174	4.9
Total	3,539	100

Source: TsGADA, f. 1262, op. 1, ch. 1, ed. khr. 889, 1819–20; 1129, 1820–21; op. 4, ch. 1, ed. khr. 345, 1826–27; 380, 1827–28; 408, 1828–29; 428, 1829–30; 447, 1830–31; 463, 1831–32; 479, 1832–33; 503, 1833–34; op. 1, ch. 1, ed. khr. 2419, 1839–40; op. 4, ch. 2, ed. khr. 824, 1856–57; 843, 1857–58.
Note: In some cases two offenses were committed at the same time. The total number of offenses is 3,539, with 3,331 incidents of punishment.

tinually guarding the forests. Together these three acts constituted one-third of all the offenses for which the serfs of Petrovskoe were punished.

Whatever the punishment for cutting down estate trees without permission or stealing estate grain, these offenses persisted in having a high rate of frequency, almost 1,200 incidents during the thirteen years for which estate records are complete. Nineteenth-century ethnographers have suggested that the peasants did not see cutting down trees on private property as theft, since the forest itself was not a product of human labor. Logs belonged to those who felled them. Frederick Law Olmsted, a highly praised contemporary observer of American slavery, noted in 1856 when commenting on slave attitudes toward grain theft: "It is told to me as a singular fact, that everywhere on the plantations, the agrarian notion has become a fixed point of the negro system of ethics: that the result of labor

166

belongs of right to the laborer."[12] Similarly, as writers dealing with other peasant societies have suggested, one might expect that stealing estate grain upset the economic equilibrium in the village much less than theft from other peasants. It was simply viewed as enlarging the total pie rather than carving a bigger slice for oneself. Thus stealing from the estate, one might think, may have been risky but did not offend social morality. When caught and punished, a peasant might have felt unfortunate but not guilty. Eugene Genovese notes that American slaves made such a distinction: "They stole from each other but merely took from their masters." Even some slaveowners shared this attitude, punishing their hands not for stealing, but for getting caught.[13]

But the theft of estate property did engender considerable conflict among the serfs at Petrovskoe. Forest guards were responsible for turning in fellow serfs found stealing wood. If the bailiff discovered that a substantial number of trees had been cut but no one caught, the guards were whipped for negligence. Often both the thief and the guard were beaten, the first for the theft and the second for catching the thief only after the act. Fights frequently ensued between thieves and forest guards. If a guard tried to do a serf a favor and was caught, the punishment could be severe.

> Peasant Trofim Fedotov, a guard in the estate forest, permitted estate peasants from the village of Rodionovka to cut down an oak for poles and to sell [them] to nonestate peasants, for which he was whipped with a birch rod, had half his head shaved, and was dismissed from his post.[14]

12. A. Efimenko, "Trudovoe nachalo v narodnom obychnom prave," *Slovo,* no. 1 (1878):145–46; P. Chubinskii, "Ocherk narodnykh iuridicheskikh obychaev," 681. See also Aleksandrov, *Sel'skaia obshchina,* 160–62. Frederick Law Olmsted, *A Journey in the Seaboard States* (New York, 1856), 117. Cited in Genovese, *Roll, Jordan, Roll,* 602.
13. Edward C. Banfield, *The Moral Basis of a Backward Society* (New York, 1958); George M. Foster, "Peasant Society and the Image of the Limited Good," *American Anthropologist* 67, no. 2 (1965):296–97; Genovese, *Roll, Jordan, Roll,* 602, 604.
14. TsGADA, f. 1262, op. 4, ch. 1, ed. khr. 345, l. 17–19 (March 1827).

Even serfs who were not forest guards were supposed to report thefts of wood to the bailiff:

> Peasants Timofei Vorob'ev and Prokhar Kashirin: the first thievishly felled four logging oaks and sold them to a Moiseev *odnodvorets* [smallholder], and the latter knew of this matter and did not inform the estate authorities; for this, Vorob'ev was whipped with a birch rod and had half his head shaved, and Kashirin owing to old age was left unwhipped but had half his head shaved, and upon the discovery of this offense twenty rubles were taken from the odnodvorets.[15]

But one did not even have to be a witness to be punished. In early June 1828 Akim Dmitriev, Timofei Efimov, and Foma Golitsyn were working an estate field together sowing buckwheat. Golitsyn stole some seed that was later found in his home, but when Dmitriev and Efimov claimed they did not see him take it, they were beaten "for not seeing the above concealment," a good example of collective responsibility.[16]

Theft of estate property turned witnesses into either informers or accomplices. For disciplinary action to be taken, thefts of estate property had to be reported to the bailiff by other serfs. The bailiff had no other way of knowing of such offenses except the few he might discover himself. In some instances the records have such notations as "according to the testimony given against him by field peasant" so and so, or "the forest guard who clearly saw them with the stolen rye." In addition, there were at least sixteen cases of serfs' being punished for giving false testimony against other peasants. Informing must have been widespread at Petrovskoe, and in such circumstances it is hard to see how an atmosphere of animosity, ill-will, and vengeance would not have prevailed.

Approximately 15 percent of all the thefts cited in the manuals of discipline involved peasant property (see table 33). It was considerably harder for serfs to steal from each other than from the estate. Seed grain was easy to pilfer from the

---

15. TsGADA, f. 1262, op. 4, ch. 1, ed. khr. 308, l. 8–9 (January 1826).
16. TsGADA, f. 1262, op. 4, ch. 1, ed. khr. 380, l. 26–27.

TABLE 33

Theft, by Ownership of Stolen Item (Complete Data Years Only)

Items Stolen	Peasant Property	Estate Property	Unknown	Total
Wood or timber	14	633	1	648
Clothes	27	1	—	28
Horses	19	0	1	20
Other livestock	5	6	—	11
Hay	11	22	—	33
Grain	25	152	2	179
Money	3	0	—	3
Miscellaneous	44	40	2	86
Total	148	854	6	1,008

Source: See table 32.

estate when working the demesne, but the peasants did not work each other's strips. Peasant huts, granaries, and outbuildings were completely enclosed by a fence, making it rather difficult to enter undetected. Most thefts of peasant property recorded in the manuals involved items of significance and value. Stealing livestock, usually horses, made up 16 percent of the thefts. Food grain and major items of clothing accounted for approximately 18 percent each. The remainder included such miscellaneous but not insignificant articles as household implements, farm tools, beehives, and garden vegetables.

The loss of a horse could bring about the immediate ruin of a household as well as prevent it from fulfilling its estate labor obligations and paying its taxes. Consequently, horse stealing was the most severely punished offense on the estate. All horse thieves were flogged, and over half had their heads and beards shaved, the highest frequency of this punishment for any single offense. If the horse had been sold, fines were levied, often two or three times the value.

> Village of Kanin and Petrovskoe peasants Pavel Krytaev and Efim Nikulin stole a horse from Petrovskoe peasant Rodion Petrov and gave it to the son of the Kanin priest, who in turn sold the horse in Tambov for twenty-four

rubles. From the above Krytaev and Nikulin it was decided to recover by appraisal thirty-five rubles, in all seventy rubles, and beyond this they were flogged with severity with a birch rod and had half their heads shaved.[17]

In late summer, after the grain was cut and tied, it was easy to steal sheaves of cereal from another's strip of land. On occasion whole cartloads would disappear. In spite of fences, peasant homes were still vulnerable.

> Peasant Vasili Prokharov stole from the house of Timofei Kandratev of the same village a woolen rug, six empty beehives, one empty cask, and one tub, for which he was whipped, and the stolen items were returned to the owner.[18]

The punishment for a theft did not vary whether it was estate or serf property that was stolen. Though thefts from the estate included primarily timber and feed grain, while from other serfs food, livestock, and clothing were the most common, this was simply the result of the goods each had and the ease of stealing them. Any wood or lumber the peasants possessed would have been stored inside the fenced household enclosure, whereas the estate had over 6,100 acres of open forest to protect. Peasants' livestock grazing on communal pastures was an easy target. Estate grain in the fields after harvest was often guarded. Although peasant fields adjacent to estate lands consequently enjoyed some measure of protection, many strips of peasants' arable land were isolated and vulnerable to theft. Individuals could do little to protect their scattered stacks of grain.

Anthropologists studying peasant communities have found theft and the fear of theft widespread. In Vasilika, Greece, "a watchdog is a common addition to a household's collection of farm animals. The people there believe thievery is a constant danger to be guarded against and prefer, if possible,

---

17. TsGADA, f. 1262, op. 4, ch. 1, ed. khr. 248, l. 1 (October 1823).
18. TsGADA, f. 1262, op. 4, ch. 1, ed. khr. 380, l. 18–21 (March 1828).

not to leave their household compound totally unguarded."[19] Similarly, in the Mexican village of Tzintzuntzan, to prevent theft "house doors usually are kept closed all day long, and at night they are wedged shut with heavy poles. . . . Nearly all homes have dogs that are beaten and abused, taught to hate man, and trained to attack anyone who comes to the door."[20] Peasants in southern Italy are themselves disturbed that "theft . . . is a disastrously common occurrence."[21] In a highland community in Peru, serfs in the early 1960s exhibited behavior quite similar to that of the inhabitants of Petrovskoe. "Theft was far from limited to manor possessions. Vicos serfs robbed one another, so they built guardhouses in the fields as harvest time approached, locked their storerooms, etc." Slaves' stealing from each other was a problem on some plantations in America, and they often "either locked their cabins during the day or locked closets or sleeping rooms inside their cabins in order to keep out thieves."[22] It seems likely that attitudes at Petrovskoe toward theft and property were the same, and the serfs shared their feelings with persons who were not in servitude.

Subsistence crises did not cause a sudden increase in the number of thefts, but stealing wood and feed grain (73 percent of all theft and 28 percent of all offenses) did reflect chronic need. The serious shortage of forests throughout the entire region surrounding the Petrovskoe estate, and the limitations placed on pastureland by the three-field system of crop rotation, created a demand that outweighed the inevitable consequences of impermissibly drawing on these resources so necessary for survival and an improved quality of life.[23] The

19. Ernestine Friedl, *Vasilika: A Village in Modern Greece* (New York, 1962), 31.
20. George M. Foster, *Tzintzuntzan: Mexican Peasants in a Changing World* (Boston, 1967), 103.
21. Joseph Lopreato, *Peasants No More: Social Class and Social Change in an Underdeveloped Society* (Scranton, Pa., 1967), 104.
22. Allan R. Holmberg, "Algunas relaciones entre la privación psicobiológica y el cambio cultural en los Andes," *América Indígena* 27, no. 1 (1967):12; and Genovese, *Roll, Jordan, Roll*, 606–7.
23. Forests made up only 7 percent of the land in the district of Borisoglebsk. TsGADA, f. 1355, op. 1, ed. khr. 1575; and TsGVIA, f. Voenno-uchenyi arkhiv, ed. khr. 19079. See also Confino, *Systèmes agraires*, 72.

peasants obviously felt that the benefits compensated for the risks, something one bailiff had to admit: "In spite of carefully guarding the forests, the peasants of the village of Petrovskoe and Kanin continually steal wood, which neither fines nor punishment restrain."[24]

By its very nature, the theft of wood or feed grain entailed a comparatively low risk of getting caught. Still, given the frequency of punishment for these offenses, flogging had become as much a part of life as was the need to pilfer wood, willfully graze livestock in prohibited places, or steal feed. And the bailiff, when confronted by this behavior, had few choices. But punishment could not overcome ecological disadvantages and material shortages, and attempts at stricter control, given the structure of authority at Petrovskoe, might only have meant greater discord. Punishment was already the product of malice, mistrust, and fear among the peasants. The use of more severe forms of punishment might have made it harder to control more damaging types of theft. Consequently, as the pattern of punishment in table 34 shows, the bailiff saw a need to distinguish serious theft from the mere pilfering of wood or feed.

But nothing did more to create animosity between serfs than estate corvée, and here we enter the realm of a virtual slave regime. The world of obligatory labor was violent, and the enmity between peasant functionaries and field peasants was enormous.

Village of Varvarina *starosta* [elder] Vasili Fedorov has lodged a complaint against Matvei Katykhov, a field peasant of the same village who, when designated for work, went out to plow the lower fallow field and without waiting for the drawing of lots began to work by himself on a desiatina that was easier than others. After the distribution to everyone of his desiatina, Katykhov was ordered by the elder to go to that desiatina he had received by lot, upon which Katykhov disobeyed the elder and swore at him. For such disobedience and swearing the elder hit him once with a knout, and then the above-men-

24. TsGADA, f. 1262, op. 4, ch. 2, ed. khr. 846, l. 2 (17 October 1857).

TABLE 34

Form of Punishment by Offense (Complete Data Years Only)

Offenses	Total Frequency of Offenses	Number Punished by Shaving			Number Punished by Fining		
		N	%	Column %	N	%	Column %
Theft							
Wood or timber	625	43	6.9	25.0	24	3.8	22.4
Other theft	330	83	25.2	48.3	42	12.7	39.3
Intentionally allowing livestock in estate or peasant fields	318	7	2.2	4.1	13	4.1	12.1
Social offenses (violent or disorderly behavior)	221	16	7.2	9.3	8	3.6	7.5
Domestic offenses	73	4	5.5	2.3	0	0.0	0.0
Work-related offenses	1,279	1	0.1	0.6	1	0.1	0.9
Watch-duty offenses	183	9	4.9	5.2	15	8.2	14.0
Miscellaneous offenses	93	9	9.7	5.2	4	4.3	3.7
Total	3,122	172	—	100.0	107	—	99.9

Source: See table 32.
Note: To establish the relation between offenses and punishment, those incidents when two offenses were committed at the same time have been eliminated.

tioned field peasant, seizing a pole from the plow, beat the starosta's head bloody until he was too exhausted to hit the elder any more, and then he went away, leaving him alone. The elder lodged a complaint against the above-mentioned field peasant, and he brought forth witnesses of the same village, who were summoned to the estate office for the investigation of this, and upon the testimony of these peasants, Katykhov was found to be guilty, for which he was whipped severely with a birch rod.[25]

In September 1820 a peasant carting buckwheat to the threshing floor refused to pick up some straw that had fallen. The

25. TsGADA, f. 1262, op. 1, ch. 1, ed. khr. 889 (July 1820).

overseer struck the peasant with a knout, and the peasant responded by beating him with the handle of a pitchfork.[26] When starosta Buziukin punished a field serf for laziness, the peasant and his brother "beat Buziukin with their fists and tore out hair from his head and beard."[27] In all, the bailiffs punished serfs seventy-seven times for violent, disorderly conduct against peasant functionaries, fifty-six times for insolence, forty-one times for fighting, and eleven times for assault. And these do not include all the incidents that were handled by the serf overseers themselves and not reported to the bailiff. One might expect that if the peasant functionary got the upper hand in any violent dispute, he was less likely to inform the bailiff of the fight.

Far more often the serfs of Petrovskoe responded to obligatory work not with force or rage, but with indifference (see table 35). Yet this did little to ease the tension between overseers and drivers, on the one hand, and field peasants on the other. Peasant functionaries were responsible for getting the required number of serfs out to work and seeing that the work was done properly and on time. Caught between the bailiff who wanted work obligations carried out well and the field serfs who had little enthusiasm for corvée, serf functionaries were in a wretched position. If a serf failed to show up for work, frequently the driver (nariadchik) was held responsible and punished. Just as often the field serfs themselves were flogged, and it was not at all unusual for both to be whipped. In December 1839 "village of Petrovskoe driver Rodion Semenov was whipped with a rozga for not sending peasant women out on schedule." But in June 1831 it was the women who were beaten "for not going out to estate work according to the schedule." And in yet a third instance, "driver Sidar Gaglov [was whipped] for not sending field peasants to estate work, and field peasants of the same village, Andrei Poliakov and Abram Poliakov were whipped in the office with a rozga for not going out to estate work according to schedule."[28] Finally

26. TsGADA, f. 1262, op. 1, ch. 1, ed. khr. 1129.
27. TsGADA, f. 1262, op. 4, ch. 1, ed. khr. 429, l. 15–16.
28. TsGADA, f. 1262, op. 1, ch. 1, ed. khr. 2419; op. 4, ch. 1, ed. khr. 463, l. 16–18 (April 1832).

TABLE 35

Frequency of Work Offenses (Complete Data Years Only)

Offenses	Frequency	Percentage of Total Work Offenses	Percentage of Total Offenses
Improperly working or plowing fields	457	32.4	12.9
Absent from fieldwork	290	20.6	8.2
Irresponsible regarding work	142	10.1	4.0
Careless or negligent in supervising field peasants	138	9.8	3.9
Failing to send required number of field peasants out to work	109	7.7	3.1
Careless or negligent in processing grain	108	7.7	3.1
Disobedient	100	7.1	2.8
Lazy	29	2.1	0.8
Late for work	23	1.6	0.6
Failing to complete work on schedule	14	1.0	0.4
Total	1,410	100.1	39.8

Source: See table 32.

driver Sidar Arkhipov, unable to force a number of women out to work and probably fearful of the consequences, "got himself drunk, tied their braids together, and led them around the village."[29]

To prevent the serfs from plowing the furrows too shallow or too far apart or from passing over a number of spots in the field required the constant attention of serf functionaries in the spring and late summer. Massive floggings in the field were not unusual. One day in May 1829 one elder, seven drivers, and seventy field peasants were whipped for poor plowing of estate fields. The next month fifty-three serfs were beaten for tilling the buckwheat fields improperly. And on a day in late

29. Ibid., ed. khr. 463, l. 13–15 (March 1832).

July four drivers, twenty-eight field peasants with their wives, and twenty-two other males were whipped "for carelessness in the harvest of estate rye allotted by tiaglo." The following May, sixty-eight peasants were flogged at various times during the month for negligently preparing the spring fields. One day in June, a year later, one driver and forty field serfs felt the lash for carelessly plowing a fallow field. The next June another thirty-one were beaten.[30] Similarly, mass absenteeism resulted in mass punishment. And in one rather unusual instance, a driver and twenty-five peasants were flogged when they failed to show up in the fields to offer a special prayer for rain.[31] The serfs, of course, were experienced cultivators and knew how to farm properly. Yet whatever the task, the manuals of discipline reveal widespread noncooperation, insubordination, negligence, intransigence, laziness, and mischief making.

The situation of peasant functionaries was hardly enviable. Though often abused by those they supervised, overseers, drivers, and forest guards received a substantial proportion of all punishments. In almost one out of every four work offenses it was the peasant functionary who was flogged, though as a group they constituted only 8 percent of the adult male work force. Since field peasants' disobedience, carelessness, or apathy were often the cause, resentment must have been great. In addition, while the bailiff might be able to check up on the fifty to sixty functionaries himself, he had to rely on overseers and drivers to report to him those field serfs who were negligent or lazy. Thus serf officials were in a position to either punish or be punished, only adding to the tension between them and the ordinary serfs.

Not surprisingly, peasant functionaries abused their authority. Without permission they exempted certain peasants from estate labor obligations, or they divided tasks unfairly. They dealt more leniently with some individuals than with oth-

30. TsGADA, f. 1262, op. 4, ch. 1, ed. khr. 413, l. 15–20; ed. khr. 429, l. 17–18; ed. khr. 447, l. 19–20; ed. khr. 463, l. 21–22.
31. TsGADA, f. 1262, op. 4, ch. 1, ed. khr. 479, l. 15–16 (April 1833). See also ed. khr. 345, l. 24–26 (June 1827); ed. khr. 429, l. 7–8 (November 1829); ed. khr. 447, l. 19–20 (June 1831); ed. khr. 463, l. 16–24 (April, May, and July 1832).

ers. In one case a driver sought sexual favors from a woman he supervised.[32] In all, distrust, suspicion, and social conflict were basic strains and disruptive aspects of serf life, and violence was the usual method of alleviating these tensions.

Although the bailiffs became involved in domestic matters only reluctantly, they commonly had to intervene in violent disputes between serfs who were members of different households. Generally the manuals of discipline give few details of conflicts between serfs not related to work, but the records reveal sixty-two incidents of fighting, thirty of quarreling, seventeen of assault, and twelve of violent, disorderly behavior. Again, one must expect that only a fraction of the total, probably the most serious cases, came to the attention of the bailiffs.

Surprisingly, there were no cases of murder cited in the records, but serf violence did lead to serious injury, as the following two examples show:

> Peasant Mikhail Kozmin and his son fractured the skull of a peasant of the same village, Gardei Savel'ev, such that they almost killed him. Upon the investigation by the Petrovskoe estate administration it turned out that peasant Kozmin probably had some sort of grudge against Savel'ev, persuaded him to come into his house, and along with his son began beating him without reason. For this crime the above-mentioned culprits have been left unpunished awaiting special instructions from the main office, and at the same time the administration humbly requests that in order to curtail similar unruly, riotous conduct among the peasants some kind of exemplary punishment be permitted.[33]

> Peasant Zot' Fedorov Medenov came to blows with Filip Kulikov, a peasant of the same village, and fractured his skull, for which he was whipped with a birch rod, with a fine of five rubles going to the estate for the doctor to

32. TsGADA, f. 1262, op. 4, ch. 1, ed. khr. 558, l. 8 (6 June 1836).
33. TsGADA, f. 1262, op. 4, ch. 2, ed. khr. 846, l. 14 (22 October 1857).

treat Kulikov, and for the injury to Kulikov five rubles, in all ten rubles.[34]

Pranks often got out of hand. In March 1828 three peasants on their way home from winnowing estate grain met Ul'iana Alekseeva, "and for their amusement tied her to the back of a sled," which they ran around the village until it crashed into the gate of the manor house.[35] Others had bad relations with their neighbors and fought repeatedly. Accusations of theft often ended in violence.[36]

Domestic tensions were at their highest during the summer, when the pressure of field work caused considerable strain within peasant households. June and August, the two months of peak field labor, saw 40 percent of all punishments for domestic reasons. In July, August, and September two-thirds of the incidents of dividing a household without permission occurred. Late fall, however, was a far more convenient time for households to split, when the harvest was in and the amount of field work greatly reduced. Serfs were also flogged, most likely at the request of family members, for tilling their own fields poorly or renting them out to other peasants.

In nineteenth-century France and Germany there were high rates of violence in the countryside, and violence was an accepted way of dealing with rural tension. As Zehr writes, "Interpersonal violence, in other words, was a traditional outlet for frustration, an expression of social conflict. In fact, interpersonal violence was often recognized and tolerated as such by villagers and authorities."[37] Similar comments have been made regarding rural England in the sixteenth and seventeeth centuries.[38] Anthropologists have also found quarrelsomeness

34. TsGADA, f. 1262, op. 4, ch. 1, ed. khr. 447, l. 5–6 (November 1830).
35. TsGADA, f. 1262, op. 4, ch. 1, ed. khr. 380, l. 18–20 (May 1828).
36. TsGADA, f. 1262, op. 1, ch. 1, ed. khr. 887 (20 August 1820); op. 4, ch. 1, ed. khr. 380, l. 24–25 (May 1828); ed. khr. 413, no *list* (April 1829); ed. khr. 429, l. 21–22 (July 1830).
37. Howard Zehr, *Crime and the Development of Modern Society* (Totowa, N.J., 1976), 134.
38. Lawrence Stone, *The Family, Sex, and Marriage in England, 1500–1800* (New York, 1977), 93–102.

and violence common in peasant communities.[39] But at Petrovskoe the bailiffs could not tolerate violence. It frequently had economic repercussions, and it always had the potential for creating broader social disorder. Petrovskoe, after all, was not a self-regulating community. Yet to limit violence implied the use of violence, for there were no other effective forms of punishment. Consequently, as the data from the manuals of discipline make clear, the bailiffs were forced to distinguish between major property crimes, which were severely punished, and crimes of violence, which were dealt with more leniently, usually by flogging alone. But in the end manorial violence only added to the violent behavior common to peasants generally.

A number of petty regulations were employed to control serf behavior. Some landlords and bailiffs went so far as to introduce Hussar military rules on their estates, requiring "a strict execution of everything; discipline was almost unlimited, and meant extending the rules of military subordination, where one is punished for the slightest slip, where there is the same regimen, the same work."[40] At Petrovskoe, though this was not the case, the peasants could not go fishing without permission. The sale of many goods required the bailiff's approval. Serfs were punished for having "unauthorized" people, usually non-estate peasants, in their homes. Of course, one needed permission to leave the estate. These restrictions are typical of many slave regimes.

A number of questions emerge from this analysis of punishment. First, did it deter crime, limit violence, and encourage better work habits? As table 34 shows, fining serfs and shaving half their heads and beards were punishments essentially for serious thefts. The same was true with recruitment and exile. Thus, along with the rod, the bailiff had a number of responses to major thefts, acts that were potentially very harmful to the estate or a serf household. But for pilfering

39. Oscar Lewis, *Life in a Mexican Village: Tepoztlán Restudied* (Urbana, Ill., 1951), 428–29; George M. Foster, "Interpersonal Relations in Peasant Society," *Human Organization* 19 (Winter 1960–61):175; Joseph Lopreato, "Interpersonal Relations in Peasant Society: The Peasants' View," *Human Organization* 21 (Spring 1962):22.

40. Letter of E. F. Suslin, bailiff to landlord M. S. Lunin, 8 August 1825. Cited in Grekov, "Tambovskoe imenie," 486.

wood or grazing livestock in cereal fields, high-frequency offenses, the birch rod was the main form of discipline. And work offenses, though the most common, were the least severely punished, weakening the bailiff's ability to maintain a strict work regime.

Data from the years for which the exact number of lashes was recorded make it possible to establish the seriousness with which the bailiff viewed different types of offenses. For work offenses, serfs received the fewest lashes, an average of thirty-one blows. For the theft of wood or timber the serfs got an average of thirty-four lashes; for negligence during watch, which usually meant a theft had taken place, thirty-eight lashes; for intentionally letting animals feed in the fields or for serious theft, forty lashes; and for insolence or fighting, forty-nine lashes.

The bailiff had to establish a clear hierarchy of offenses. Consequently, breaches in the work routine, even though obligatory labor was the essential purpose of serfdom, were more leniently punished than all other kinds of offenses the serfs committed. The serfs did work, albeit grudgingly and inefficiently, but the bailiffs' power to alter their behavior or attitudes was severely restricted. In addition, the random yet inevitable nature of punishment for many offenses, especially for theft, certainly encouraged the serfs to separate misfortune from guilt and to inure themselves to corporal punishment.

The serfs of Petrovskoe might well have viewed flogging for theft or for negligence during work, 78 percent of all offenses, as random, unavoidable, and simply part of life. Given the way the bailiffs maintained discipline, luck as much as guilt, necessity as much as inevitability were key factors affecting punishment. From the peasants' perspective, to survive one could not escape the rod. Wood was in short supply. Livestock was a form of insurance and savings, more valuable than most family members. To the bailiff, widespread noncompliance, insubordination, and theft of estate property required the liberal use of the rozga. Flogging therefore was a necessary consequence of serf life. Yet to the degree that serfs saw corporal punishment as inevitable, it could not have been a very effective method of control.

What were the effects of this violence on serf children?

For American Negro slaves, Blassingame writes, "the shock of seeing their parents flogged was an early reminder to many black children of what slavery was."[41] At Petrovskoe children did not have to witness such horrors. Virtually all floggings took place in the estate office, occasionally in the fields. Formal public whippings were extremely rare, 2.5 percent of all cases, and were held before village elders, not the entire village. But with the number of blows averaging in the thirties, children must certainly have been aware of it when their parents were beaten. Moreover, exile, recruitment, and shaving half of the head and beard were obvious to all. In America, "learning to accept personal abuse and the punishment of loved ones passively was one of the most difficult lessons for the slave child."[42] Though the records of the Petrovskoe estate and nineteenth-century Russian ethnographers are silent on children's reaction to this aspect of their social environment, young serfs probably underwent a process of socialization in some ways similar to that of young black slaves, who learned obedience to avoid pain and suffering.[43] But black slaves were not instructed by their parents to be unconditionally submissive, whereas at Petrovskoe peasant patriarchs as well as the bailiffs needed compliant serfs. Thus submission to authority must have been one of the early lessons for serf children.

How parents at Petrovskoe treated their children is unknown, but the Vicos serfs in highland Peru offer an interesting, if only speculative, analogy. Neither infancy nor preadolescence was a happy time for Vicos children, who were whipped by their parents for such offenses as fighting with siblings over food.

> Cattle constituted the most valued form of property owned by the manor serfs. Yet the task of herding livestock often was or had to be delegated to very young, untrained children, because the male parent owed half a week's obligatory labor to the manor. . . . So the high

41. John W. Blassingame, *The Slave Community: Plantation Life in the Antebellum South,* 2d ed. (Oxford, 1979), 186.
42. Ibid., 187.
43. Ibid., 188.

property value of stock came into frequent conflict with affection toward offspring in determining parental behavior. The overriding childhood memories of many a Vicos serf consist of rejection—feelings colored by remembrances of parental physical chastisement for losing a highly valued animal. Typical punishment for losing a charge seems to have been to beat the child, and/or roundly berate it for the carelessness assumed to have occurred, and to send it back out into the frightening dark night to search for the lost property, cold, supperless, and fearful of ghosts.[44]

It should be stressed that there is no evidence to support any similarities between Vicos and Petrovskoe serfs in their behavior toward children. But there is a parallel. At Petrovskoe, children often tended livestock, since their parents and elders were busy in the fields six days a week for much of the summer. Not only was there danger of losing an animal, but if it wandered off into the fields often the parent or head of household was held responsible and beaten, only adding to the problem. Though not conclusive, traditional lullabies reveal evidence of parental neglect.[45] One nineteenth-century observer of peasant life in Perm' province noted that parents were little concerned with the moral upbringing of their children.[46] Russian parents have been characterized as negligent and even hostile toward their children, having "power assertive" rather than loving relationships.[47] But these are at best hints of parental attitudes, since the quality of the studies these statements derive from can easily be challenged. Nevertheless, in light of the patriarchal exploitation of household members, such behavior would not be surprising.

44. Holmberg, "Algunas relaciones," 6.
45. Antonina Martynova, "Life in the Prerevolutionary Villages as Reflected in Popular Lullabies," in *The Family in Imperial Russia,* ed. D. L. Ransel (Urbana, Ill., 1978), 175–81.
46. N. Rogov, "Materialy dlia opisaniia byta permiakov, *ZhMVD,* no. 4 (1858):72–73.
47. Patrick Dunn, "'That Enemy Is the Baby': Childhood in Imperial Russia," in *The History of Childhood,* ed. Lloyd deMause (New York, 1974), 385, 393.

Why were women so infrequently disciplined? As mentioned previously, females committed fewer than 5 percent of the offenses recorded in the manuals. With the exception of two instances when women were forced to wear an iron collar, flogging was the only form of punishment. That women did not fell trees, plow estate fields, have watch duty, or serve as functionaries is part of the reason. When women were punished it was primarily for work offenses, over 80 percent of the time. For males, work offenses constituted only 40 percent of the total. It remains unclear why the manuals record so few incidents of females being punished for theft, quarreling, or fighting. Whether females were less likely to commit such acts, whether their punishment was left to husbands and fathers, or whether their husbands or heads of household were personally held responsible for them is unknown.

How could the bailiff flog as many as eighty people in one day and yet maintain order? Why did the serfs not revolt? No doubt the rift between field peasants on the one hand and, on the other hand, serf functionaries, heads of household, and village elders with the power of the commune behind them made revolts difficult to organize. The interests of the likely leaders of any disturbance often clashed with those of the ordinary field peasant. A driver flogged for not being able to get certain peasants out to work might well be more resentful toward them than toward the bailiff. Serf patriarchs benefited primarily from the exploitation of the other members of their household, and this generational stratification certainly limited effective action against estate authorities.

Organized resistance was not one of the serfs' responses to their plight. At Petrovskoe there was only one uprising during the nineteenth century, and that was related to the sale of a number of families to Siberia, itself a unique incident. Flight was an alternative for a few. Between December 1815 and April 1832, thirty-three serfs fled the estate, twenty-nine males and four females. Some departed to avoid conscription. Others left because of problems within their households, conflicts that may have been only partially attributable to serfdom. Often serfs who had taken flight returned voluntarily, and the authorities were successful in returning most others.

The manuals of discipline convincingly show that noncooperation, indiscriminate violence, and apathy were commonplace and constituted the basic serf response to servitude. Historians have noted quite similar behavior in American slaves. Although a number of interpretations have been put forth, analogies with total institutions have been the most incisive. Prisons, concentration camps, mental hospitals, armies, monasteries, convents, slave plantations, and serf estates are all examples of total institutions, which aspire to provide for the inhabitants' total welfare, however defined. In terms of their situation, the residents of total institutions are very similar. They live a routinized, if not regimented existence and are largely cut off from the wider society. Some of the literature analyzing total institutions, especially slave plantations and prisons, provides interesting parallels that can help us in understanding Russian serfdom.[48]

George M. Fredrickson and Christopher Lasch have argued that on American slave plantations power was not based upon a rightful or legitimate authority and so did not inspire in the slaves an internalized sense of duty and a willingness to obey and cooperate.[49] The same has been shown for prison inmates. As Sykes writes, "Apathy, sabotage, and the show of effort rather than the substance—the traditional answers of the slave—rise in prison to plague the custodian-manager and his limited means of coercion cannot prevent them from occurring."[50] Thus, as at Petrovskoe, such total institutions use rewards, incentives, punishments, and coercion to make people work and behave. But they are at best only partially successful. The basic response of the inmates in total institutions is "playing it cool."[51] They are master opportunists, unwilling to volunteer and constantly trying to beat the system at its own game.[52] Their intransigence is "hedonistic rather than political, accommodationist rather than revolutionary."[53] Generally there is little group loyalty and little organized resistance.[54]

48. Goffman, *Asylums*, xiii, 4–5.
49. Fredrickson and Lasch, "Resistance," 230–32.
50. Sykes, *Society of Captives*, 28.
51. Goffman, *Asylums*, 64; Sykes, *Society of Captives*, 42.
52. Fredrickson and Lasch, "Resistance," 241.
53. Ibid., 237.
54. Goffman, *Asylums*, 61.

Holmberg, writing on the Vicos in Peru, has suggested that the fears and punishments the serfs experienced created a distinctive "culture of repression," marked by "danger-avoidance" and "defensive ignorance" where "innovation was equated with bad character and even perversion, and idiosyncrasy was regarded as pathological."[55]

The usefulness of these analogies (they are only that and suffer from all the limitations of any such comparisons) is that they offer a broad sociological and theoretical basis for understanding the social structures at Petrovskoe and serf behavior. It is hard to see how the serfs of Petrovskoe would have developed any internalized sense of obligation toward their landlord. In fact, the manuals of discipline at Petrovskoe read like the records of a disciplinary court in a New Jersey state prison.[56] In both institutions, priority was given to maintaining order, especially to limiting theft and violence. Yet the maintenance of order inherently clashed with the need for work tasks to be performed correctly. To quote from Sykes: "The use of force is actually grossly inefficient as a means for securing obedience, particularly when those who are to be controlled are called on to perform a task of any complexity. A blow with a club may check an immediate revolt, it is true, but it cannot assure effective performance on a punch-press."[57] As in prisons, on serf estates and slave plantations "rigid standards of discipline tend to give way before the need to keep things running smoothly without undue effort on the part of the custodians."[58] Though the managers of such institutions fear disorder in the absence of controls, nonetheless absolute power yields to compromise and a corruption of authority. At Petrovskoe the exercise of total power was never feasible either financially or technologically. Thus power was not compromised as much as in a maximum-security prison. Rather, collective responsibility was fostered by elaborate social structures and sanctions that were the very basis of serf life.

The rewards and punishments at Petrovskoe provided

---

55. Holmberg, "Algunas relaciones," 14–16.
56. Sykes, *Society of Captives*, 42–44.
57. Ibid., 49.
58. Fredrickson and Lasch, "Resistance," 232.

adequate incentives and coercion to establish the authority of the bailiff, especially among the peasant patriarchs and serf functionaries, who received a disproportionate share of both the good and the bad. But as with prisoners and slaves, the subjugation of the serfs was incomplete.[59] Peasant patriarchs and the bailiffs themselves had a particularly difficult time maintaining their authority over young adult males for whom life offered little but exploitation for a generation. Yet the young had few alternatives except to face the risks of flight. If they were unduly recalcitrant, recruitment into the army was their lot. As Fredrickson and Lasch conclude, "slaves could have accepted the legitimacy of their masters' authority without feeling any sense of obligation to obey it."[60] It was precisely this tension that caused the bailiffs at Petrovskoe to see the serfs as lazy, irresponsible, and negligent. Yet it would be difficult to explain why the serfs should have behaved otherwise. It is in this sense that the rozga, the birch rod, whatever its efficacy, was seen as a necessary tool of serfdom.

59. Sykes, *Society of Captives,* 48; Fredrickson and Lasch, "Resistance," 233–34.
60. Ibid.

CONCLUSION

THE CENTRAL PURPOSE OF THE PETROVSKOE ESTATE WAS TO exploit serf labor, and thus the overriding need was for a structure of authority to coerce and cajole the peasants into working. In this sense exploitation was largely a social problem resolved by a conjunction of interests fusing the power of serf patriarchs and functionaries with the authority of the bailiff. This not only provided the fundamental basis of social control but structured serf agriculture much to the detriment of agronomic development. If agricultural improvement were given any consideration at all, it was clearly secondary to labor management.

Serfdom was, of course, economically exploitative, but it was far more socially oppressive than economically onerous. This is not to say that the serfs of Petrovskoe would not have been appreciably better off materially had they worked six days a week for themselves instead of having to give three to the Gagarins. But if pre-1800 Europe is taken as a yardstick, then the overall standard of living at Petrovskoe was quite comparable. There is no evidence that serfdom had an adverse effect on the peasants' material conditions or life expectancy. The means of exploiting peasants in western Europe may have been quite different from those at Petrovskoe and the environments dissimilar. But in the end the material, though not social or psychological, quality of life was much the same. These Russian serfs simply were not poorer than peasants elsewhere.

In a traditional agricultural society the equitable distribution of wealth does not require, reflect, or raise up a spirit of communalism. Unfettered individualism or unshackled familism may readily coexist with elaborate mechanisms seeking to limit socioeconomic differentiation and maintain the status quo.[1] Although property relations define and structure peasant society, the link between property and *mentalité,* wealth and

1. Foster, *Tsintzuntzan,* 133–43; Foster, "Peasant Society," 302–6.

187

behavior, is not simple or straightforward. There is no necessary logic tying the radical egalitarianism in wealth observed at Petrovskoe with an attitude of communality, indigenous socialism, or even communism. There is no evidence either.

The community at Petrovskoe may have shared the risks of an uncertain environment, but this did not require considerable cooperation. The redistribution of arable land may have avoided the kinds of conflicts over land common in peasant societies, but the regulation of household fission, recruitment, and communal concerns with tax defaulters were all potential sources of tension. Moreover, it was primarily in the interest of the landlord to equalize wealth, since this maximized output, ensured the optimal productivity of serf labor, and minimized the risk that any individual household, the basic unit of production, would be unable to fulfill its obligations. In all this was a different, but not necessarily more harmonious response to the environment and political order.

In fact many of the functions of the Petrovskoe commune seem little different from the activities of village communities throughout Europe in the modern period. Strip farming, the periodic redistribution of land, and the collective responsibility for the payment of taxes and dues were hardly unique to Russian communes, though these practices may have disappeared from much of Europe by the mid-nineteenth century.[2] These are common risk-avoiding techniques among peasants.[3] The commune at Petrovskoe did much less than many village organizations. Though the serfs were not worse off than many European peasants, they maintained their two parish churches rather poorly. The only communal institution, the granary for storing emergency reserves, was required by law. Lack of cooperation seems to be characteristic of most peasant societies, and Petrovskoe was no exception.[4] Serfdom was responsible for the

2. Jerome Blum, "The Internal Structure and Polity of the European Village Community from the Fifteenth to the Nineteenth Century," *Journal of Modern History* 43, no. 4 (1971):541–52.

3. Scott, *Moral Economy*, 2–5.

4. Foster, "Peasant Society," 301; Banfield, *Moral Basis*, 83–90; Lewis, *Life in a Mexican Village*, 428; Lopreato, *Peasants No More*, 116–25; Lopreato, "Interpersonal Relations," 21; E. G. Friedman, "The World of 'La Miseria,'" *Partisan Review* 20, no. 2 (1953); reprinted in *Peasant Society: A Reader* ed. Jack M. Potter et al. (Boston, 1967), 330.

radical egalitarianism, and there is no need to romanticize these social or economic arrangements.[5]

Life in Petrovskoe was hostile, violent, vengeful, quarrelsome, fearful, and vituperative. The patriarchal household held the society together, employing punishment to coerce the serfs into submission and using recruitment or exile to rid the estate of those who would not adjust. The process of socialization was painful, though most came to accept the norms of serf life. Yet the frequent recourse to flogging, a violent form of coercion, meant rule violation was a persistent problem and submission was incomplete.

With coercion an inherently inefficient and dangerous way of obtaining compliance, it is not difficult to understand why reward and collective responsibility as reflected in patriarchy came to play an important role in serf life. Patriarchy broke serf society up into manageable units for control, and to patriarchs, those powerful intermediaries in the institution of serfdom, went wealth and status by peasant standards. With competition among households for access to productive resources limited, wealth and status depended on a patriarch's ability to exploit the other members of his household and manage their affairs, especially marriage, to his own advantage. The rewards were meaningful, real, and considerable.

Though the patriarchs were a distinct generational stratum with many rights and privileges, support for their authority came primarily from the bailiff. Thus patriarchy did not require substantial cooperation among the heads of household. Each patriarch pursued his own interests individually, stealing, lying, cheating, and fighting when necessary or convenient. This accounts for the considerable tension between households in spite of the radical economic egalitarianism and the equitable distribution of land.

Serf behavior and attitudes were an integrated human response to the ecological constraints at work in the society and the inhuman degradation of being reduced to property. Life was wretched and fearful, and the causes were natural. But it

5. See Scott, *Moral Economy*, 5.

was the social oppression of serf over serf that distinguished the structure of authority. And to free these peasants would require a social, behavioral, and attitudinal revolution demolishing the foundations of authority and the *mentalitiés* erected on them.

ABBREVIATIONS USED IN
FOOTNOTES AND BIBLIOGRAPHY

ch.	chast' [part]
ed. khr.	edinitsa khraneniia [storage unit]
ES	*Etnograficheskii sbornik*
f.	fond [archival record group]
l.	list [folio, leaf, sheet]
op.	opis' [inventory]
TsGADA	Tsentral'nyi Gosudarstvennyi Arkhiv Drevnikh Aktov (Moscow) [Central State Archive of Ancient Acts]
TsGVIA, f. VUA	Tsentral'nyi Gosudarstvennyi Voenno-istoricheskii Archiv (Moscow), fond Voenno-uchenyi Arkhiv [Central State Military History Archive, Military Science Archive]
ZhMGI	*Zhurnal Ministerstva gosudarstvennykh imushchestv*
ZhMVD	*Zhurnal Ministerstva vnutrennikh del*
ZLOSKh	*Zapiski Lebedianskago obshchestva sel'skago khoziaistva*

BIBLIOGRAPHY

Archival Sources

Note: All references are to TsGADA, f. 1262 (Gagarinykh), op. 4 unless noted. Titles in the original frequently have orthographic or grammatical errors. They appear here as they are on the documents.

Household Lists and Inventories

"Podvornye spiski ['vedomosti'] tiaglykh i netiaglykh krest'ian muzhskago i zhenskago polu po selu Petrovskomu s derevniami s ukazaniem ikh imushchstvennago polozheniia i kolichestvo u nikh skota, khleb, i stroenii." (Titles vary slightly.)
- ch. 1, ed. khr. 41 (October 1813–April 1814).
- ch. 1, ed. khr. 59 (April–May 1814).
- ch. 1, ed. khr. 121 (1 January 1818).
- ch. 1, ed. khr. 186 (April 1821).
- op. 1, ch. 1, ed. khr. 1495 (10 May 1824).
- ch. 1, ed. khr. 344 (May 1826).
- ch. 1, ed. khr. 357 (May 1827).
- ch. 2, ed. khr. 822 (1 November 1856).

Monthly Registration Data of Births and Deaths

"Vedomost' Borisoglebskikh votchin sel Petrovskago i Kanina s derevniami o pribyli i ubyli nakhodiashchikhsia v onykh votchinakh muzheska i zhenska polu dusham za [month], [year] goda." (Titles vary slightly.)
- ch. 1, ed. khr. 28 (January–December 1812).
- ch. 1, ed. khr. 42 (January–August 1813).
- ch. 2, ed. khr. 652 (September 1854–August 1855).
- ch. 2, ed. khr. 800 (September 1855–August 1856).
- ch. 2, ed. khr. 823 (September 1856–August 1857).
- ch. 2, ed. khr. 842 (September 1857–August 1858).

Financial Records of the Peasant Commune

"Kniga Petrovskago votchinnago pravleniia o prikhode i raskhode mirskoi denezhnoi summy." (Titles vary slightly.)

ch. 1, ed. khr. 76 (September 1815–August 1816).
ch. 1, ed. khr. 115 (September 1817–August 1818).
ch. 1, ed. khr. 139 (September 1819–August 1820).
ch. 1, ed. khr. 160 (September 1820–August 1821).
ch. 1, ed. khr. 189 (September 1821–August 1822).
ch. 1, ed. khr. 214 and 215 (September 1822–August 1823).
ch. 1, ed. khr. 235 and 236 (September 1823–August 1824).
ch. 1, ed. khr. 275 (September 1824–August 1825).
ch. 1, ed. khr. 313 and 314 (September 1825–August 1826).
ch. 2, ed. khr. 722 and 723 (September 1826–August 1827).
ch. 1, ed. khr. 384 (September 1827–August 1828).
ch. 1, ed. khr. 414 (September 1828–August 1829).
ch. 1, ed. khr. 433 (September 1829–August 1830).
ch. 1, ed. khr. 451 and 452 (September 1830– August 1831).
ch. 2, ed. khr. 750 and 751 (September 1831–August 1832).
ch. 1, ed. khr. 483 (September 1832–August 1833).
ch. 1, ed. khr. 507 and 508 (September 1833–August 1834).
ch. 1, ed. khr. 527 and 528 (September 1834–August 1835).
ch. 1, ed. khr. 546 (September 1835–August 1836).
ch. 1, ed. khr. 564 (September 1836–August 1837).
ch. 2, ed. khr. 782 (September 1838–August 1839).
ch. 1, ed. khr. 548 (September 1839–August 1840).
ch. 1, ed. khr. 593 (September 1840–August 1841).
ch. 1, ed. khr. 601 (September 1841–August 1842).
ch. 1, ed. khr. 608 (September 1842–August 1843).
ch. 1, ed. khr. 656 (September 1854–August 1855).
ch. 2, ed. khr. 805 (September 1855–August 1856).
ch. 2, ed. khr. 828 (September 1856–July 1857).
ch. 2, ed. khr. 848 (September 1857–August 1858).
ch. 2, ed. khr. 868 (September 1858–August 1859).
ch. 2, ed. khr. 887 (September 1860–August 1861).

Financial Records of the Estate

"Kniga Borisoglebskikh ikh Siiatel'stve Kniazei Nikolaia i Sergeia
    Sergeevichev Gagarinykh Votchin Sel Petrovskago i Kanina s
    derevniami o prikhode i raskhode ekonomicheskoi denezhnoi
    summy." (Titles vary slightly.)
ch. 1, ed. khr. 20 (September 1811–August 1812).
ch. 1, ed. khr. 29 (September 1812–August 1813).
ch. 1, ed. khr. 44 (September 1813–August 1814).
ch. 1, ed. khr. 61 (September 1814–August 1815).
ch. 1, ed. khr. 74 (September 1815–August 1816).
ch. 1, ed. khr. 94 (September 1816–August 1817).

ch. 1, ed. khr. 101 (September 1817–August 1818).
ch. 1, ed. khr. 123 (September 1818–August 1819).
ch. 1, ed. khr. 137 (September 1819–August 1820).
ch. 1, ed. khr. 190 (September 1821–August 1822).
ch. 1, ed. khr. 210 (September 1822–August 1823).
ch. 1, ed. khr. 233 (September 1823–August 1824).
ch. 1, ed. khr. 273 (September 1824–August 1825).

Manuals of Discipline

"Shtrafnaia kniga Petrovskago votchinnago pravleniia na zapisku
  nakazannye za raznye prestuplenii dvorovykh i krest'ian." (Titles vary.)
op. 1, ch. 1, ed. khr. 889 (September 1819–August 1820).
op. 1, ch. 1, ed. khr. 1129 (September 1820–August 1821).
op. 4, ch. 1, ed. khr. 212 (September 1822–August 1823).
ch. 1, ed. khr. 248 (September 1823–August 1824).
ch. 1, ed. khr. 269 (September 1824–August 1825).
ch. 1, ed. khr. 308 (September 1825–August 1826).
ch. 1, ed. khr. 345 and 347 (September 1826–August 1827).
ch. 1, ed. khr. 380 and 381 (August 1827–August 1828).
ch. 1, ed. khr. 408 and 413 (September 1828–August 1829).
ch. 1, ed. khr. 428 and 429 (September 1829–August 1830).
ch. 1, ed. khr. 447 (September 1830–August 1831).
ch. 1, ed. khr. 463 (September 1831–August 1832).
ch. 1, ed. khr. 479 (September 1832–August 1833).
ch. 1, ed. khr. 503 (September 1833–August 1834).
ch. 1, ed. khr. 523 (September 1834–August 1835).
ch. 1, ed. khr. 542 (September 1835–August 1836).
ch. 1, ed. khr. 561 (September 1836–August 1837).
op. 1, ch. 1, ed. khr. 2419 (September 1839–August 1840).
op. 4, ch. 2, ed. khr. 824 (September 1856–August 1857).
ch. 2, ed. khr. 843 (September 1857–August 1858).
ch. 2, ed. khr. 863 (September 1858–August 1859).

Bailiff's Reports

"Raporta iz Petrovskago votchinnago pravleniia v Glavnuiu votchin-
  nuiu kontoru o sostoianii votchinnago i krest'ianskago
  khoziaistva v selakh Petrovskom i Kanine s derevniami." (Titles vary.)
ch. 1, ed. khr. 474 (September 1832–August 1833).
ch. 1, ed. khr. 496 (September 1833–August 1834).
ch. 1, ed. khr. 518 (September 1834–August 1835).
ch. 1, ed. khr. 539 (September 1835–August 1836).

ch. 1, ed. khr. 558 (September 1836–August 1837).
ch. 1, ed. khr. 649 (September 1854–August 1855).
ch. 1, ed. khr. 666 (September 1855–August 1856).
ch. 2, ed. khr. 846 (September 1857–August 1858).
ch. 2, ed. khr. 866 (September 1858–August 1859).
ch. 2, ed. khr. 884 (September 1860–August 1861).
ch. 2, ed. khr. 897 (September 1861–August 1862).

Other Documents

op. 1, ch. 1, ed. khr. 187 (31 October 1804), "Kopiia resheniia Borisoglebskago suda o nezakonorozhdenii."

ch. 1, ed. khr. 256 (1 May 1810), "Vedomost' Tambovskoi Gubernii Borisoglebskoi Okrugi, Sela Petrovskago s derevniami o sostoiashchikh vo onykh votchinakh zemliakh, dvorovykh i krest'ianskikh muzheska i zenska polu dush, i ikh imushchestvakh."

ch. 1, ed. khr. 18 (1811), "Petrovskoe imenie: Revizskie skazki."

ch. 1, ed. khr. 58 (1814), "Polozhenie denezhnomu zhalovan'iu i pochemu soderzhanie dvorovym sem'iam sela Petrovskago i Kanina s derevniami na 1814 god."

ch. 1, ed. khr. 150 (September 1819), "Opis' Sely Petrovskago i Kanina s derevniami imeiushchimusia pri kazhdom otdelenii stroeniiu, s oznacheniem kakoi mery v dlinu i shirinu."

ch. 2, ed. khr. 906 (September 1819), "Proshenie krest'ian S. Petrovskago i Kanina s derevniami o novom rasporiadke pakhotnykh zemliakh."

ch. 1, ed. khr. 135 (27 September 1819–18 July 1820), "Registr' Sela Petrovskago i Kanina s derevniami neimushchim i bezloshadnym krest'ian."

op. 1, ch. 1, ed. khr. 1063 (23 February 1820), "Registr' Petrovskago votchinnago pravleniia kto imenno otdan v rekruty v nyneshnei 88 nabor iz kakikh semeistvakh i kakikh povedenikh."

ch. 1, ed. khr. 161 (19 July 1820), "Zapiska o imeushcheisia raspashnoi zemle," and "Kratkaia vypiska Sela Petrovskago i Kanina s derevniami skol'ko v kotorom otdelenii sostoit na krest'ianakh po knigam raznago roda khleba, v to chislo skol'ko na krest'ianine pokazano chto sostoiat dolzhny, i zatem skol'ko ostaetsia na umershikh i vybylykh iz votchin i krest'iane otkazyvaetsia nevedeniem."

ch. 1, ed. khr. 249 (1823–24), "Vypiska iz podvornye vedomosti skol'ko imeetsia muzheska i zhenska pola dush krest'ian i imeiushchemusia pri nego raznomu skotu i pchely."

ch. 1, ed. khr. 291 (1824–25), "Vypiska iz podvoynye vedomosti krest'ianam, s kogo imianno slozheny tiagly za buych'no, starastiiu let i ne sposobnosti k rabote i vmesto onykh na kogo nalozheno."

ch. 2, ed. khr. 727 (September 1826–August 1827), "Zhurnal Petrovskago Votchinnago Pravleniia smotriteliam i kantorskim sluzhiteliam o ispravlenii dolzhnostei i o povedenii."

ch. 1, ed. khr. 377 (September–October 1827), "Registr' Petrovskago votchinnago pravleniia bezdolzhnostnym dvorovym liudiam, vdovam, i vzroslym devkam s pokazaniem proizvodstva godovago i mesiachnago polozheniia," and "Registr' Petrovskago votchinnago pravleniia dolzhnostnym dvorovym liudiam s pokazaniem proizvodstva godovago i mesiachnago polozheniia."

ch. 1, ed. khr. 415 (September 1828–September 1829), "Votchinaia khlebnaia kniga."

ch. 1, ed. khr. 396 (29 April 1829), "Registr' Sela Petrovskago i Kanina z derevniami bezloshadnym i malokonnym krest'ianam, a skol'ko v kakom otdelenii takovykh imeetsia."

ch. 2, ed. khr. 753 (12 January and 28 September 1831), "Imiannoi Spisok, Sela Petrovskago i Kanina s derevniami, krest'ianam otdannykh v nyneshnii 95 nabor v rekruty, so opisaniem ikh semeistv i so oznacheniem za chto postupili na sluzhbu," and "Imiannoi Spisok Petrovskago Votchinnago Pravleniia iz podvornykh vedomostei krest'ianskim semeistvam, iz koikh naznachaiutsia za raznyia prestuplenii v rekrutskuiu otdachu."

ch. 2, ed. khr. 754 (26 October 1831), "Registr' Petrovskago Votchinnago Pravleniia, Sel Petrovskago i Kanina s derevniami krest'ianskim devkam kotoryia po sovershennym letam dolzhny postupit' v zamuzhestva."

ch. 1, ed. khr. 484 (1832), "Vedomost' Sela Petrovskago Votchiny Ego Siiatel'stva Gospodina deistvitel'nago statskago sovetnika Kammergera i Kavalera Nikolaia

Sergeevicha Gagarina, urozhainaia i umoltnaia, urozhainomu sego 1832 goda, raznomu khlebu."

ch. 1, ed. khr. 515 (February 1834), "Podvornaia opis' Petrovskago votchinnago pravleniia imeushchemusia u krest'ian raznago vida skota i khleba."

ch. 1, ed. khr. 521 (27 January 1835), "Vypiska Petrovskomu Imeniiu bezloshadnym i khudokonnym krest'ianam."

ch. 1, ed. khr. 541 (24 November 1835 and 29 June 1836), "Registr' Petrovskago votchinnago pravleniia khudokonnym i bezloshadnym krest'ianam."

ch. 1, ed. khr. 589 (February 1839), "Vypiska iz dekliplikatsii mezhevago plana, po selu Petrovskomu i Kaninu s derevniami o znachaiushchaia vladenie krest'ian sennymi polosami."

ch. 1, ed. khr. 605 (22 July 1841), "Spisok Petrovskago Votchinnago Pravleniia, krest'ianam neradeuishchim o domostroitel'stve, voram, p'ianitsam, i buntovshchikam, dolzhenstvuiushchim postupit' v prodazhu na Sibirskiia zavody."

ch. 1, ed. khr. 598 (1841–42), no title [two letters: (1) from a soldier's wife and (2) from the village priest, to the Moscow estate office].

ch. 1, ed. khr. 615 (December 1843–April 1844), "Vedomosti o sostoiane vsekh vidov votchinnago i krest'ianskago khoziaistva Petrovskago imeniia."

ch. 2, ed. khr. 902 (1848, 1862), "Eksplikatsiia k planu sel Petrovskago, Koshelevo tozh', i Kanina, Bobrova tozh' s derevniami . . . sostavlennaia v 1862 godu chastnym zemlemerom Mikhailovym," and "Eksplikatsiia izvlechennaia iz Plana sostavlennago v 1848 godu po Petrovskomu imeniiu."

op. 1, ch. 1, ed. khr. 2813a (1848), "Kopii opisaniia imenii pereshedshiia vo vladeniia kniazia N. N. i A. N. Gagarinykh posle smerti Kn. N. S. Gagarina."

op. 1, ch. 1, ed. khr. 2833 (7 December 1848–29 January 1849), "Svedenie Petrovskago Imeniia, o zemle, zavodakh, mel'nitsakh, i o prichem s pokazaniem vo chto onyia otseneny po mestnym polozheniem," and "Svedenii Petrovskago imeniia, imeushchemusia Gospodskomy Stroeniiu, s pokazaniem vo chto onoe otsenena."

op. 1, ch. 1, ed. khr. 2830a (1849), "Statisticheskoe opisanie imenii Kn. N. N. Gagarina."

ch. 2, ed. khr. 863 (12 October 1850), "Sela Petrovskago,
    Revizskaia Skazka 1850 goda Oktiabriia 12 dnia
    Tambovskoi Gubernii, Borisoglebskago uezda, Votchina
    Ego Siiatel'stva Gvardii Otstavnago Poruchika Kniazia
    Nikolaia Nikolaevicha Gagarina, Sela Petrovskago o
    sostoiashchikh muzheskago i zhenskago pola dvorovykh
    liudiakh i krest'ianakh."
ch. 1, ed. khr. 861 (1 May 1858), "Revizskaia skazka 1858
    Goda Maiia 1 go Dnia, Tambovskoi Gubernii,
    Borisoglebskago uezda, Votchiny Ego Siiatel'stva
    Gvardii otstavnago Poruchika Kniazia Nikolaia
    Nikolaevicha Gagarina, Sela Petrovskago o
    sostoiashchikh muzheska i zhenska pola dvorovykh
    liudiakh i krest'ianakh."
ch. 2, ed. khr. 869 (7 July 1858), "Poverka imeiushchimsia po
    Petrovskomu imeniiu v nalichnosti raznomu khlebu,
    materialam, instrumentu, i veshcham."
ch. 2, ed. khr. 862 (June–August 1862), "Svedeniia o
    dvorianskom imenii Borisoglebskago uezda, ego
    Siiatel'stva Kniazia Nikolaia Nikolaevicha Gagarina, po
    Selu Petrovskomu s derevniami."
ch. 2, ed. khr. 934 (14 January 1904), "Svidetel'stvo o razdele
    zemli s krest'ianami Petrovskago imeniia posle reformy
    1861 g. i mezhdu naslednikami N. N. Gagarina."
TsGADA, f. 1355, op. 1, ed. khr. 1575 (1780s),
    "Ekonomicheskoe Primechanie Goroda Borisoglebska i
    Ego Uezda."
TsGVIA, f. VUA, ed. khr. 19078 (1787), "Atlas Tambovskago
    namestnichestva soderzhashchei v sebe topograficheskoe
    opisanie General'nuiu v sei gubernii i dvenattsami
    uezdov karty tak zhe dvenattsati godov plany i piati
    soedinennykh sudokhodnykh rek."
TsGVIA, f. VUA, ed. khr. 19079 (1839), "Ekonomicheskoe
    primechanie Borisoglebskago uezda."
TsGADA, f. 1357, op. 1, ed. khr. 1/211 (1850s),
    "Ekonomicheskoe primechanie chast' dach'
    Borisoglebskago uezda."
TsGADA, f. 1357, op. 1, ed. khr. 222 (1850s),
    "Ekonomicheskie primechaniia Mende po
    Borisoglebskomu, Tambovskomu, Usmanskomu
    uezdam."

Published Sources

A. B. "Brit'e pomeshchikami polgolovy krest'ianam dlia presecheniia samovol'nykh otluchek. In *Arkhiv istorii truda v Rossii*, 2:151–52. Petrograd, 1921.

A. M. "Narodnye iuridicheskie obychai i deistvuiushchee zakonodatel'stvo." *Delo*, no. 8 (1870): 24–43.

A. P. "Opisanie uluchsheniia byta krest'ian (Moskovskoi gubernii, Podol'skago uezda, v imenii AVP)." *Zhurnal zemlevladel'tsev*, no. 13, part 5 (1858):1–18.

Abramovich, D. M. "Selo Kosnishche, Vladimir-Volynskogo uezda, Volynskoi gub." *Zhivaia starina* 2, part 2 (1898):184–202; 3–4, part 2 (1898):385–96.

Afanas'ev, A. "Dedushka domovoi." In *Arkhiv Istoriko-iuridicheskikh svedenii, otnosiashchikhsia do Rossii*, 1, part 6, 13–29. Moscow, 1850.

_____. "Kritika: Etnograficheskii sbornik." *Otechestvennye zapiski*, nos. 9–10, part 4 (1853):1–26.

Akademiia Nauk SSSR, Geograficheskoe obshchestvo. *Russkie geografy i puteshestvenniki: Fondy arkhiva geograficheskogo obshchestva*. Leningrad, 1971.

Akademii Nauk SSSR, Institut etnografii im. N. N. Miklukho-Maklaia. *Trudy*, n.s., *Selo Viriatino v proshlom i nastoiashchem*, 41. Moscow, 1958.

Albritton, E. C., ed. *Standard Values in Nutrition and Metabolism*. Washington, D.C., 1954.

Aleksandrov, V. A. *Sel'skaia obshchina v Rossii (XVII–nachalo XIX v.)*. Moscow, 1976.

_____. "Vologodskaia svad'ba." *Biblioteka dlia chteniia*, no. 5 (1863):1–44; no. 6 (1863):1–45.

Aleksandrov, V. A., et al., eds. *Russkie: Istoriko-etnograficheskii atlas*. 2 vols. Moscow, 1967–71.

Apostol'skii, P. M. "Krest'ianskaia svad'ba v Mtsenskom uezde." *Izvestiia Imperatorskago obshchestva liubitelei estestvoznaniia, antropologii, i etnografii* 28 (1877):139–45.

Aristov, N. "Ocherk krest'ianskoi svad'by." *Volga*, no. 13 (1862):49–50; no. 14 (1862):53–54; no. 15 (1862):61–62.

Arkhangel'skii, A. "Selo Davshino, Iaroslavskoi gubernii, Poshekhonskago uezda." *Etnograficheskii Sbornik* 2, (1854):1–80.

Astrov, P. I. "Ob uchenii sverkh-estestvennoi sily v narodnom sudoproizvodstve krest'ian Elatomskago uezda, Tambovskoi gub." *Izvestiia Imperatorskago obshchestva liubitelei es-*

testvoznaniia, antropologii, i etnografii, vol. 61; *Trudy etnograficheskago otdela*, 9 (1889):49–57.

Babarykin, V. "Sel'tso Vasil'evskoe, Nizhegorodskoi gubernii, Nizhegorodskago uezda." *Etnograficheskii sbornik* 1 (1853):1–24.

Banfield, E. C. *The Moral Basis of a Backward Society*. New York, 1958.

Barykov, F. "Obychai nasledovaniia u gosudarstvennykh krest'ian (Po svedeniiam, sobrannym ministerstvom gosudarstvennykh imushchestv)." *Zhurnal Ministerstva gosudarstvennykh imushchestv* 91, part 1 (1862):1–33, 232–59, 353–76, 456–69.

Blassingame, J. W. *The Slave Community: Plantation Life in the Antebellum South*. 2d ed. Oxford, 1979.

Bloch, M. *Feudal Society*. Trans. L. A. Manyon. 2 vols. Chicago, 1961.

Blum, J. *The End of the Old Order in Rural Europe*. Princeton, 1978.

―――. "The Internal Structure and Polity of the European Village Community from the Fifteenth to the Nineteenth Century." *Journal of Modern History* 43, no. 4 (1971):541–76.

―――. *Lord and Peasant in Russia from the Ninth to the Nineteenth Century*. Princeton, 1961.

Bohac, R. "Family, Property, and Socioeconomic Mobility: Russian Peasants on Manuilovskoe Estate, 1810–1861." Ph.D. dissertation, University of Illinois, 1982.

Bondarenko, V. "Pover'ia krest'ian Tambovskoi gubernii." *Zhivaia starina* 1, part 1, no. 3 (1890):115–21.

Boserup, E. *Women's Role in Economic Development*. London, 1970.

Brzheskii, N. K. *Ocherki iuridicheskago byta krest'ian*. Saint Petersburg, 1902.

Caldwell, J. C. "A Theory of Fertility: From High Plateau to Destabilization." *Population and Development Review* 4, no. 4 (1978):553–57.

Chambers, J. D. *Population, Economy, and Society in Pre-Industrial England*. Oxford, 1972.

Chayanov, A. V. *The Theory of Peasant Economy*. ed. D. Thorner et al. Homewood, Ill., 1966; originally published 1926.

Cheremisinov, A. "Prikaz pomeshchika A. M. Cheremisinova, Kovrovskoi votchiny, derevni Elokhova, staroste Egoru Vasil'evu i vsemu miru." In *Arkhiv istoricheskikh i prakticheskikh svedenii, otnosiashchikhsia do Rossii,* 3:15–30. Saint Petersburg, 1862.

Chubinskii, P. "Ocherk narodnykh iuridicheskikh obychaev i poniatii v Malorossii." *Zapiski Imperatorskago russkago geograficheskago obshchestva po otdeleniiu etnografii,* 2 (1896):677–716.

Clark, C., and M. Haswell. *The Economics of Subsistence Agriculture.* New York, 1967.

Coale, A. J., and P. Demeny. *Regional Model Life Tables and Stable Populations.* Princeton, 1966.

Cockburn, J. S., ed. *Crime in England, 1550–1800.* Princeton, 1977.

Confino, M. *Domaines et seigneurs en Russie vers la fin du XVIIIe siècle.* Paris, 1963.

_____. *Systèmes agraires et progrès agricole.* Paris, 1969.

Crisp, O. *Studies in the Russian Economy before 1914.* London, 1976.

D. I. "Zametki o krest'ianskoi sem'e v Novgorodskoi gubernii." In *Sbornik narodnykh iuridicheskikh obychaev,* 18:261–76. *Zapiski Imperatorskago russkago geograficheskago obshchestva po otdeleniiu etnografii,* 2 (Saint Petersburg, 1900).

Dal', V. *Poslovitsy russkago naroda.* Moscow, 1862.

deMause, L., ed. *The History of Childhood.* New York, 1974.

Demos, J. *A Little Commonwealth: Family Life in Plymouth Colony.* Oxford, 1970.

Diakonov, V. N. "Opisanie khoziaistva V. N. Diakonova, Tambovskoi gub., Spasskago u. (Sel'tso Tarbeevka)." *Zapiski Lebedianskago obshchestva sel'skago khoziaistva za 1851, 1852,* 390–401.

Dilaktorskii, K. "Svadebnye obychai i pesni v Totemskom uezde Vologodskoi gubernii." *Etnograficheskoe obozrenie* 42, no. 3 (1899):160–65.

Dmitriukov, A. "Nravy, obychai, i obraz zhizni v Sudzhanskom uezde, Kurskoi gubernii." *Moskovskii telegraf,* no. 10 (1831):255–71; no. 11 (1831):359–77.

Dobrozrakov, I. "Selo Katunki s ego prikhodskimi derevniami." *Nizhegorodskii sbornik* 1, part 2 (1867):169–89.

_____. "Selo Ul'ianovka, Nizhegorodskoi gubernii, Lukoianovskago uezda." *Etnograficheskii sbornik* 2 (1853):25–60.

Druzhinin, N. M. *Gosudarstvennye krest'iane i reforma P. D. Kiseleva.* 2 vols. Moscow and Leningrad, 1946–58.

Dubasov, I. "K istorii krepostnago prava." *Drevniaia i novaia Rossiia,* no. 4 (1877):399–401.

_____. "Kholernyi god v Tambove, 1830." *Russkaia starina*, no. 12 (1875):742–47.

_____. "Krest'ianskie bezporiadki v Tambovskoi gubernii v tsarstvovanie imperatora Pavla I." *Drevniaia i novaia Rossiia*, no. 3 (1877): 307–9.

_____. "Tambovskaia kholernaia smuta v 1830–1831 godakh." *Istoricheskii vestnik* 29 (1887):620–28.

Dunn, Stephen P., and Ethel Dunn. *The Peasants of Central Russia.* New York, 1967.

Efimenko, A. "Krest'ianskaia zhenshchina." *Delo*, no. 2 (1873):173–206; no. 3 (1873):57–99.

_____. "Narodnye iuridicheskie vozzreniia na brak." *Znanie*, no. 1 (1874):1–45.

_____. "Semeinye razdely." In *Izsledovaniia narodnoi zhizni*, 1:125–35. Moscow, 1884.

_____. "Trudovoe nachalo v narodnom obychnom prave." *Slovo*, no. 1, (1878):146–73.

Efimenko, P. *Pridanoe po obychnomu pravu krest'ian Arkhangel'skoi gubernii.* Saint Petersburg, 1872.

_____. "Sem'ia Arkhangel'skago krest'ianina po obychnomu pravu." *Sudebnyi zhurnal*, July–August 1873, 32–114.

Fedorov, V. A. *Pomeshchich'i krest'iane tsentral'no-promyshlennogo raiona Rossii kontsa XVIII–pervoi poloviny XIX v.* Moscow, 1974.

Filipov, A. "Narodnoe obychnoe pravo, kak istoricheskii material." *Russkaia mysl'*, no. 9 (1886):56–71.

Fogel, Robert W., and Stanley L. Engerman. *Time on the Cross: The Economics of American Negro Slavery.* Boston, 1974.

Food and Agriculture Organization of the United Nations. *Production Yearbook, 1970.* Rome, 1971.

Forster, E., and R. Forster, eds. *European Diet from Pre-Industrial to Modern Times.* New York, 1975.

Forster, R., and O. Ranum, eds. *Food and Drink in History: Selections from the Annales, E.S.C.* Baltimore, 1979.

Foster, G. M. "Interpersonal Relations in Peasant Society." *Human Organization* 19 (Winter 1960–61):174–78.

_____. "Peasant Society and the Image of the Limited Good." *American Anthropologist* 67, no. 2 (1965):293–315.

_____. *Tzintzuntzan: Mexican Peasants in a Changing World.* Boston, 1967.

Fredrickson, G., and C. Lasch. "Resistance to Slavery." *Civil War History*, December 1967. Reprinted in *The Debate over Slavery*, ed. A. Lane, 223–44. Urbana and Chicago, 1971.

Friedl, E. *Vasilika: A Village in Modern Greece.* New York, 1962.
Friedman, E. G. "The World of 'La Miseria,'" *Partisan Review* 20, no. 2 (1953). Reprinted in *Peasant Society: A Reader,* ed. J. M. Potter et al., 324–36. Boston, 1967.
Galentorn, N. "Svad'ba v Saltykovskoi volosti, Morshanskago uezda, Tambovskoi gubernii." In *Materialy po svad'be i semeino-rodovomu stroiu narodov SSSR,* 1:171–195. Leningrad, 1926.
Genovese, E. G. *Roll, Jordan, Roll: The World the Slaves Made.* New York, 1974.
Gerschenkron, A. "Agrarian Policies and Industrialization: Russia, 1861–1917." In *The Cambridge Economic History of Europe,* vol. 6, part 2, 706–800. Cambridge, 1965.
Glass, D. V., and D. E. C. Eversley, eds. *Population in History.* London and Chicago, 1965.
Glavnyi General'nyi Shtab. *Materialy dlia geografii i statistiki Rossii, sobrannye ofitserami General'nago Shtaba.* 25 vols. Saint Petersburg, 1859–69.
Goffman, E. *Asylums: Essays on the Social Situation of Mental Patients and Other Inmates.* Garden City, N.Y., 1961.
Golitsyn, N. S. "O merakh k ustroistvu statisticheskikh istochnikov i rabot v Rossii." *Zhurnal Ministerstva vnutrennikh del,* no. 5 (1860): 1–48.
Goode, W. J. *World Revolution and Family Patterns.* New York, 1963.
Goody, J., ed. *The Developmental Cycle in Domestic Groups.* Cambridge, 1977.
Goody, J., and S. J. Tambian. *Bridewealth and Dowry.* Cambridge, 1973.
Grekov, B. D. "Tambovskoe imenie M. S. Lunina v pervoi chetverti XIX v." *Izvestiia,* Akademiia Nauk SSSR, *Otdelenie obshchestvennykh nauk,* ser. 7, no. 6 (1933):481–520; no. 7 (1933):623–48.
Gross, F. *Il Paese: Values and Social Change in an Italian Village.* New York, 1973.
Gruzinov, I. R. "Byt krest'ianina Tambovskoi gubernii." *Zhurnal zemlevladel'tsev* 2, no. 5, part 6 (1858):1–18.
————. "Vozmozhnost' uluchsheniia byta pomeshchich'ikh krest'ian (Tambovskoi gubernii)." *Zhurnal zemlevladel'tsev* 4, no. 13, part 4 (1858):20–24.
Halpern, J. M., and B. K. Halpern. *A Serbian Village in Historical Perspective.* New York, 1972.
Heer, D. M. "The Demographic Transition in the Russian Empire

BIBLIOGRAPHY

and the Soviet Union." *Journal of Social History* 1
(1968):193–240.
Henry, L. *Manuel de démographie historique*. 2d ed. Paris, 1970.
Hilton, R. H. *The English Peasantry in the Later Middle Ages*. Ox-
ford, 1975.
Hollingsworth, T. H. *Historical Demography*. London, 1969.
Holmberg, A. R. "Algunas relaciones entre la privación
psciobiológica y el cambio cultural en los Andes." *América
indígena* 27, no. 1 (1967):3–24.
Iakunin, I. "Kholera v Tambove v 1830-om godu: Po razskazam
ochevidtsev." *Vestnik Evropy* 55, no. 10 (1875):204–23.
Iatsunskii, V. K. "Izmeneniia v razmeshchenii zemledeliia v Evro-
peiskoi Rossii s kontsa XVIII v. do pervoi mirovoi voiny." In
*Voprosy istorii sel'skogo khoziaistva, krest'ianstva, i revoliut-
sionnogo dvizheniia v Rossii*. Moscow, 1961.
Indova, E. I. *Krepostnoe khoziaistvo v nachale XIX veka po mate-
rialam votchinnogo arkhiva Vorontsovykh*. Moscow, 1955.
Isaev, A. "Znachenie semeinykh razdelov krest'ian." *Vestnik Evropy*
63, no. 7 (1883):333–49.
Kagarov, E. G. "Sostav i proiskhozhdenie svadebnoi obriadnosti." In
Sbornik Muzeia antropologii i etnografii AN SSSR, 152–93.
Leningrad, 1929.
Kalachov, N. "Iuridicheskie obychai krest'ian v nekotorykh mest-
nostiakh." In *Arkhiv istoricheskikh i prakticheskikh svedenii,
otnosiashchikhsia do Rossii*, 2:15–28. Saint Petersburg, 1859.
Kalinovskii, G. "Opisanie svadebnykh ukrainskikh prostonarodnykh
obriadov v Maloi Rossii i v Slobodskoi Ukrainskoi gubernii."
Khar'kovskii sbornik 3 (1889):160–74.
Keller, L. R. "Opisanie krest'ianskoi izby s glinosolomennymi ste-
nami i svodom." *Zhurnal Ministerstva gosudarstvennykh
imushchestv* 29, no. 4, part 2 (1848):1–3.
Khozikov, A. "Statisticheskii ocherk Tambovskoi gubernii." *Zhurnal
Ministerstva gosudarstvennykh imushchestv* 31, no. 2, part 2
(1849):137–54; no. 3, part 2 (1849):153–68.
Kishkin, M. N. "Dannye i predpolozheniia po voprosu ob uluchshenii byta krest'ian v Kirsanovskom uezde, Tambovskoi
gubernii." *Sel'skoe blagoustroistvo*, no. 1 (1859):225–62.
Kostolovskii, I. V. "Iz svadebnykh i drugikh poverii Iaroslavskoi
gubernii." *Etnograficheskoe obozrenie*, nos. 1–2 (1911):248–
52.
Kostrov, N. "Svadebnye obriady Minusinskikh krest'ian." *Illiustratsiia*, no. 176, (1861):10–11; no. 177 (1861):26–27.
Koval'chenko, I. D. *Krest'iane i krepostnoe khoziaistvo Riazanskoi i*

Tambovskoi gubernii v pervoi polovine XIX veka. Moscow, 1959.

————. *Russkoe krepostnoe khoziaistvo v pervoi polovine XIX veka.* Moscow, 1967.

Kozlov, Kh. "Sel'sko-khoziaistvennaia statistika Borisoglebskago uezda." *Izvestiia Tambovskoi Uchenoi Arkhivnoi Komissii* 29 (1890):77–101.

————. "Tseny raznykh produktov v 1796–1856 godakh." *Ekonomicheskii ukazatel'*, no. 35 (1857):805–12.

"Krest'ianskaia svad'ba v Iaroslavskoi gubernii." *Vsemirnaia illiustratsiia*, no. 12 (1878):201–2; no. 13 (1878):214–15.

Krivoshapkin, M. "Russkaia svad'ba s eia obriadami i pesniami." *Svetoch* 2 (1860):1–110.

Kusheva, E. N. "Khoziaistvo Saratovskikh dvorian Shakhmatovykh v XVIII veke." *Izvestiia, Akademiia Nauk SSSR, Otdelenie gumanitarnykh nauk,* ser. 7, no. 7 (1929):575–604; no. 8 (1929):673–93.

Kushner, P. I., ed. *The Village of Viriatino.* Trans. Sula Benet. New York, 1970.

Kuz'min. *Voenno-statisticheskoe obozrenie Rossiiskoi Imperii.* Vol. 13, part 1. *Tambovskaia gubernia.* Saint Petersburg, 1851.

Kuznetsov, Ia. "Svad'ba v Kremlevskom prikhode Vetluzhskago uezda, Kostromskoi gubernii." *Zhivaia starina,* no. 4, part 2 (1899):531–35.

Laslett, P., ed. *Household and Family in Past Time.* Cambridge, 1972.

Lebedev, N. "Byt krest'ian Tverskoi gubernii, Tverskago uezda." *Etnograficheskii sbornik* 1 (1853):174–202.

Lebrun, F. *La vie conjugale sous l'Ancien Régime.* Paris, 1975.

Lee, R. D. "Methods and Models for Analyzing Historical Series of Births, Marriages, and Deaths." In *Population Patterns in the Past.* New York, 1977.

Lenskii, B. "Semeinye razdely." *Delo,* no. 11 (1881):17–48.

Le Roy Ladurie, E. *The Peasants of Languedoc.* Trans. John Day. Urbana, Ill., and Chicago, 1974.

Lewis, O. *Life in a Mexican Village: Tepoztlán Restudied.* Urbana, Ill., 1951.

Liashchenko, P. I. *Istoriia narodnogo khoziaistva SSSR.* 2 vols. Moscow, 1947–48.

Lichkov, L. S. "Krest'ianskie semeinye razdely." *Severnyi vestnik,* no. 1, part 2 (1886):84–108.

Litvak, B. G. *Ocherki istochnikovedeniia massovoi dokumentatsii XIX nachala XX v.* Moscow, 1979.

———. *Russkaia derevnia v reforme 1861 goda: Chernozemnyi tsentr, 1861–98 gg.* Moscow, 1972.

Lopreato, J. "Interpersonal Relations in Peasant Society: The Peasants' View." *Human Organization* 21 (1962):21–24.

———. *Peasants No More: Social Class and Social Change in an Underdeveloped Society.* Scranton, Pa., 1967.

Lorimer, F. *Culture and Human Fertility.* New York, 1958.

Malykhin, P. "Byt krest'ian Voronezhskoi gubernii Nizhnedevitskago uezda." *Etnograficheskii sbornik* 1 (1853):203–34.

Mashkin. "Byt krest'ian Kurskoi gubernii, Oboianskago uezda." *Etnograficheskii sbornik* 5 (1862):1–119.

Matveev, P. A. "Ocherki narodnago iuridicheskago byta Samarskoi gubernii." In *Sbornik narodnykh iuridicheskikh obychaev,* 8:11–46. *Zapiski Imperatorskago russkago geograficheskago obshchestva po otdeleniiu etnografii,* 1 (Saint Petersburg, 1878).

Mechnikov, I. "Vozrast vstupleniia v brak." *Vestnik Evropy,* no. 1 (1874):232–83.

Mikhailov, S. "Svadebnye obriady v Kozmodemianskom uezde, Kazanskoi gubernii." *Russkii dnevnik,* no. 12 (1859): no. 13 (1859).

Mikheev, M. E. "Opisanie svadebnykh obychaev i obriadov v Buzulukskom uezde, Samarskoi gubernii." *Etnograficheskoe obozrenie* 42, no. 3 (1899):144–59.

Mukhin, V. P. *Obychnyi poriadok nasledovaniia u krest'ian.* Saint Petersburg, 1888.

Myl'nikova, K., and V. Tsintsius. "Severno-velikorusskaia svad'ba." In *Materialy po svad'be i semeino-rodovomu stroiu narodov SSSR,* 1:17–170. Leningrad, 1926.

N. —R. "Svadebnye obychai krest'ian Kostromskoi gubernii." In *Sbornik narodnykh iuridicheskikh obychaev,* 2:243–60. *Zapiski Imperatorskago russkago geograficheskago obshchestva po otdeleniiu etnografii,* 18 (Saint Petersburg, 1900).

N. R-v. "Svadebnye obychai v Ostashkovskom uezde v polovine XIX veke." *Tverskaia starina,* no. 2 (1913):39–47.

Nasonov, A. N. "Iusupovskie votchiny v XIX–om veke." *Doklady. Akademiia Nauk SSSR,* ser. B (January–February 1926):1–4.

———. "Iz istorii krepostnoi votchiny XIX veka v Rossii." *Izvestiia. Akademiia Nauk SSSR,* ser. 6 (1926), nos. 7–8 (1926):499–526.

———. "Khoziaistvo krupnoi votchiny nakanune osvobozhdeniia

krest'ian v Rossii." *Izvestiia*, Akademiia Nauk SSSR, *Otdelenie gumanitarnykh nauk*, ser. 7, nos. 4–7 (1928):343–74.
"Neskol'ko slov o zemledel'cheskikh orudiiakh." *Sel'skoe khoziaistvo*, part 2 (February 1861):35–38.

Nifontov, A. S. *Zernovoe proizvodstvo Rossii vo vtoroi polovine XIX veka*. Moscow, 1974.

Nikolaev, A. "Krest'ianskaia svad'ba v Zvenigorodskom uezde, Moskovskoi gubernii." *Severnaia pchela*, no. 209 (1863):921–22; no. 210 (1863):925–26.

————. "Svadebnye obriady Malorossov, Sudzhanskago uezda." *Moskvitianin* 2, no. 7 (1854):73–92; no. 8 (1854):121–40.

"Ocherki Tambovskoi gubernii v statisticheskom otnoshenii." *Zhurnal Ministerstva vnutrennikh del*, no. 7, part 3 (1858): 1–88.

Okhrimovich, V. "Znachenie malorosskikh svadebnykh obriadov i pesen v istorii evoliutsii sem'i." *Etnograficheskoe obozrenie*, no. 4 (1891):44–105.

Ordin, N. G. "Svad'ba v podgorodnykh volostiakh Sol'vychegodskago uezda." *Zhivaia starina*, no. 1 (1896):51–121.

Osokin, S. "Sel'skaia svad'ba v Malmyzhskom uezde." *Sovremennik* 61, part 4 (1857):54–87.

Otto, N. "Iz narodnago byta: Novgorodskaia svad'ba." *Severnaia Pchela*, no. 137 (1862):545–46; no. 138 (1862):549–50.

Pakhman, S. V. *Obychnoe grazhdanskoe pravo v Rossii*. 2 vols. Saint Petersburg, 1877.

Pfeller, A. I. "Khoziaistvennyi otchet po imeniiam g. Vitse-Prezidenta A. I. Pfeller v guberniiakh Tul'skoi, Riazanskoi, Orlovskoi, i Kurskoi." *Zapiski Lebedianskago obshchestva sel'skago khoziaistva za 1848*, (1849), 102–27; *za 1849* (1850), 102–20.

Plakans, Andrejs. "Seigneurial Authority and Peasant Family Life: The Baltic Area in the Eighteenth Century." *Journal of Interdisciplinary History* 5 (1975):626–54.

Polanyi, K. *The Great Transformation*. Boston, 1957.

Polnaia entsiklopediia russkago sel'skago khoziaistva i soprikasaiushchikhsia s nim nauk. 12 vols. Saint Petersburg, 1900–1912.

Potter, J., et al., eds. *Peasant Society: A Reader*. Boston, 1967.

Pr. V. E-iu. "Opisanie sel'skoi svad'by v Sengileevskom uezde, Simbirskoi gubernii." *Etnograficheskoe obozrenie* 42, no. 3 (1899):108–44.

Preobrazhenskii, A. "Prikhod Stanilovskii na Siti, Iaroslavskoi guber-

nii, Molozhskago uezda." *Etnograficheskii sbornik* 1
(1853):125–73.
———. "Volost' Pokrovsko-Sitskaia, Iaroslavskoi gubernii, Mo-
lozhskago uezda." *Etnograficheskii sbornik* (1853):61–124.
Priklonskii, S. A. "Krest'ianskii mir i prikhodskii pricht." *Severnyi
vestnik,* no. 1, part 2 (1885):42–64; no. 2, part 2 (1885):77–
95.
*Prilozheniia k trudam Redaktsionnykh komissii dlia sostavleniia Pol-
ozheniia o krest'ianakh, vykhodiashchikh iz krepostnoi
zavisimosti. Svedeniia po pomeshchich'im imeniiam.* 6 vols.
Saint Petersburg, 1860.
Rabb, T. K., and R. I. Rotberg, eds. *The Family in History.* New
York, 1973.
Ransel, D. L., ed. *The Family in Imperial Russia.* Urbana, Ill., 1978.
Razumikhin, S. "Selo Bobrovki i okruzhnyi ego okolotok, Tverskoi
gubernii, Rzhevskago uezda." *Etnograficheskii sbornik* 1
(1853):235–82.
Redfield, R. *The Little Community* and *Peasant Society and Culture.*
Chicago, 1960.
Robinson, G. *Rural Russia under the Old Regime.* New York, 1932.
Rogov, N. "Materialy dlia opisaniia byta permiakov." *Zhurnal Min-
isterstva vnutrennikh del,* no. 4 (1858):45–127.
Rubinshtein, N. A. *Sel'skoe khoziaistvo Rossii vo vtoroi polovine
XVIII v.* Moscow, 1957.
Rudnev, A. "Selo Golun' i Novomikhailovskoe, Tul'skoi gubernii,
Novosil'skago uezda." *Etnograficheskii sbornik* 2 (1854):98–
110.
"Russkaia prostonarodnaia svad'ba v derevne." *Kaleidoskop,* no. 46
(1862):824–26; no. 47 (1862):830–40.
Samaha, J. *Law and Order in Historical Perspective: The Case of
Elizabethan Essex.* New York, 1974.
Samokvasov, D. "Semeinaia obshchina v Kurskom uezde." In *Sbor-
nik narodnykh iuridicheskikh obychaev* 1:11–15. *Zapiski
Imperatorskago russkago geograficheskago obshchestva po ot-
deleniiu etnografii,* 8 (Saint Petersburg, 1878).
Savel'ev, A. "Ocherki lichnykh i imushchestvennykh otnoshenii
mezhdu suprugami, po russkim zakonam i obychnomu
pravu." *Iuridicheskii vestnik,* no. 12 (1878):767–87; no. 7
(1879):120–56.
Scott, J. C. *The Moral Economy of the Peasant: Rebellion and Subsistence in Southeast Asia.* New Haven, 1976.
Semenov, M. "Khoziaistvennyia oshibki ot neurozhaia."
Zemledel'cheskii zhurnal, no. 6 (1840):443–50.

BIBLIOGRAPHY

Semenova-Tian-Shanskaia, O. P. *Zhizn' "Ivana." Ocherki iz byta krest'ian odnoi iz chernozemnykh gubernii.* Zapiski Imperatorskago russkago geograficheskago obshchestva po otdeleniiu etnografii, 39 (Saint Petersburg, 1914).

Semevskii, V. I. "Domashnii byt i nravy krest'ian vo vtoroi polovine XVIII v." *Ustoi,* no. 1 (1882):90–132; no. 2 (1882):63–108.

———. *Krest'iane v tsartsvovanie Imperatritsy Ekateriny II.* Saint Petersburg, 1881–1901.

———. "Sel'skii sviashchennik vo vtoroi polovine XVIII veka." *Russkaia starina,* no. 8 (1877):501–38.

Shanin, T. *The Awkward Class.* Oxford, 1972.

Shchepetov, K. N. *Krepostnoe pravo v votchinakh Sheremetevykh.* Moscow, 1947.

Shelekhov, D. P. *O nastoiashchem polozhenii sel'skago khoziaistva v Rossii i prichinakh prodolzhaiushchikhsia neurozhaev.* Saint Petersburg, 1842.

Shishkov, A. N. "Mysli o khoziaistve i otchetnosti." *Zapiski Lebedianskago obshchestva sel'skago khoziaistva za 1855 god,* part 2 (1856):104–227.

Shorter, E. *The Making of the Modern Family.* New York, 1975.

Shpilevskii, M. "Materialy dlia istorii narodnago prodovol'stviia v Rossii." *Zapiski Imperatorskago Novorossiiskago universiteta* 14, part 1 (1874):1–35.

Shternberg, N. "Novye materialy po svad'be." In *Materialy po svad'be i semeino-rodovomu stroiu narodov SSSR,* 1:6–16. Leningrad, 1926.

Sivkov, K. V. *Ocherki po istorii krepostnogo khoziaistvo i krest'ianskogo dvizheniia v Rossii v pervoi polovine XIX veke.* Moscow, 1951.

Slavutinskii, S. T. "Otryvki iz vospominanii: Krest'ianskie volneniia v Riazanskoi gubernii s 1847 po 1858." *Drevniaia i novaia Rossiia,* no. 9 (1878):38–53; no. 10 (1878):135–56.

Slicher van Bath, B. H. *The Agrarian History of Western Europe, A.D. 500–1800.* London, 1963.

"Sloboda Trekhizbianskaia." *Etnograficheskii sbornik* 2 (1854):1–18.

Smirnov, A. G. "Narodnye sposoby zakliucheniia braka." *Iuridicheskii vestnik,* no. 5 (1878):661–93.

———. "Obychai i obriady russkoi narodnoi svad'by." *Iuridicheskii vestnik,* no. 7 (1878):981–1015.

———. *Ocherki semeinykh otnoshenii po obychnomu pravu russkago naroda.* Moscow, 1878.

Smirnova, M. "Rodil'nye i krestil'nye obriady krest'ian sela Golitsyna, Kurganskoi volosti, Serdobskago uezda, Saratovskoi gubernii." *Etnograficheskoe obozrenie*, nos. 1–2 (1911):252–56.

Smith, R. E. F. *Peasant Farming in Moscovy.* Cambridge, 1977.

Southworth, H. M., and B. F. Johnston, eds. *Agricultural Development and Economic Growth.* Ithaca, N.Y., 1967.

Stone, L. *The Family, Sex, and Marriage in England, 1500–1800.* New York, 1977.

Stroev, V. N. "Ubiistvo kniazia N. S. Gagarina." *Istoricheskii vestnik* 104 (March 1906):955–59.

Sukhov, P. M. "Neskol'ko dannykh po narodnomu kalendariu i o svadebnykh obychaiakh krest'ian." *Etnograficheskoe obozrenie*, nos. 2–3 (1892):239–45.

Sumtsov, N. F. *O svadebnykh obriadakh, preimushchestvenno russkikh.* Kharkov, 1881.

"Svadebnye obriady Malorossiian slobody Vorontsovki, Pavlovskago uezda." *Voronezhskaia beseda*, 1861, 167–78.

Sykes, G. *The Society of Captives.* Princeton, 1958.

Tengoborskii, L. V. *O proizvoditel'nykh silakh Rossii.* Moscow, 1854.

Terner, F. G. "Tri publichnyia lektsii po statistike Rossii." *Ekonomist* 3, no. 1 (1860):1–76.

Tilly, L., and J. Scott. *Women, Work, and Family.* New York, 1978.

Tiutriumov, I. "Krest'ianskaia sem'ia: Ocherki obychnago prava." *Russkaia rech'*, no. 4 (1879):270–94; no. 7 (1879):123–56; no. 10 (1879):289–318.

———. "Krest'ianskoe nasledstvennoe pravo." *Slovo*, no. 1 (1881):42–75; no. 2 (1881):46–85.

Tobias, J. J. *Crime and Industrial Society in the Nineteenth Century.* New York, 1967.

Troitskii, P. "Selo Lipitsy i ego okrestnosti, Tul'skoi gubernii, Koshirskago uezda." *Etnograficheskii sbornik* 2 (1854):81–97.

Trudy komissii po preobrazovaniiu volostnykh sudov. Vols. 1–7. Saint Petersburg, 1873–74.

V. B. "Simbirskie obychai pokupat' nevest." *Otechestvennyia zapiski* 9, no. 7 (1840):28–29.

V. V. "Semeinye razdely i krest'ianskoe khoziaistvo." *Otechestvennye zapiski*, no. 1 (1883):1–22; no. 2 (1883):137–61.

Veselovskii, K. S. "Neskol'ko dannykh dlia statistiki urozhaev i neurozhaev v Rossii." *Zhurnal ministerstva gosudarstvennykh imushchestv* 62 part 2 (1857):23–38.

Vil'son, I. I. *Ob'iasneniia k khoziaistvenno-statisticheskomu atlasu Evropeiskoi Rossii.* 4th ed. Saint Petersburg, 1869.

Vinogradov, N. "Narodnaia svad'ba v Kostromskom uezde." *Trudy Kostromskago nauchnago obshchestva po izucheniiu mestnago kraia* 8 (1917):71–152.

Volkonskii, V. P. "Ocherki khoziaistva po imeniiu V. P. Volkonskago." *Zhurnal sel'skago khoziaistva i ovtsevodstva,* no. 7 (1846):9–12.

Vucinich, W., ed. *The Peasant in Nineteenth Century Russia.* Stanford, 1968.

Wallace, D. M. *Russia on the Eve of War and Revolution.* ed. C. E. Black. New York, 1961.

Wallace, S. E. *Total Institutions.* New Brunswick, N.J., 1971.

Wharton, C. R., ed. *Subsistence Agriculture and Economic Development.* Chicago, 1969.

Wheaton, R. "Family and Kinship in Western Europe: The Problem of the Joint Family Household." *Journal of Interdisciplinary History* 5 (1975):601–28.

Winner, I. *A Slovenian Village: Zerovnica.* Providence, R.I., 1971.

Wolf, E. *Peasants.* Englewood Cliffs, N.J., 1966.

Wrigley, E. A. *Population and History.* New York, 1969.

Zaionchkovskii, P. A. *Otmena krepostnogo prava v Rossii.* Moscow, 1968.

Zaloskin, A. "Khoziaistvennye statisticheskie zamechaniia po selu Abakumovo, Riazanskoi gubernii, Pronskago uezda, pomeschika G. . . na," *Zhurnal zemlevladel'tsev* 2, no. 6 (1858): 40–42.

Zapiski Lebedianskago obshchestva sel'skago khoziaistva, 1847–57. Moscow, 1848–58.

Zehr, H. *Crime and the Development of Modern Society.* Totowa, N.J., 1976.

Zelenin, D. K. *Opisanie rukopisei uchenago arkhiva Imperatorskago russkago geograficheskago obshchestva.* 3 vols. Petrograd, 1914–16.

Zhuravskii, D. P. *Ob istochnikakh i upotreblenii statisticheskikh svedenii.* Kiev, 1846.

Zvonkov, A. P., "Sovremennye brak i svad'ba sredi krest'ian Tambovskoi gubernii, Elatomskago uezda." In *Izvestiia Imperatorskago obschestva liubitelei estestvoznaniia, antropologii, i etnografii,* 61: 24–48. *Trudy etnograficheskago otdela,* 9 (Moscow, 1889).

INDEX

Made in the USA
Lexington, KY
23 August 2012